Z GUIDE FOR BEGINN

COMPUTER SCIENCE TEXTS

Z GUIDE FOR BEGINNERS

MIKE McMORRAN
BSc

and

STEVE POWELL
BA

OXFORD
BLACKWELL SCIENTIFIC PUBLICATIONS
LONDON EDINBURGH BOSTON
MELBOURNE PARIS BERLIN VIENNA

To Annie and Ann, whose patience enabled us to complete this book.

© 1993 by Mike McMorran & Steven Powell

Blackwell Scientific Publications
Editorial offices:
Osney Mead, Oxford OX2 0EL
25 John Street, London WC1N 2BL
23 Ainslie Place, Edinburgh EH3 6AJ
238 Main Street, Cambridge,
  Massachusetts 02142, USA
54 University Street, Carlton
  Victoria 3053, Australia

Other Editorial Offices:
Librairie Arnette SA
2, rue Casimir-Delavigne
75006 Paris
France

Blackwell Wissenschafts-Verlag
Meinekestrasse 4
D-1000 Berlin 15
Germany

Blackwell MZV
Feldgasse 13
A-1238 Wien
Austria

First published 1993

Typeset using BookMaster™ and the
IBM 3800 printing system
Printed and bound in Great Britain by
Hartnolls Ltd, Bodmin, Cornwall

DISTRIBUTORS

Marston Book Services Ltd
PO Box 87
Oxford OX2 0DT
(*Orders:* Tel: 0865 791155
         Fax: 0865 791927
         Telex: 837515)

USA
Blackwell Scientific Publications, Inc.
238 Main Street
Cambridge, MA 02142
(*Orders:* Tel: 800 759-6102
           617 876-7000)

Canada
Oxford University Press
70 Wynford Drive
Don Mills
Ontario M3C 1J9
(*Orders:* Tel: 416 441-2941)

Australia
Blackwell Scientific Publications
Pty Ltd
54 University Street
Carlton, Victoria 3053
(*Orders:* Tel: 03 347-5552)

A catalogue record for this book is available
from the British Library.

Library of Congress
Cataloging in Publication Data
McMorran, Mike.
    Z guide for beginners/Mike McMorran
    and Steve Powell.
       p.   cm.
    Includes index.
    ISBN 0–632–03117–4
    1. Z (Computer program language)
    I. Powell, Steve, B.A.
    II. Title.
    QA76.73.Z2M35   1992
    005.13′3—dc20   91-43363
                                          CIP

Contents

Preface

'Let's have Z first, and football afterwards!'
Lewis Carroll, What the Tortoise Said to Achilles

In our experience Z has an academic reputation. Not that this is such a bad thing, since it lends respectability to the notation and encourages fine minds to take it seriously. However, it does discourage some people from learning Z and, with it, the principles and benefits of formal methods. Most existing publications aim to be complete and rigorous, and this is quite natural in the precision-sensitive climate in which Z flourishes. As a consequence they suffer by being difficult for the beginner, whose aims are more practical and immediate than academic. And really there is no need for this, as Z is basically a simple notation. Many people in industry, with no especial mathematical prowess, have been pleasantly surprised by its clarity and utility and their own facility with it. In fact, and this may surprise many readers, there is good reason to believe that people *without* strong mathematical backgrounds can and do make better Z specifiers than most.

Initially, those parts of industry that wanted to use Z wrote their own in-house guides. At that time there were no reference books easily available in the public domain. That is no longer the case, but there is still no simple introduction for the beginner. One of the authors produced a manual that served as a guide to Z for the IBM United Kingdom Development Laboratories at Hursley Park, Winchester. That manual provided the inspiration for this book.

You will notice that examples figure strongly throughout, and we have tried to introduce some that are slightly out-of-the-ordinary. You may also notice that there is no attempt anywhere to give a complete BNF (Backus-Naur Form) definition of the syntax of Z; nor is there a mathematical semantics. These are quite deliberate omissions. It is not that these could not be given, although, since Z evolves even as we write, it is doubtful that such descriptions would long survive. Instead, we feel that these formal devices are, in a sense, irrelevant. Syntax very definitely, and semantics significantly, bows to practical consideration in the Z world. From the first, utility and clarity have determined the extent of the notation and it is these that we aim to demonstrate. The wonder is how few organizing ideas are necessary to achieve such great expressive power.

We intend the book to be self-contained. We start by explaining some of the background and context of formal methods in Chapter 1 and introduce the main Z constructs in Chapter 2. We then give an explanation of predicate logic and basic set theory in Chapters 3 and 4.

In Chapters 5 and 6 we explain how *relations* and Z schemas are used to model real world data, and Chapter 7 shows how Z schemas can be used to describe the behaviour of these data. At this point in the book, all the major Z constructs have been demonstrated and the reader should be able to understand and construct specifications of many possible systems. The remaining chapters develop these ideas, introducing more complex data models, the technique called "promotion" and the "schema calculus". Appendix A brings together an informal summary of the notation and the various constructs we describe, suitable for quick reference.

Throughout the book each concept is illustrated in terms of earlier notions and reinforced by simple *exercises*. We recommend that you tackle exercises as you reach them — they often embody some point which may not be explicit in the text. They are not supposed to be difficult: we expect them to take from 3 to 30 minutes each. There are sample answers to these exercises at the end of each chapter.

From Chapter 4 onwards, each chapter is followed by a collection of *specification problems* for which solutions are provided at the end of the book. These represent more substantial tasks (from an hour to three days, perhaps?) and will give you a flavour of practical Z. The problems cover a wide range, including not only some traditional computer system problems but also a car-radio and the games of Checkers and GO. A clear understanding is not found by simply "doing" problems — they need to be explored. The answers, such as they are, provide only *sample* solutions and do not pretend to be the best: looking for alternative and better expressed solutions will give you an authentic taste of real specification. It will also help you to form an opinion about good specification *style*. This is very difficult alone. Though you can try these problems by yourself, they are best appreciated with a colleague. A note of caution is in order here — strong feelings can arise when criticising style. There is no precisely defined notion of "simplicity" and though a particular case may seem clear cut to you, others can (and will) see it differently. In seeking simple expression of ideas we need diplomacy, clarity of thought and sensitive communication skills — all of which have little to do with formal mathematics but, we hope you will come to agree, everything to do with good specification.

The book may be self-contained but it is not complete. More can be said about the use of Z for specification and there is much more to say about its application to design. We concentrated only on using Z for *specification* and we stopped when we felt we had illustrated the notation in nearly all of its conceptual areas, at a point where a newcomer could confidently begin useful work.

We are indebted to those who gave freely of their time to review all or part of the drafts of this book. What they suggested caused us to rework many sections. In some details we may have trampled upon their explicit comments while benefiting enormously from them. We hope they will forgive us for ignoring some of what they said. IBM deserves much credit, not only for the opportunities we have enjoyed in its ranks, but also for practical and enlightened support of formal methods over several years.

We apppreciate IBM's permission to use the *Z User Manual (IBM Technical Report 12.274)* as the starting point for this book, and to use IBM BookMaster and IBM 3800 printing subsystems to produce the masters.

We appreciate, too, the indulgence and support of our long-suffering families.

M.A.M. and S.P. 1992

Chapter 1
Introduction – Why Formal?

'I said it in Hebrew – I said it in Dutch –
    I said it in German and Greek:
But I wholly forgot (and it vexes me much)
    That English is what you speak!'

Lewis Carroll, The Hunting of the Snark, Fit the Fourth

Why do we need to use a 'formal' notation to write a computer system specification when English is what we speak? In this chapter we explain the concerns that have given rise to the growth of formal methods.

SIMPLICITY AND SURPRISE

The computer chip is everywhere these days – in traffic lights, video recorders, ovens and electric kettles. Chips seem to control much of society. Of course this is not true; control rests with people and the chip is simply the *means* of their control. Their intentions are expressed and replayed by software: choreography carefully planned beforehand.

So, the traffic light embodies a 'traffic cop', the video recorder a skilful engineer, the electric kettle... (we are assured that some electric kettles *do* have chips in them). Everywhere there are complex machines making life more friendly and more relaxing; the skills of experts distilled into mechanisms so that life holds few surprises. Or does it?

Complex machines *fail* in complex ways. Such failures surprise users (you and me) and designers, too. For along with comparatively small increases in complexity of construction come enormous increases in complexity of behaviour; the number of possible configurations of a computer-controlled video recorder is many more than might be anticipated from the instruction booklet. The successful design keeps many configurations hidden so that most of the time we are not aware of this sea of possibility. Just ask yourself these questions about a video cassette recorder:

What does it do if I am replaying a tape when the timer indicates another programme to record?

What if I set two programme times that overlap? Three?

What if I set the start time to be *after* the end time for a recording?

What happens if the end of the tape is reached during a recording?

If the power fails during a recording, but not long enough for the memory to be lost, or the timer fails, what happens to the recording when power resumes?

Of course the VCR does *something* in these cases, perhaps depending on other conditions, but the point of the questions is that we do not know what it is supposed to do unless we try it. The instruction book does not appear to help much – can it be that the *designers* did not know either? Some other true stories suggest that this might be so.

There is the story of the fly-by-wire jet fighter plane that, during tests, was taken across the equator on automatic pilot where it promptly flipped upside down. The programmer (who lived in the Northern Hemisphere) had assumed that a certain data value would always be positive. Happily this was a simulation flight.

Then there was the intelligent torpedo that steered itself after launch, tracking its target by detecting engine noise. One of the primary sources of engine noise was the submarine that fired it, and submarine commanders were naturally concerned that the torpedo did not turn on them by mistake. The weapons designers therefore built in a safety mechanism so that, if the torpedo sensed it had turned through 180 degrees after launch, it would automatically detonate and harmlessly explode. Proper tests had to be conducted, and a submarine duly went to the testing range. The first two torpedoes went unerringly to target but the third got stuck in the launch tube. It proved impossible to free it so the submarine commander decided to abandon the test. One can imagine him chuckling about boffins who could not get even simple things right as he gave the order to turn about...

Such examples show that, even in 'life and death' applications, where designers and implementers take extraordinary care, it is still possible to make elementary mistakes. This is because, in designing complex mechanisms, ultimately we rely upon one of the most complex mechanisms known: the human brain. Yet the brain has the same failure characteristics as any complex machine – so much so that experimental studies show a limit upon *reliable* behaviour. It can be summed up thus: 'you cannot think about more than seven things at once (give or take two)'. The brain can handle about seven things simultaneously: any more and it makes mistakes. So consistent is this limit that, in 1956, George A. Miller published a paper in the *Psychological Review* called *The Magical Number Seven, Plus or Minus Two* in which he identified it. Surprisingly, however, we seem to be able to build reliable structures with far more than seven independent pieces – so how do we do it? Miller pointed out the phenomenon known as 'chunking' which allows us to group together many items and treat them as a single one of the seven things we can recall. So, in a sequence of letters drawn from the alphabet at random, we would be hard pressed to recall more than about nine without error, and our recall limit for sequences of *words* is also about nine. This is true even though the total number of letters in the sequence of words is itself much larger than nine. If we remember words instead of letters we can recall more than nine letters in perfect sequence. The words are treated as single entities, from which we reconstruct the individual letters.

Starting with just *letters* it takes insight to group them and discover *words*. Rising to the word level can, if the groups of letters are chosen well, lead to great expressive power. We call this 'rising up' process *abstraction*. The objects on the higher level (in this case *words*) are called the 'abstractions'. Abstraction allows us to build thousands of co-operating parts reliably provided only that, at each stage of design, we deal with a small number of things at once. By designing in this way we obtain highly reliable structures. But given any one mechanism there may be many designs for it and in describing these designs there may be many ways to group pieces reliably. That is, in describing behaviour there are many ways to abstract. Choosing a good abstraction is an art; precise, reliable mechanisms owe much more to matters of style and good taste than they do to mindless computery. Far more than complex safety mechanisms or layers of backup systems, or exhaustive testing, a system owes its reliability to simple, straightforward, *understandable* design.

SOFTWARE ENGINEERING

This book is about a notation for writing specifications of complex mechanisms – usually software systems.

In general, engineering is about being systematic in producing reliable mechanisms meeting complex needs. Software engineering is the same, except that the mechanisms produced are largely software ones. Software mechanisms have proved extremely difficult to produce because of the potential for complexity in software construction. Software, too, comes with no natural abstractions, whereas traditional engineering has physical *form* to guide the abstraction process. Thus, plan elevations of a building, circuit diagrams and physical chip layout drawings are all natural abstractions in which to work. They are, in essence, representations of what we see with our eyes. As abstractions they are simple and *iconic*: codified forms that resemble what they represent. In software systems such natural representations do not arise. Software corresponds to no physical manifestation; it has been called 'pure thought-stuff'. The diagrams used in software design usually represent by analogy and either lack precision or else have limited application. They are certainly not an 'artist's impression' of what you might eventually see.

There are some commonly accepted abstractions—*procedures* for instance—which are extensively used but suffer from being so flexible that unless carefully constrained they provide little in the way of organization in themselves. Abstractions like these occur at such a low level that they do not help in the early stages of system design.

In the absence of natural abstractions new ones are invented. This is another difference between software engineering and other kinds of engineering. In building a bridge the abstractions in which the design and construction are expressed are largely determined beforehand. No architect would invent completely new concepts in which to design a building—this would be professional suicide. Besides, good abstractions for this are already well understood and accepted. In designing a software system, however, new concepts, forms and abstractions and wholly novel entities are often fabricated, invented especially for the system being designed.

With few commonly accepted universal forms to develop and study, the software engineering discipline has turned instead to the act of design itself. Traditionally we delineate *phases* in the construction of software systems. These might be: requirements gathering; system specification; high- and low-level design; implementation; testing and maintenance. A central intention of such phases is that they *separate* large-scale construction into smaller parts. If the parts are self-contained and coherent each phase may be considered independently as a single unit. However, a rigorous definition of each phase is not possible and in practice phases overlap and the boundaries are blurred.

Given a particular partition of system construction into phases we can measure many things: the number of errors found in each phase; the amount of 'effort' required for each phase; the predictability of later 'effort' from measurements of early phases; the relative duration of each phase. We can (and do, above all) measure the *cost* of each phase. Because of the expense involved the bulk of the information is gathered *in situ*, from actual commercial development. Developing theories of this process and formulating its principles is a scientifically risky business for a number of reasons. First of all, there is no general agreement about what phases *are* anyway and no guarantee that a particular project will stick to them. Secondly, there are a huge number of variables involved and no 'experiment' is repeated, even approximately. Futhermore, measurement costs money and commercial pressures tend to detract from careful recording of events for later study. Lastly, commercial information tends to be proprietary and gathering enough relevant information for analysis can be difficult.

Given this environment it might be supposed that there would be little published material, but due to the enormous potential benefits the opposite is true. Books, papers and seminars abound, many advancing theories about development; we suffer from having too many general principles and too few data with which to test them.

There are two observations that seem generally useful, however. The first is that a problem found early in the process is much cheaper to correct than one found later. Once a system is being used by customers it could cost 100 times more to fix a problem than it would if the same problem had been found during specification. Formal specification exposes logical errors very early on and this is an important justification for using it.

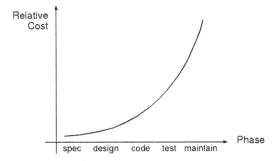

Fig 1.1. Relative cost of fixing problems.

The second observation is that efficient communication is vital to any team effort. In this context 'efficient' means relevant and precise. Completely isolated phases are obviously useless (no communication); everybody knowing everything is equally absurd (too much communication). Choosing an efficient and effective means to communicate is not easy and this is one of the most significant problems of any large project. In complex engineering it is not surprising to find formal notations, both pictorial and textual, aiming to describe facets of the system for the benefit of others.

As a brief aside, lest there be any confusion, we must clearly contrast these notations with computer programming languages. Computer programs are formal statements, the intent of which is to communicate with a machine – they are directly expressed in a mechanism. This is entirely different from formality that aims to communicate with another person. In the former case the criterion for success is that the mechanism has the 'correct behaviour'. In the latter case the criterion is that the person understands something. A choice of names, layout and procedural abstraction makes little difference to a computer — to a person they are crucial. Badly chosen the description is useless; well-chosen it becomes highly valuable.

Of course, for many years the computer program has been forced to serve both masters. People actually *do* read computer programs, and to be useful they had better be written for people as well as compilers. To be *really* useful a programming language has to be designed for people to read as well as compilers to translate, and inevitably this gives rise to conflicts. The organizing principles for good understanding may not be the same as for good compilation and execution.

In summary, software engineering aims to make systematic the reliable production of software systems. In this activity there is necessarily precise communication between phases and people occurring at many levels. Formal notations based upon essentially human needs have arisen over the last decade. One of these is Z.

FORMALITY

There are many *methodologies*, such as SSADM (Structured Systems Analysis and Design Method), JSD (Jackson System Design) and HOOD (Hierarchical Object-Oriented Design), being used in the software industry at the moment. These might all be called 'formal methods'. They are methodical for they have defined stages and procedures. They are also formal for they employ notations and nomenclatures that admit only certain forms and arrangements. This enables their practice to be controlled and analyzed, facilitating adherence to the precepts of the method. They generally employ 'formal' diagrammatic techniques, for example data-flow diagrams and entity-relationship diagrams, having syntax rules and an associated semantics. They also have 'formal' phases into which activities are partitioned, there being a set of official rules which determine which phases have been completed and which are next to commence. These uses of the word formal are valid but we use it in another sense entirely.

Where we use the term 'formal method' we mean the application of mathematics and logic to the description and design of systems behaviour. The term 'formal' comes from formal logic, and from attempts to mechanize logical reasoning. It is this that has given us insight into the nature of systems description and, ironically, led a school of thought away from mechanical reasoning toward greater human understanding. To place a formal notation like Z into this context, then, it might form a part of a methodology, but in no way *prescribes* a development process.

Z has a lot to say about the development process, however. In some ways its strong bias towards strict mathematical meaning throws some of the traditional problems into stark relief. It is far easier to see the distinction between a specification and a design with a clear and unambiguous definition of both, and the possiblity of a well-defined relationship between them. However, the nature of formality is often not clear, and the contrast between a formal and informal development can often seem strongest in the detail of one and the vagueness of the other. Let us then, for a moment, contrast the opposite ends of the development trail.

A computer program can be thought of as purely formal. It is one of a well-defined and fixed set of *forms*; it has a specific (intended) meaning; and it may be manipulated using rules that preserve its meaning. These are characteristics of formality.

At the other extreme, a typical set of requirements for a system is anything but formal. It could take many forms and new forms are often invented for new cases; its meaning can be unclear and is occasionally intentionally so; if it is manipulated there is no guarantee that the meaning is preserved, there are no rules to help us preserve its meaning.

We could regard systems development as a journey from this vague and informal description to a precise and pernickety description – for a precise and pernickety machine to follow. At some point along the route complete formality and precision appears and from then on a developer may claim that 'it's plain sailing'. From this perspective the recent development of programming and design languages has been to bring forward the point where formality can 'take over'. Higher and higher level programming languages allow the magic formality to occur earlier and earlier in the project. Presumably the aim is to formalize development altogether. The machine and all of the design will then follow precise and unambiguous rules and procedures – the user's requirements will be simply and immediately expressed in formal terms.

But is this possible? Is not 'requirements' simply computer-speak for 'what the clients want'? And is it not commonly held that clients never know what they want? How can we formalize that which is not known? Perhaps we cannot, and the totally formal development is a myth.

If we accept that the start of the journey is in a vague place and the end is in a precise one, then it seems inescapable that there is some sort of discontinuity encountered along the way – a magical point where vague informal ideas are transformed into precise and specific notations. If this point is not when requirements are expressed then it must occur later. How is the transfer negotiated? Is this the most dangerous step of the whole trip?

It might be, if it were necessary. But there is another view.

Rather than being opposites or rivals, informal and formal expressions are complementary. Rather than a formal description *displacing* an informal one it should *support* it. The formal and informal descriptions of *anything* are inseparable. This point of view holds that there is no cutover from natural languages to 'unnatural' ones – instead both co-exist at all places where there are people to view them. Both are essential. Neither formal notation alone, nor informal text by itself, can do justice to design. This is illustrated in Figure 1.2.

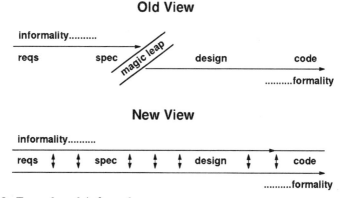

Fig 1.2. Formal and informal.

Earlier and earlier in design there have been notations used to support informal explanations; these, in turn, have explained the notations. The two explanations are mutually reinforcing at all points of contact; there is no need of a 'cutover'. This reinforcement can be seen occurring spontaneously in computer programs. The *comment* is a heavily-used mechanism that blends informal explanation with formal program text. When used best, comments bind a program into an amalgam which conveys intent much better than either comments or program alone.

Z has grown with a style which supports this view. Each piece of formal text is usually preceded and followed by explanation in informal text. The informal text is a necessary bridge between the mathematics and the living, breathing world. In Z we might say:

$$\forall \mathit{fn} : \mathit{FileName} \bullet \#\mathit{fn} < 9$$

literally: 'for all *fn* in *FileName*, the size of *fn* is less than 9'. In the explanation this might appear as 'each *FileName* is less than nine characters long'.

Even in this tiny fragment we see formal text nouns (*FileName*) used freely in the informal explanation, and also how easily the mathematics is read after consulting the informal text. In a larger document the full story becomes apparent; formal text is explained by informal, which, in turn, uses notions named and defined formally. The two explanations reinforce each other like the warp and weft of a cloth – going in different directions and relying entirely on one another for support. Each new piece of formal text is a mystery without the simultaneous development of the reader's informal understanding. Each new informal explanation is ambiguous without the preceding formal base, and a formal expression.

In short, the nature of formality is such that purely technically correct mathematics is of little use – the proper use of formal notations is as an *underpinning* to understanding.

THE FINAL SURPRISE

While learning formal notations and teaching software engineering we discovered something that surprised us: 'Complexity is easy and simplicity hard'. It continues to surprise us.

Complexity is easy: Of course it is easy – if it were difficult we would not see so much of it! This is at once glib and irrefutable.

There is other evidence: we have frequently observed a reaction to formal specification in the first stages of using Z. It can be named the 'mathematical syndrome'. It is recognized by an easy grasp of the notation, followed by withdrawal for anything up to a month. The sufferer then reappears, triumphant, holding The Definitive Specification: several pages of hand-written Z with (and this clinches the diagnosis) absolutely no informal explanation whatsoever. From this point the symptoms develop into aggressive defence of the document, accompanied by the claim that the specifying has been done and we should all proceed immediately to implementation. Mild cases can simply produce rather more predicate logic than we would like, but this is still painful for colleagues and friends.

Despite the name, do not think that the mathematical syndrome affects only mathematicians.

Simplicity is hard: Any specification can be improved and formal ones are no exception. 'Improved' here means 'made more understandable' and 'made simpler'. Over and again apparently stable and elegant specifications are simplified, long after one would think that this is impossible. Sometimes simpler implies smaller, often it does not. The simplest explanations turn out to be the most difficult to find. After all, they are in the last place we look for them.

This is not always appreciated by those who commission specification work.

Let us imagine some time in the near future, after we have been using Z to describe a system. We have made false starts; we have filled wastebaskets with rejected expressions; we have finally produced a simple and precise description which is easy to read and understand — and, just at this point, our boss looks over our shoulder and says:

'But of course! Why did it take you so long just to say *that*?'

This could be a very depressing moment. But do not despair, for now is the time to celebrate! We have just received our first accolade and our specification is already a wild success!

Chapter 2
A Z Document

'If there is no meaning in it,' said the King, 'that saves a
world of trouble, you know, as we needn't try to find any.'
Lewis Carroll, Alice in Wonderland

Faced with some Z, how do we set about finding the meaning in it? In
this chapter we introduce the main parts of a Z *document* – a form in
which coherent Z specifications often come.

A Z DOCUMENT

A Z document is usually a specification for or design of a computer
system of some sort. It is a combination of mathematical text and
English. There are no rules defining the style of Z we must use,
though in the course of this book we will recommend some. Thus we
cannot describe for you a 'typical' Z document; there are almost as
many different styles as there are authors!

One common use of Z is to specify the behaviour of a system under
the action of various commands (or 'operations'). In Figure 2.1 we
show the main parts of such a document. Each part is explained
briefly and we expand these explanations in the remainder of this
chapter. On the left we show the chapter number in which a detailed
explanation will be given, and on the right we show an illustration of
the sort of Z text that might appear in that part of a document.

For simplicity, we have shown each part as if it were a coherent
whole. In fact, within a document we can introduce any of the constructs at any place that we choose: there is no need to follow a particular order. Typically, we choose to build each part on what went
before, so we often start by introducing some given sets.

GIVEN SETS

A *given set* is a collection of objects we wish to use but whose values
we do not yet need to discuss. For example, in the specification of a
computer system for keeping a doctor's records, we might expect to
deal with patients and so we introduce them as a given set like this:

[*PATIENT*]

This says that the set *PATIENT* contains objects we wish to discuss but says nothing about their characteristics. Often, at some level of abstraction, we wish to defer discussion of the details of such a collection; that is what a given set lets us do.

Given sets will be explained further in Chapter 4.

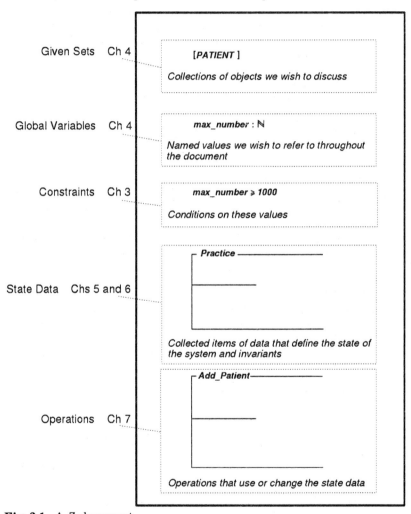

Fig 2.1. A Z document.

VARIABLES

A *variable* is a named value. The *scope* of a variable is that part of the document in which the variable is *known*. At any point in the document, we can refer only to those variables that are known there. A *global variable* is a variable known throughout the whole document.

We must *declare* each variable we wish to use (though its declaration need not precede its use). For example, in a doctor's system, we might need to discuss the maximum number of patients a doctor is permitted, so we declare it like this:

max_patients : $\mathbb{N}$

($\mathbb{N}$ is the set of numbers *0,1,2,3,....*) We will explain how to write declarations in the next section.

It is important to realise that, in Z, the value of a variable is never modified. This means that a Z variable differs from a programming variable in that throughout a Z document all occurrences of the same variable refer to the same value.

An *identifier* used as a variable name is a sequence of letters, digits and underscore characters. Uppercase letters are distinct from lowercase letters and the first character must be a letter. In Chapter 7, we shall see how identifiers can be 'prefixed' and 'decorated'. The syntax rules for identifiers are summarized in Appendix A.

DECLARATIONS

A *declaration* introduces a variable, names it and says what sort of value it has. We can introduce several variables in one declaration. For example,

x,y,z : *100..999*

declares *x*, *y* and *z* each to be a number between *100* and *999*.

pat1, pat2 : *PATIENT*

declares *pat1* and *pat2* to be patients (that is, to be members of the set *PATIENT*).

Two or more declarations can be written on one line separated by semi-colons, like this:

max_patients : $\mathbb{N}$; *x, y, z* : *100..999*; *pat1, pat2* : *PATIENT*

This is called a *declaration list*.

┌─ **Exercise 2.1** ──┐
│ Introduce a set of doctors and three variables to represent particular
│ doctors.
└──┘

EXPRESSIONS

We can write an ***expression*** using variables. For instance, if we
declare x and y as numbers:

   $x, y : \mathbb{N}$

then we can write an expression such as

   $x + 2*y - 5$

The functions $+$, $-$ and $*$ used here are the usual arithmetic ones
(*addition*, *subtraction* and *multiplication*), and we will explain how we
can use them in Chapter 5.

ABBREVIATIONS

If a particular expression occurs frequently, we may want to name it.
We can use an ***abbreviation*** (indicated by the symbol $==$) to introduce a new variable to stand for the value of an expression, thus:

   polyfun $== x^2+5*x*y+y^2$

which introduces a global variable called *polyfun*. Wherever *polyfun* is
used, we could replace it by $x^2+5*x*y+y^2$ without changing the meaning
of the specification.

Often, we use an abbreviation to give a meaningful name to a real
world concept. For instance, suppose we need to discuss *dates*, such as
'17 January 1991'. We may not be interested in the precise format but
want to compare dates (to subtract two dates to determine elapsed days
for example). So we decide to represent them with numbers (the
number of days since the start of the century, perhaps), thus:

   Date $== \mathbb{N}$

Now we can declare variables, such as

   birth, marriage, death : *Date*

which means the same as

   birth, marriage, death : $\mathbb{N}$

but is more readable.

CONSTRAINTS

A *constraint* is a condition we wish to place on some data values. To express a constraint, we write an expression called a *predicate*. For instance, we might decide that the limit on the size of a practice must be at least *1,000* patients, so we say

max_patients $\geq$ *1000*

A constraint can be very simple, like this one, or it can be quite complicated, such as:

$(x^2+y^2 < 42*x+y) \wedge (x-y \bmod 27 = 2) \vee (x^3-y^3 < 200)$

(The usual arithmetic comparison operators are available and are written $=, <, >, \leq, \geq$ and $\neq$.)
The symbol $\wedge$ is read 'and' and $\vee$ is read 'or', so we read this constraint as:

'x squared plus y squared is less than 42 times x plus y and
x minus y modulo 27 is 2 or
x cubed minus y cubed is less than 200'.

The predicates that make up a constraint, and the logical operators for combining them, such as 'and' and 'or', will be explained in Chapter 3. We can introduce a constraint when we declare a variable, like this:

$\begin{array}{|l}
\textit{max_patients} : \mathbb{N} \\
\hline
\textit{max_patients} \geq \textit{1000}
\end{array}$

or like this:

max_patients : $\mathbb{N}$ | *max_patients* $\geq$ *1000*

This is called an *axiomatic definition*. In the horizontal form, the symbol | is called a *constraint bar* and is read 'such that'.
Several constraints can be written in one axiomatic definition, for instance

$\begin{array}{|l}
\textit{max_patients} : \mathbb{N} \\
\hline
\textit{max_patients} \geq \textit{1000} \\
\textit{max_patients} \leq \textit{9999}
\end{array}$

When predicates are written on adjacent lines like this, they are assumed to be joined by an 'and' symbol, so this axiomatic definition says that *max_patients* lies between *1000* and *9999*. In fact, we can write this constraint without using 'and' as:

1000 ≤ max_patients ≤ 9999

Exercise 2.2

Write a predicate that states that the three doctors introduced in Exercise 2.1 are all different from each other.

STATE DATA AND SCHEMAS

State data are items of data grouped together and identified by a name. The grouping construct is called a *schema*. We normally include the *state invariants* in the schema; these are constraints on the data values. A schema is commonly drawn in an open-sided 'E-shaped little box' with a label at the top and a line separating the data and constraints like this:

```
┌─Practice ─────────────────────────────────────
│ pat : ℙ PATIENT
│ doc : ℙ DOCTOR
│ reg : PATIENT ⇸ DOCTOR
│──────────────────────────
│ #pat ≤ max_patients
│ dom reg = pat
│ ran reg = doc
└────────────────────────────────────────────────
```

This introduces a joint practice named *Practice* containing a set of patients named *pat*, a set of doctors named *doc*, and a relationship between the patients and doctors named *reg*. (ℙ means 'set of' and # means 'number of' and these will be explained in Chapter 4.)

The state invariants say that there are no more than *max_patients* patients and that the *reg* relationship relates the set *pat* to the set *doc* (we will explain the dom and ran functions in Chapter 5).

The variables *pat*, *doc* and *reg* are **local** to *Practice*; they are not known outside it. We say that *pat*, *doc* and *reg* have **local scope** as opposed to *max_patients*, *DOCTOR* and *PATIENT* which have **global scope**. We will say more about the scope of schema variables in Chapter 6.

The use of schemas for describing state data will be explained in Chapter 6 and the data models for describing relationships will be explained in Chapters 5 and 8.

---- **Exercise 2.3** ----------------------------------

Introduce appropriate given sets and write the declaration part of a schema that represents the state of a simple house agent's business.

OPERATIONS

Operations on the state are also described by schemas. For instance, an operation to add a new patient to the practice might look like this

```
┌─ AddPatient ──────────────────────────
│ ΔPractice
│ newpat? : PATIENT
│ doctor? : DOCTOR
│ ────────────
│ reg′ = reg ∪ {newpat? ↦ doctor?}
└───────────────────────────────────────
```

ΔPractice (read 'delta practice') says that this operation may change the state of the *Practice*.

The variables ending in a question mark, *newpat?* and *doctor?*, are input parameters to the operation.

The *reg* relation after the operation is denoted *reg′* (read 'reg dashed' or 'reg primed'). It consists of the relation *reg* with the addition of the pair (*newpat?, doctor?*).

The use of schemas for describing operations will be explained in Chapter 7.

---- **Exercise 2.4** ----------------------------------

Write the declaration part of a schema to add a new house to the house agent's lists.

THE BASIC LIBRARY

The Z notation is used in conjunction with a ***basic library*** or ***mathematical toolkit***. This is simply a collection of definitions that can be used in any document.

The basic library is (theoretically) itself a Z document containing these definitions. Any group of people using Z specifications must agree what is in their basic library, and the best way to do this would be to produce a Z document defining it. However, in some groups, the library is agreed informally. In theory, different groups could use totally different libraries. In practice, however, there will be a great deal that is common in such libraries. The definitions that we assume to be in our basic library are summarized in Appendix A. They include + − * and the set of natural numbers, $\mathbb{N}$. Note that it is rarely necessary to use real numbers (such as 2·743) in Z specifications, so they are not provided in the basic library.

ANSWERS TO EXERCISES

Answer 2.1

[*DOCTOR*]
doc1, doc2, doc3 : *DOCTOR*

Answer 2.2

doc1 ≠ *doc2*
doc1 ≠ *doc3*
doc2 ≠ *doc3*

which can also be written as

doc1 ≠ *doc2* ≠ *doc3* ≠ *doc1*

Answer 2.3

There are, of course, many different ways we might answer this. Here is one very simple model.

[*HOUSE*]
[*CLIENT*]

```
┌─ Agent ─────────────────────────────────
│ houses : ℙ HOUSE
│ vendors : ℙ CLIENT
│ purchasers : ℙ CLIENT
└─────────────────────────────────────────
```

Answer 2.4

```
┌─ AddHouse ──────────────────────────────
│ ΔAgent
│ house? : HOUSE
│ vendor? : CLIENT
└─────────────────────────────────────────
```

Chapter 3
Logic

'Contrariwise,' continued Tweedledee, 'if it was so, it
might be; and if it were so, it would be; but as it isn't, it
ain't. That's logic.'
Lewis Carroll, Through the Looking Glass

The formal text of a Z document consists of phrases written in mathematical notation. In this chapter we introduce *logic*, which provides rules for combining and manipulating statements, and for describing the properties of a system.

PREDICATES

A **predicate** is a statement which can be either *True* or *False*. For instance,

9 < 16

is *True*, while

$8 \geq 3^2$

is *False*, and

amount ≤ 100

is either *True* or *False* depending on the value of the variable *amount*.

A predicate may appear inside another expression, inside a schema or as an axiomatic definition. If we write a predicate as an axiomatic definition, then we assert that its value is *True* and we constrain the values of the global variables in the predicate.

Exercise 3.1

Write declarations and a predicate asserting that the number *r* is a square root of the number *n*.

CONSISTENCY

Suppose somewhere in our specification we wrote

amount ≤ 100

and elsewhere we assert

  amount > 200

then we have written a contradictory or *inconsistent* specification. We are likely to notice such a simple contradiction without mechanical help, but in a more complex case a contradiction could be difficult to spot. Consider the following predicates:

  $(a>b \Rightarrow s=1) \lor (a<b \Rightarrow x=4)$

'*a* greater than *b* implies *s* equals 1 or *a* less than *b* implies *x* equals 4', and

  $(a-b=2) \land (s=3) \land (x=6)$

'*a* minus *b* equals 2 and *s* equals 3 and *x* equals 6'.

Are these two predicates inconsistent? A software tool that could check for consistency might be helpful here!

The study of logic is concerned with rules for making valid inferences from predicates. In defining computer systems, the variables correspond to the data of the system being defined, and we use mathematical logic to reason about them. Mathematical reasoning and proof are beyond the scope of this book, but we hope that the reader will appreciate that, by *formalizing* the specification, it becomes possible to reason about it.

COMBINING PREDICATES

A predicate can be negated by the **logical operator**

¬ (not),

and two predicates can be combined by the following *logical operators*:

∧ (and)
∨ (or)
⇒ (implies)
⇔ (equivalent to).

If we write

  $(amount \leq 100) \land (balance > amount)$

then we are asserting that both predicates are *True*, that is, that *amount* does not exceed *100 and balance* is greater than *amount*.

Some notations use a three-valued logic: *True*, *False* or *Undefined*. Z uses a two-valued logic and, if a predicate value cannot be determined, we simply accept that we do not know its value, though it must be either *True* or *False*. For instance, this occurs when a function is applied to a value not in its domain – see Chapter 5. This point of view has two advantages. It allows us to deduce the logical value of predicates even when parts of the predicate are undetermined, and, more significantly, it preserves all the usual logical equivalences that we can derive by inference.

In this chapter we will illustrate the meaning of each basic logical operator by a *truth table* which contains a 'Don't Know' row and column, and, in these tables, '?' will stand for *Don't Know*. When verifying logical equivalences, however, there is never any need to consider the 'Don't Knows' since they can always be inferred from the *True*s and *False*s.

With each operator we will also provide a *circuit diagram* which illustrates the operator. Switches in the circuit correspond to the predicates in the expression (P and Q). The light in the circuit will be *on* precisely when the expression is *True*. (We will not develop the correspondence between circuits and logic further but use it only for illustration.)

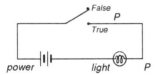

Fig 3.1. The circuit for the 'expression' P.

To set the scene, Figure 3.1 shows one of the simplest circuits, that for no logical operator at all. The light in this circuit is on if and only if P is *True*. In all our circuits, when a switch is 'down' the corresponding unknown is *True*, and when it is 'up' the unknown is *False*.

Negation (not)

A statement, P, can be negated by the logical operator ¬ to form a *negation*, written ¬P and read 'not P'. For example,

¬(3 ∈ *evens*)

states that the number 3 is *not* in the set *evens* (the symbol ∈ means 'is a member of'). The circuit for negation is shown in Figure 3.2.

We can explain negation in words as follows:

- ¬P is *True* if P is *False* and *False* if P is *True*.

- If the value of P cannot be determined, then the value of ¬P cannot be determined.

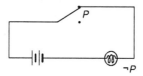

Fig 3.2. The circuit for ¬P.

The truth table for negation is given in Table 3.1.

Table 3.1. ¬P (not).

P	¬P
True	*False*
False	*True*
?	?

Conjunction (and)

Two statements, P and Q, can be combined by the logical operator ∧ to form a ***conjunction***, written P∧Q and read 'P and Q'. For example,

(3 ∉ evens) ∧ *(5 ∈ primes)*

states that the number *3* is not in the set *evens and 5* is in the set *primes*. The circuit for conjunction is shown in Figure 3.3.

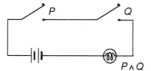

Fig 3.3. The circuit for P∧Q.

The conjunction of P and Q is defined thus:

- If both P and Q are *True*, then P∧Q is *True*.
- If either P or Q is *False*, or both are *False*, then P∧Q is *False*.
- If the value of P cannot be determined, then the value of P∧Q is *False* if Q is *False*, otherwise its value cannot be determined.
- Similarly, if Q is undetermined, then P∧Q is *False* if P is *False*, otherwise it is undetermined.

The truth table for conjunction is given in Table 3.2.

Table 3.2. And, Or, Implies and Equivalence.

P	Q	P∧Q	P∨Q	P⇒Q	P⇔Q
True	True	True	True	True	True
True	False	False	True	False	False
True	?	?	True	?	?
False	True	False	True	True	False
False	False	False	False	True	True
False	?	False	?	True	?
?	True	?	True	True	?
?	False	False	?	?	?
?	?	?	?	?	?

Disjunction (or)

Two statements, P and Q, can be combined by the logical operator ∨ to form a **disjunction**, written P∨Q and read 'P or Q'. For example,

$(3 \in evens) \lor (5 \in primes)$

states that the number 3 is in the set *evens or* the number 5 is in the set *primes* (*or both*). The circuit for disjunction is shown in Figure 3.4.

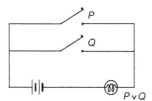

Fig 3.4. The circuit for P∨Q.

The disjunction of P and Q is defined thus:

- If either P or Q is *True*, or both are *True*, then P∨Q is *True*.
- If both P and Q are *False*, then P∨Q is *False*.
- If the value of P cannot be determined, then the value of P∨Q is *True* if Q is *True*, otherwise its value cannot be determined.
- Similarly, if Q is undetermined, then P∨Q is *True* if P is *True*, otherwise it is undetermined.

The truth table for disjunction is given in Table 3.2.

Implication (implies)

Two statements, P and Q, can be combined by the logical operator $\Rightarrow$ to form an **implication**, written $P \Rightarrow Q$ and read 'P implies Q'. For example, given $n>2$, we might write

$n \in primes \Rightarrow n \in odds$

to state that the number n is in the set of *primes implies that* the number n is in the set *odds*.

The circuit for implication is shown in Figure 3.5.

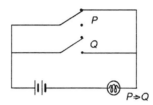

Fig 3.5. The circuit for $P \Rightarrow Q$.

The implication $P \Rightarrow Q$ is defined thus:

- If Q is *True*, then $P \Rightarrow Q$ is *True*, irrespective of the value of P.
- If P is *False*, then $P \Rightarrow Q$ is *True*, irrespective of the value of Q.
- If P is *True* and Q is *False*, then $P \Rightarrow Q$ is *False*.
- If the value of P cannot be determined, then the value of $P \Rightarrow Q$ is *True* if Q is *True*, otherwise its value cannot be determined.
- If the value of Q cannot be determined, then the value of $P \Rightarrow Q$ is *True* if P is *False*, otherwise its value cannot be determined.

The truth table for implication is given in Table 3.2.
Often an alternative definition, shown in Exercise 3.2, is easier to use.

Exercise 3.2

Show that $P \Rightarrow Q$ is logically equivalent to $(\neg P) \vee Q$.

This means that, whatever combinations of *True* and *False* that P and Q have, both expressions result in the same logical value. Rather than inventing a special symbol for this we will use an ordinary equals sign. So, this exercise is to show that:

$P \Rightarrow Q = (\neg P) \vee Q$

It is easiest to show this using a truth table.

The definition of 'implies' may conflict with our intuitive expectation. For instance, it is easy to mis-interpret the old saw 'a tidy desk implies a tidy mind' to mean that the owner of an untidy desk has an untidy mind (whereas, actually, we can infer nothing about the owner's mind in this case). We have more to say about implication on page 29.

Equivalence (if and only if)

Two statements, *P* and *Q*, can be combined by the logical operator ⇔ to form an ***equivalence***, written *P*⇔*Q* and read '*P* is equivalent to *Q*', or '*P* if and only if *Q*'. For example,

> *n* ∈ *evens* ⇔ *n* ∉ *odds*

states that *n* is in the set *evens* *if and only if* *n* is not in the set *odds*. Notice that this statement says both that an even number is not odd *and* that a number that is not odd is even. Exercise 3.5 formalises this observation.

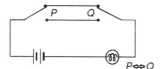

Fig 3.6. The circuit for *P*⇔*Q*.

The circuit for equivalence is shown in Figure 3.6 and the truth table is in Table 3.2. (You probably have a circuit like that of Figure 3.6 near the stairway of your house.)

The equivalence *P*⇔*Q* is defined thus:

- If both *P* and *Q* are *True*, then *P*⇔*Q* is *True*.
- If both *P* and *Q* are *False*, then *P*⇔*Q* is *True*.
- If *P* is *True* and *Q* is *False*, then *P*⇔*Q* is *False*.
- If *P* is *False* and *Q* is *True*, then *P*⇔*Q* is *False*.
- If the value of either *P* or *Q* cannot be determined, then the value of *P*⇔*Q* cannot be determined.

Exercise 3.3
Show that *P*⇔*Q* = (*P*⇒*Q*) ∧ (*Q*⇒*P*).

MANIPULATING LOGICAL EXPRESSIONS

The exercises in this section should reinforce the concepts explained above. In each exercise, you may use truth tables to demonstrate the result.

Exercise 3.4

(Commutative Laws) Show that $P \wedge Q = Q \wedge P$ and that $P \vee Q = Q \vee P$.

Exercise 3.5

(Associative Laws) Show that $(P \wedge Q) \wedge R = P \wedge (Q \wedge R)$ and that $(P \vee Q) \vee R = P \vee (Q \vee R)$.

(Thus we may write $P \wedge Q \wedge R$ and $P \vee Q \vee R$ without ambiguity.)

Exercise 3.6

(Distributive Law) Show that $P \wedge (Q \vee R) = (P \wedge Q) \vee (P \wedge R)$.

UNIVERSAL QUANTIFIER

Sometimes we need to express a constraint that applies to each member of a collection of objects. For this, we can use the **universal quantifier**, written $\forall$ (upside down A) and read 'for all'.

For instance, to say that all file names are less than 9 characters long, we might write:

$\forall fn : FileName \bullet \#fn < 9$

We can read the bullet ($\bullet$) as 'it is the case that', so this phrase can be read:

'*For all fn* in *FileName it is the case that* the size of *fn* is less than 9'.

The variable *fn* is a placeholder for a typical member of *FileName*. It is called a **bound variable** and its name has no significance. Thus

$\forall x : FileName \bullet \#x < 9$

is an exactly equivalent statement.

Exercise 3.7

Write a predicate that states that no member of a set of numbers, *NumSet*, is larger than 50.

The foregoing example is a simple case of the general form

$\forall$ declaration-list $\bullet$ predicate

The declaration-list can contain several variables, for example:

$\forall stu : Student; sub : Subjects \bullet stu$ *studies sub*

'All students study all subjects.'

A universally quantified expression often contains an *implication* as in

$\forall i, j : 1..100 \bullet i \neq j \Rightarrow table\ i \neq table\ j$

(where *table* is an array of 100 elements) which says that each element of *table* is distinct (different from all the others). To express such constraints, we can use the more general form:

∀ declaration-list | constraint • predicate

For example,

$\forall i, j : 1..100 \mid i \neq j \bullet table\ i \neq table\ j$

Here we read the constraint bar (|) as 'such that', so this phrase can be read:

'For all *i* and *j* in *1..100 such that i* not equal to *j it is the case that table i* is not equal to *table j* .'

The two forms

∀ declaration • constraint ⇒ predicate

and

∀ declaration | constraint • predicate

are precisely equivalent. We usually choose the second form if the declaration and constraint are closely related. Together they define a collection (the members of declaration which satisfy constraint) and the quantified predicate is true of all members of this collection.

Exercise 3.8

Write a predicate that states that the numbers in *table 1..100* are in ascending order.

Write a predicate that states that the numbers in *array 1..50* are in ascending order *and are all distinct*.

EXISTENTIAL QUANTIFIER

Sometimes we need to state that, among a collection of objects, there is at least one with a particular property. For this, we can use the **existential quantifier**, written ∃ (backward E) and read 'there exists'.

For instance, to say that at least one student is studying maths, we might write:

∃ *stu* : *Student* • *stu studies Maths*

In this context, we can read the bullet as 'for which', so this phrase can be read:

'*There exists* a *stu* in *Students for which stu* studies *Maths.*'

Once again, *stu* is a bound variable and could be replaced by another identifier.

Exercise 3.9

Write a predicate that states that there exists a member of *NumSet* less than 50.

Write a predicate that states that there does not exist a member of *IntSet* greater than 100.

Rephrase this second predicate using ∀ instead of ∃.

Write declarations and a predicate that states that the number *n* is a perfect square.

Several variables can appear in the declaration, for example:

$$\exists\, i, j : 1..100\, \bullet\, i \neq j \wedge table\, i = table\, j$$

says that *table* contains at least two values which are identical.

Such a conjunction often occurs in an existentially quantified expression, and we can use the more general form:

∃ declaration-list | constraint • predicate

for example,

$$\exists\, i, j : 1..100\, |\, i \neq j\, \bullet\, table\, i = table\, j$$

'There exist *i* and *j* in *1..100 such that i* is not equal to *j for which table i* equals *table j* .'

The two forms

∃ declaration • constraint ∧ predicate

and

∃ declaration | constraint • predicate

are precisely equivalent. We usually choose the second form if the declaration and constraint are closely related. Together they define a collection (the members of declaration which satisfy constraint) and the quantified predicate is true of at least one member of this collection.

UNIQUE EXISTENTIAL QUANTIFIER

The **unique existential quantifier**, $\exists_1$, read as 'there exists a unique', can be used in a similar way to ∃ to state that there exists *exactly one* member of the set satisfying the stated conditions. For example, given a suitable set *primes*,

$\exists_1 p : primes \bullet 1000 \le p \le 1100$

states that there is exactly one prime number between *1000* and *1100* (in fact, the value of the predicate is *False* because there are several prime numbers in this range).

NESTED QUANTIFIERS

Since a quantified predicate is a predicate in its own right, one quantifier can be nested within another. For example

$\forall n : \mathbb{N} \mid n > 2 \wedge (\exists i : \mathbb{N} \bullet n = 2*i) \bullet (\exists p, q : primes \bullet n = p + q)$

expresses the statement 'Every even number bigger than 2 is the sum of two prime numbers.' This is usually called *Goldbach's conjecture*.

Exercise 3.10

For the purposes of illustration, *Goldbach's conjecture* was not expressed very succinctly. Find a simpler way of expressing it.

BOUND VARIABLES

The bound variables used in quantified expressions are local variables known only within the quantified expression in which they are declared. So, when we write

$\exists i, j : 1..100 \bullet (i \ne j \wedge table\, i = table\, j)$

the variables *i* and *j* are known only within the phrase in parentheses. If we had also declared a *global* variable named *i*, then this would be a different variable known elsewhere in the document but not known inside the quantifier. We have created a 'hole' in the scope of the global variable *i*. (We will say more about scope in Chapter 6.) Notice that we can use the same name for different local variables inside different quantifiers.

MORE ABOUT IMPLICATION

Something that puzzles the beginner is why $P \Rightarrow Q$ should be *True* when P is *False*. To understand this, we need to look at an implication used in conjunction with another predicate.

Every Sunday, my family *drive_out* to the country, and, if the *sun_is_shining*, we *picnic*. We could capture this *FamilyRule* formally like this:

drive_out ∧ (*sun_is_shining* ⇒ *picnic*)

The first Sunday arrives, the *sun_is_shining* and we *drive_out* for a *picnic*. Clearly we are following our *FamilyRule*.

The second Sunday arrives and it is raining. What do we do? The *FamilyRule* states quite clearly that we *drive_out*, so off we go. We arrive at our local beauty spot around lunch time and are hungry. However, we don't feel like picnicing in the car, so we lunch in the local pub. Are we following the *FamilyRule*? A common-sense interpretation of the rule suggests we *are* following it. This is confirmed by the mathematical definition of 'implies' which says that the implication *sun_is_shining*⇒*picnic* is *True* because *sun_is_shining* is *False* (even though we do not *picnic*). *drive_out* is also *True*, so *FamilyRule* is *True*.

So the mathematical definition that $P \Rightarrow Q$ is *True* when P is *False* really *does* correspond to our common-sense English interpretation, though this was not immediately obvious!

By the way, if it is raining but we choose to eat our sandwiches (*picnic*) in the car, we have still satisfied the *FamilyRule*.

Because the English interpretation of 'implies' is somewhat different from its mathematical definition, we advise you to *avoid* implication unless the cases are simple and disjoint.

$(a < 0 \Rightarrow flag = -1)$ ∧
$(a = 0 \Rightarrow flag = 0)$ ∧
$(a > 0 \Rightarrow flag = 1)$

is easy to understand, but can also be expressed using disjuncts like this:

$(a < 0 \wedge flag = -1)$ ∨
$(a = 0 \wedge flag = 0)$ ∨
$(a > 0 \wedge flag = 1)$

which in a more complicated case is the style we recommend (see below).

It is tempting to use implication where we would use an **if ... then** statement in a programming language. The following example illustrates the danger in this.

Suppose we have two sets of names, *Valid*, the set of all syntactically valid names and *Known*, a subset of these. We intend *Known* to hold names that are 'known to our system'. Now imagine that we are describing an operation involving a *name* and having a *result* which can take only one of three particular values: *OK*, *unknown* and *invalid*.

To summarize the conditions that govern *result* we might try the conjunction:

(*name* ∈ *Known* ⇒ *result* = *OK*) ∧
(*name* ∉ *Known* ⇒ *result* = *unknown*) ∧
(*name* ∉ *Valid* ⇒ *result* = *invalid*)

This predicate probably does not express our intent, however, as *result* can never take the value *invalid*!

> **Exercise 3.11**
>
> Show that *result* cannot equal *invalid* by using truth tables or otherwise.

Here we can better express our intent by using disjunctive phrases, thus:

(*name* ∈ *Known* ∧ *result* = *OK*) ∨
(*name* ∉ *Known* ∧ *result* = *unknown*) ∨
(*name* ∉ *Valid* ∧ *result* = *invalid*)

> **Exercise 3.12**
>
> Compare the truth table of this expression with that of the previous exercise.

ANSWERS TO EXERCISES

Answer 3.1

$n : \mathbb{N}$
$r : \mathbb{N}$
$r * r = n$

Answer 3.2
Implication:

Table 3.3. $P \Rightarrow Q = (\neg P) \lor Q$

P	Q	$P \Rightarrow Q$	$\neg P$	$(\neg P) \lor Q$
True	True	**True**	False	**True**
True	False	**False**	False	**False**
False	True	**True**	True	**True**
False	False	**True**	True	**True**

Answer 3.3
Equivalence:

Table 3.4. $P \Leftrightarrow Q = (P \Rightarrow Q) \wedge (Q \Rightarrow P)$.

P	Q	P⇔Q	P⇒Q	Q⇒P	(P⇒Q)∧(Q⇒P)
True	*True*	**True**	*True*	*True*	**True**
True	*False*	**False**	*False*	*True*	**False**
False	*True*	**False**	*True*	*False*	**False**
False	*False*	**True**	*True*	*True*	**True**

Answer 3.4
(Commutative Laws for *and* and *or*) We can see that the truth tables for *and* and *or* are symmetric so that we can interchange *P* and *Q* and the table entries will not change.

Answer 3.5
(Associative Law for *and*)

Table 3.5. $(P \wedge Q) \wedge R = P \wedge (Q \wedge R)$.

P	Q	R	P∧Q	(P∧Q)∧R	Q∧R	P∧(Q∧R)
True	*True*	*True*	*True*	**True**	*True*	**True**
True	*True*	*False*	*True*	**False**	*False*	**False**
True	*False*	*True*	*False*	**False**	*False*	**False**
True	*False*	*False*	*False*	**False**	*False*	**False**
False	*True*	*True*	*False*	**False**	*True*	**False**
False	*True*	*False*	*False*	**False**	*False*	**False**
False	*False*	*True*	*False*	**False**	*False*	**False**
False	*False*	*False*	*False*	**False**	*False*	**False**

(Associative Law for *or*)

Table 3.6. $(P \vee Q) \vee R = P \vee (Q \vee R)$.

P	Q	R	P∨Q	(P∨Q)∨R	Q∨R	P∨(Q∨R)
True	*True*	*True*	*True*	**True**	*True*	**True**
True	*True*	*False*	*True*	**True**	*True*	**True**
True	*False*	*True*	*True*	**True**	*True*	**True**
True	*False*	*False*	*True*	**True**	*False*	**True**
False	*True*	*True*	*True*	**True**	*True*	**True**
False	*True*	*False*	*True*	**True**	*True*	**True**
False	*False*	*True*	*False*	**True**	*True*	**True**
False	*False*	*False*	*False*	**False**	*False*	**False**

Answer 3.6

Table 3.7. Distributive law (conjunction over disjunction).

P	Q	R	Q∨R	P∧(Q∨R)	P∧Q	P∧R	(P∧Q)∨(P∧R)
True	*True*	*True*	*True*	**True**	*True*	*True*	**True**
True	*True*	*False*	*True*	**True**	*True*	*False*	**True**
True	*False*	*True*	*True*	**True**	*False*	*True*	**True**
True	*False*	*False*	*False*	**False**	*False*	*False*	**False**
False	*True*	*True*	*True*	**False**	*False*	*False*	**False**
False	*True*	*False*	*True*	**False**	*False*	*False*	**False**
False	*False*	*True*	*True*	**False**	*False*	*False*	**False**
False	*False*	*False*	*False*	**False**	*False*	*False*	**False**

Answer 3.7

$\forall n : numSet \bullet n \leq 50$

Answer 3.8

$\forall i, j : 1..100 \mid i < j \bullet table\ i \leq table\ j$

$\forall i, j : 1..50 \mid i < j \bullet array\ i < array\ j$

Answer 3.9

$\exists n : NumSet \bullet n < 50$

$\neg \exists (m : IntSet \bullet m > 100)$

$\forall i : IntSet \bullet i \leq 100$

$n : \mathbb{N}$
$\exists r : \mathbb{Z} \bullet r^2 = n$

Answer 3.10
One slightly simpler statement is:

$\forall n : \mathbb{N} \mid n > 1 \bullet (\exists p, q : primes \bullet 2*n = p + q)$

However, the reader may find others. Note that simplicity depends upon context; if *even* were the set of positive even integers we might say:

$even \subseteq \{2\} \cup \{p, q : primes \bullet p + q\}$

as a cryptic but admittedly shorter version.

Answer 3.11

Let us label the three parts of the conjunct $C1, C2$ and $C3$, thus:

$C1 = (name \in Known \Rightarrow result = OK)$
$C2 = (name \notin Known \Rightarrow result = unknown)$
$C3 = (name \notin Valid \Rightarrow result = invalid)$

Clearly, either *name ∈ Known* or *name ∉ Known*, so for both *C1* and *C2* to be *True*, either *result = OK* or *result = unknown* must be *True*. Hence *result = invalid* cannot occur. Consider the truth table (Table 3.8).

Table 3.8. Conjunct $C1 \wedge C2 \wedge C3$.

known	valid	result	C1	C2	C3
True	*True*	**OK**	*True*	*True*	*True*
True	*True*	**unknown**	*False*	*True*	*True*
True	*True*	**invalid**	*False*	*True*	*True*
True	*False*	**OK**	*True*	*True*	*False*
True	*False*	**unknown**	*False*	*True*	*False*
True	*False*	**invalid**	*False*	*True*	*True*
False	*True*	**OK**	*True*	*False*	*True*
False	*True*	**unknown**	*True*	*True*	*True*
False	*True*	**invalid**	*True*	*False*	*True*
False	*False*	**OK**	*True*	*False*	*False*
False	*False*	**unknown**	*True*	*True*	*False*
False	*False*	**invalid**	*True*	*False*	*True*

The table shows that only two combinations allow all three conjuncts to be simultaneously *True*:

name ∈ Known ∧ name ∈ Valid ∧ result = OK
name ∉ Known ∧ name ∈ Valid ∧ result = unknown

That is, *result = invalid* cannot occur.

In fact, we could have omitted the second block of values: *name∈Known* and *name∉Valid* cannot occur together because *Known* is a subset of *Valid*.

Notice that the *order* that the implications appear in the predicate does not affect the result. This is another way in which implication differs from **if ... then** in programming languages.

Answer 3.12

We label the three parts of the disjunct $D1, D2$ and $D3$, thus:

$D1 = (name \in Known \wedge result = OK)$
$D2 = (name \notin Known \wedge result = unknown)$
$D3 = (name \notin Valid \wedge result = invalid)$

We consider the truth table again (Table 3.9) but this time we can omit the section where *name* $\in$ *Known* and *name* $\notin$ *Valid* as this cannot occur.

Table 3.9. Disjunct *D1* $\vee$ *D2* $\vee$ *D3*.

known	valid	result	D1	D2	D3
True	*True*	**OK**	*True*	*False*	*False*
True	*True*	**unknown**	*False*	*False*	*False*
True	*True*	**invalid**	*False*	*False*	*False*
False	*True*	**OK**	*False*	*False*	*False*
False	*True*	**unknown**	*False*	*True*	*False*
False	*True*	**invalid**	*False*	*False*	*False*
False	*False*	**OK**	*False*	*False*	*False*
False	*False*	**unknown**	*False*	*True*	*False*
False	*False*	**invalid**	*False*	*False*	*True*

Now there are four combinations that give rise to at least one of the disjuncts being *True*:

name $\in$ *known* $\wedge$ *name* $\in$ *valid* $\wedge$ *result* = *OK*
name $\notin$ *known* $\wedge$ *name* $\in$ *valid* $\wedge$ *result* = *unknown*
name $\notin$ *known* $\wedge$ *name* $\notin$ *valid* $\wedge$ *result* = *unknown*
name $\notin$ *known* $\wedge$ *name* $\notin$ *valid* $\wedge$ *result* = *invalid*

precisely two more than were allowed before, including one with *result* = *invalid*, as we intended. Notice that, if *name* $\notin$ *valid* (and also *name* $\notin$ *known* then of course) either *result* = *unknown* or *result* = *invalid* would satisfy the condition. The value of *result* is not completely determined by the other values and this condition.

Chapter 4
Sets, Tuples and Types

And you'd best be unpacking the things that you need
To rig yourselves out for the fight.

Lewis Carroll, The Hunting of the Snark, Fit the Fourth

In this chapter we explain 'the things we need for the fight', namely sets and tuples and functions that can be applied to them.

Sets and tuples are of fundamental importance, because mathematical structures that we use to model data, namely *relations*, *functions* and *sequences*, are defined as sets of tuples.

A *set* is a homogeneous collection of objects and a *tuple* is an ordered, possibly non-homogeneous collection of objects. In order to explain precisely what we mean by 'homogeneous' we need also to introduce the notion of *type*.

SETS

In naive set theory, a **set** can be a collection of *disparate* objects, such as the names of each member of a football team, and their boots, and the ties of each Tory MP. Any collection of objects can be a set, just so long as we can tell whether an element is, or is not, a member of the set. By contrast, Z is based on **typed set theory** in which a set is a collection of elements *all of the same type*. This corresponds to the way we think about systems, in that the objects we use to model a system tend to fall naturally into collections of like objects.

In Z, a set has the following properties:

- It is completely defined by the values it contains (its *elements*).
- A value is either a member or not (it cannot be twice in nor half in).
- Elements have no intrinsic order in the set.
- Each element is of the same type.

Given sets

A **given set** is a set whose values we do not yet need to discuss. For instance, suppose we are writing a specification for a file management system, and we do not yet know (or care) precisely what form the file names take. We can write the specification in a way that is independent of the format of file names, defining *FILENAME* to be a given set for that specification by enclosing it in **given set brackets** (square brackets) thus:

[*FILENAME*]

This introduces the identifier *FILENAME* as the name of a given set and makes no assumptions about the contents of the set *FILENAME*, though the rest of the specification may impose some, such as

#*FILENAME* < 1000

which says that there are fewer than one thousand elements in the set *FILENAME*.

By using given sets we can concentrate on certain aspects of a specification and defer decisions on other aspects. This is a powerful technique for communicating just those properties that we wish to emphasise and suppressing unnecessary detail. We can introduce several given sets with one definition, for example,

[*USERID, PASSWORD, FILENAME*]

introduces three global variables, *USERID, PASSWORD* and *FILENAME* as given sets for this specification. These three sets are distinct; it is not possible, for instance, for *USERID* and *FILENAME* to have common elements. In fact, this question never arises, for the rules of type (see later) prohibit it. In this book, we will use upper case for given set names.

The set of **integers** $\{..., -2, -1, 0, 1, 2, ...\}$, named $\mathbb{Z}$, is defined as a given set in the *basic library*.

We can construct a set from elements of other sets either by simply listing its members (*set enumeration*) or by describing a typical member (*set comprehension*).

Enumeration

To enumerate a set we simply list the elements, separated by commas, and enclose them in **set brackets**, like this: $\{5, 3, 7, 19, 13\}$. This describes a set with 5 members. If we wish, we could give a name to this set using an *abbreviation*:

someprimes == $\{5, 3, 7, 19, 13\}$

The order in which we list the elements is not significant, so $\{5, 3, 7, 19, 13\}$ and $\{3, 5, 7, 13, 19\}$ and $\{19, 13, 7, 5, 3\}$ are all the same set. Moreover, repeating an element has no effect, so $\{3, 5, 7, 13, 19\}$ and $\{3, 5, 5, 3, 7, 13, 19\}$ and $\{3, 3, 3, 3, 5, 7, 13, 19\}$ are all the same set too.

The expression $\{\ \}$ is an empty or **null set**, for which the symbol $\emptyset$ can also be used.

As a convenient shorthand, the expression *m..n* is the set of integers between *m* and *n* inclusive, called the **number range** from *m* to *n*. So $-2..2$ is the set $\{-2, -1, 0, 1, 2\}$ and *10..15* the set $\{10, 11, 12, 13, 14, 15\}$. If *m*>*n* then *m..n* is defined to be empty.

Comprehension

Usually, we describe a set by stating the properties of its members, for example,

kindergarten $== \{age : \mathbb{N} \mid 3 \le age \le 6\}$

This introduces *kindergarten* as the set $\{3, 4, 5, 6\}$. This way of describing a set is called **set comprehension**.

Exercise 4.1

Describe the set $\{2, 4, 6, 8\}$ using set comprehension.
Write three different expressions for the empty set of integers.

The general form of a set comprehension expression is written:

{declaration-list | constraint • expression}

The declaration-list introduces one or more variables, whose values may be constrained by the constraint, and the expression describes a typical member of the set. For example

sqr $== \{x : \mathbb{N} \mid 6 \le x \le 11 \bullet (x-1)^2\}$

Which could be read as 'take an *x* in $\mathbb{N}$ such that *x* is between *6* and *11* and form the set of values given by $(x-1)^2$'. This defines *sqr* as the set $\{25, 36, 49, 64, 81, 100\}$.

Exercise 4.2

Describe the set $\{2, 4, 6, 8\}$ using the above form of comprehension.
List some members of the set:

pythag_number $== \{a,b,c : \mathbb{N} \mid a^2 + b^2 = c^2 \bullet c\}$

The constraint can be omitted from the general form of set comprehension, giving us the form:

{declaration-list • expression}

For example,

$\{x : \mathbb{N} \bullet x*x\}$

is the set of squares $\{0, 1, 4, 9, ...\}$.

Exercise 4.3

Describe the set $\{2, 4, 6, 8\}$ using this form of comprehension.
List the members of $\{x : \{-1,1\}; \ y : 1..3 \bullet 4*y + x\}$.

Similarly, the expression can be omitted from the general form, giving us:

$\{$declaration-list | constraint$\}$

then the shape of the typical member is determined by the declaration-list. For example, $\{x : \mathbb{N} \mid x < 7\}$ is another way to denote the set $0..6$, and

$\{n : \mathbb{N} \mid (\exists\, m : \mathbb{N} \mid 2*m = n)\}$

is the set of even natural numbers.

The *kindergarten* example is of this form. (We will see more interesting examples when we have dealt with *tuples* later in this chapter.)

The variables introduced in the declaration part of a set comprehension expression are *bound variables* whose scope is the set comprehension expression and the constraint. For instance, in the *kindergarten* example, the variable *age* is a bound variable known only in the phrase $3 \le age \le 6$.

Data-types

When we introduce a given set, we know nothing about the values in the set. Sometimes, though, we want to introduce a set of specific values. For example, we might want to introduce a collection of values called *AddOK*, *InvalidName* and *InvalidAccount*, distinct from all other values. We can do this by using a ***data-type*** definition which introduces a given set, its members and some constraints on these members. In this case

Result $::=$ *AddOK | InvalidName | InvalidAccount*

which says that the given set called *Result* consists of just three values with those names and that the three values are distinct. The symbol | is called a ***branch separator*** (it is the same symbol as the constraint bar, but the context always determines which is meant).

A data-type definition can be regarded as a convenient shorthand; it adds no new capability to the notation. The above definition is pre-cisely equivalent to

[*Result*]

$AddOK, InvalidName, InvalidAccount : Result$

$AddOK \neq InvalidName \neq InvalidAccount \neq AddOK$
$Result = \{AddOK, InvalidName, InvalidAccount\}$

Each variable introduced by a data-type definition has global scope. So, in the example above, *Result*, *AddOK*, *InvalidName* and *InvalidAccount* are all global variables. (A more general form of data-type definition using *constructor functions* will be explained in Chapter 8.)

Notice that, although the data-type definition is equivalent to intro-ducing a *given set*, we do not use our convention of uppercase letters for it. Instead, we will adopt the convention that the data-type name *starts* with an uppercase letter.

Sets in declarations

When we declare a variable we must identify to which set its value belongs. For example,

$tablesize : \mathbb{N}$

introduces *tablesize* as a member of the set of natural numbers (we can read this as '*tablesize* is a member of $\mathbb{N}$' or simply '*tablesize* is a natural number'). The set $\mathbb{N}$ happens to be one of those built-in to Z (it is defined in the basic library).

We can equally well declare a variable as a member of some set that we have introduced beforehand:

$sqr == \{x : \mathbb{Z} \mid 5 \leq x \leq 10 \bullet x^2\}$
$s1, s2 : sqr$

introduces *s1* and *s2* as members of $\{25,36,49,64,81,100\}$.

Sets of characters and strings

You may be wondering whether a set of *characters* is defined in the Z basic library. It is not. When we need characters, we could introduce a data-type like this:

$CHAR ::= a \mid b \mid c \mid d \mid ...$

but this is irksome (so tedious, in fact, that we didn't finish writing it out). In the examples in this book, we will often introduce *CHAR* as a given set of characters without enumerating its members. We will also extend the notation so that *'a'*, and *'b'*, and so on, denote individual characters. We regard a *string* as a *sequence* of characters (sequences will be explained in Chapter 5), and we will extend the notation to denote string constants by enclosing the characters in double quotes like this: *"string"*. Actually, string constants rarely occur in specifications; they tend to be used only in supporting material (examples or illustrations, for instance).

If a specification actually *is* concerned with the contents of a character set, we recommend that you do *not* use these makeshift extensions; it would be better to define the contents precisely.

TUPLES

A **tuple** is an *ordered collection* of two or more elements which are not necessarily of the same type. To enumerate a tuple we simply list the elements, separated by commas, and enclose them in **tuple brackets** (ordinary parentheses), like this: (*'Smith', 12345, '5 Acacia Drive'*).

We can construct a tuple from variables, for example (*customer, accno, addr*) is a 3-tuple, or 'triple'. Notice that this is different from the triple (*accno, customer, addr*), because *order* is significant. Also, repetition is significant, thus (*1,3*) and (*1, 3, 3*) are different tuples. A tuple that contains just two elements, such as (*'Smith', 12345*), is called an **ordered pair**.

Sets of tuples

We can introduce a set whose members are tuples all of the same type. For example,

{(*"Smith", 478921, 120*), (*"Brown", 092387, 151*), (*"Jones", 563481, 207*)}

is a set of triples. Each element might represent an employee name, his works number and weekly salary.

The example below shows a set of *ordered pairs*

$\{a : 1..3;\ b : 4..6 \mid a + b < 8 \bullet (a,b)\}$

namely the set $\{(1, 4), (1, 5), (1, 6), (2, 4), (2, 5), (3, 4)\}$.

We will see in Chapter 5 that sets of ordered pairs form the basis for the mathematical structures that we use to model many systems.

┌─ **Exercise 4.4** ──┐
│ Write a set comprehension expression for the set of all ordered pairs of │
│ integers where the first integer in each pair is greater than the second. │
└──┘

Because ordered pairs are the most common form of tuple, two functions are provided that allow us to refer to the two elements of a pair:

- first refers to the first element of a pair.
- second refers to the second element of a pair.

For instance, first(*17*,*24*) is *17*.

Characteristic tuple

We may recall that the expression can be omitted from the general
form of set comprehension, giving us:

{declaration | constraint}

where the typical member is determined by the declaration.   This
extends to sets of tuples. For instance, the previous example could be
written

$\{a : 1..3;\ b : 4..6 \mid a + b < 8\}$

In this case, the typical member defined by the set comprehension is
determined by the ***characteristic tuple*** of the declaration. This consists of the variables in the order they appear in the declaration. So
in the example above, the characteristic tuple is (*a*,*b*). We will meet
characteristic tuples again in Chapter 6. Suppose we want to represent
the coordinates in the first quadrant of a plane (Figure 4.1).

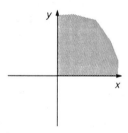

Fig 4.1. First quadrant.

We might write

$pts1q == \{x, y : \mathbb{N}\}$

where we rely on the characteristic tuple to determine the shape of the elements. This could equally well be written

$pts1q == \{x, y : \mathbb{N} \bullet (x,y)\}$

and we prefer this second form as we feel its meaning is clearer to the reader.

> **Exercise 4.5**
>
> Describe a set that could represent all the points in the first quadrant between the line $x=y$ and the x-axis.

OPERATIONS ON SETS

There are various operations that apply to sets:

- Membership.
- Equality.
- Subset.
- Power set.
- Cardinality (size).
- Cartesian product.
- Union.
- Intersection.
- Difference.
- Distributed union.
- Distributed intersection.

Membership

The predicate $x \in S$ ('x is a member of S') is *True* if x is a member of set S and is *False* if x is not a member of set S.

The predicate $x \notin S$ ('x is not a member of S') is *True* if x is not a member of set S and is *False* if x is a member of set S.

Equality

A set is completely determined by its members. Thus two sets are **equal** if and only if they contain the same members.

The predicate $A=B$ ('A equals B') is *True* if sets A and B are equal and *False* if they are not.

The predicate $A \neq B$ ('A is not equal to B') is *False* if sets A and B are equal and *True* if they are not.

For either of these predicates to make sense, A and B must be of the same type. Thus, although intuitively appealing, $CHAR \neq \mathbb{N}$ is not *True* in Z. Neither is it *False*: it is simply not possible to compare these two things.

(Note, in Z, the relations <, ≤, > and ≥ are not defined for sets, but see below.)

Subset

A *subset* of a set S is any set of elements each of which is a member of S. For example, if *evens* is $\{2, 4, 6\}$ then $\{2,4\}$ is a subset of *evens*.

The predicate $A \subseteq B$ ('A is a subset of B') is *True* if A is a subset of B and *False* if it is not.

Exercise 4.6

Write a predicate that is equivalent to the predicate $A \subseteq B$ (hint: use ∀).

Proper Subset

From the answer to Exercise 4.6, we can see that any set is a subset of itself. A *proper subset* of a set is any subset *except* the whole set itself.

The predicate $A \subset B$ ('A is a proper subset of B') is *True* if A is a proper subset of B and *False* if it is not.

Exercise 4.7

Write a predicate using ∀ and ∃ that is equivalent to the predicate $A \subset B$.

Write a predicate not using ∀ or ∃ that is equivalent to the predicate $A \subset B$.

If A is a subset of B and B is a subset of A, then sets A and B are equal:

$$(A \subseteq B) \wedge (B \subseteq A) \Leftrightarrow (A = B)$$

Exercise 4.8

State whether each of the following predicates is *True* or *False*.

$7 \in \mathbb{Z}$	$\mathbb{N} \subset \mathbb{Z}$	$\{\} \subset \{1\}$
$-2 \notin \mathbb{N}$	$\mathbb{N} \subset \mathbb{N}$	$\{\} \subset \mathbb{N}$
$\mathbb{N} \subseteq \mathbb{Z}$	$0 \in \{\}$	$\mathbb{N} \in \mathbb{Z}$

List *all* the subsets of the set $\{2, 4, 6\}$.

How many subsets are there of the set *1..10*?

Power set

The ***power set*** of a set S is the *set of all subsets* of S. It is written
$\mathbb{P}S$.

The power set of a finite set with n members contains 2^n (two 'to the
power of' n) elements, which is where the name 'power set' comes
from. This includes the set itself and the empty set.

When we wish to introduce a variable that is a *set* of elements, we
often use power set. For instance,

accnos : $\mathbb{P}\mathbb{N}$

which we read as '*accnos* is a set of natural numbers'. Similarly, if
FILENAME is a given set, then

fnset : $\mathbb{P}$*FILENAME*

declares *fnset* as a set of *FILENAME*.

Usually, the operator $\mathbb{P}$ conveys our intent well enough. However,
there are three further power set operators we can use:

$\mathbb{P}_1 S$ is the set of all subsets of S excluding {}.

$\mathbb{F}S$ is the set of all ***finite subsets*** of S.

$\mathbb{F}_1 S$ is the set of all finite subsets of S excluding {}.

Cardinality

The number of members in a finite set, S, is called the ***cardinality*** of
the set and is written #S. For example, if S is the set {3, 5, 7}, the
value of #S is 3. The cardinality of an infinite set (for instance, $\mathbb{N}$) is
not defined (in Z).

Cartesian product

If we write an expression such as

{*p* : *PERSON*; *s* : *SALARY* • (*p*, *s*)}

we have described a set of pairs each of the form (*p*, *s*) where *p* is a
PERSON and *s* is a *SALARY*. This set is called the ***cartesian product***
of the sets *PERSON* and *SALARY*. It is written *PERSON*×*SALARY* and
is sometimes called a 'cross product'.

For example, if

men == {*Joe, Bill, Fred*}
women == {*Mary, Sue*}

then *men×women* is the set of all possible mixed couples, namely

{(*Joe,Mary*), (*Joe,Sue*), (*Bill,Mary*), (*Bill,Sue*), (*Fred,Mary*), (*Fred,Sue*)}

Cartesian product can be applied to any number of sets, for instance, *A×B×C* is the set of all triples of the form (*a,b,c*) and so on. It is *not* commutative, that is, in general *A×B* ≠ *B×A*. Nor is it associative, that is, in general

(*A×B*) × *C* ≠ *A* × (*B×C*)

Although (*A×B*)×*C*, *A×*(*B×C*) and *A×B×C* each have the same number of elements, the structure of the elements is different, that is, they are all of different types.

Exercise 4.9

Given

    retcode1 ::= *a* | *b* | *c*
    retcode2 ::= *ok* | *fail*

list the elements of *retcode1×retcode2*.

Union

The **union** of two sets, *A* and *B*, is written *A∪B*. It is the set of elements that are members of *A*, or members of *B*, or both. For this to make sense, the elements of *A* and *B* must be of the same type, which, in this definition, we shall denote by *T*.

$A \cup B = \{x : T \mid x \in A \;\lor\; x \in B\}$

Set union is illustrated in Figure 4.2.

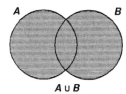

A∪B

Fig 4.2. Set union.

Note that set union is commutative, that is:

$A \cup B = B \cup A$

and associative, that is:

$A \cup (B \cup C) = (A \cup B) \cup C$

so we may write $A \cup B \cup C$ without ambiguity.

Intersection

The ***intersection*** of two sets, A and B, is written $A \cap B$. It is the set of elements that are members of both A and B. For this to make sense, the elements of A and B must be of the same type, which we shall denote by T.

$A \cap B = \{x : T \mid x \in A \wedge x \in B\}$

Set intersection is illustrated in Figure 4.3.

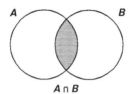

$A \cap B$

Fig 4.3. Set intersection.

Note that set intersection is commutative, that is:

$A \cap B = B \cap A$

and associative, that is:

$A \cap (B \cap C) = (A \cap B) \cap C$

so we may write $A \cap B \cap C$ without ambiguity.

Difference

The ***difference*** of two sets, A and B, is written $A \backslash B$. It is the set of elements that are members of A and *not* members of B. For this to make sense, the elements of A and B must be of the same type, which we shall denote by T.

$A \backslash B = \{x : T \mid x \in A \wedge x \notin B\}$

Set difference is illustrated in Figure 4.4.
Note that, in general, set difference is *not* commutative, that is,

$A \backslash B \neq B \backslash A$

Exercise 4.10

Using set difference, write simple expressions for $\mathbb{P}_1 S$ and $\mathbb{F}_1 S$.

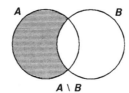

Fig 4.4. Set difference.

Distributed union

The **distributed union** of a set of sets S is written $\bigcup S$ (Figure 4.5). It is the set of elements that are members of any of the sets in S.

Fig 4.5. Distributed union.

For example, if S is $\{\{1,\ 2,\ 3,\ 4\},\ \{2,\ 3,\ 4,\ 5\},\ \{3,\ 4,\ 5,\ 6\}\}$ then $\bigcup S$ is $\{1,2,3,4,5,6\}$. This operation is often called *generalized union*.

We sometimes want to describe a data collection that is a set of sets. For example, suppose we have introduced the given set *TEAM*, and a *division* as a set of teams:

[*TEAM*]
division $==$ $\mathbb{P}\,TEAM$

We could now declare three variables:

div1, div2, div3 : *division*

then we might introduce the *league* as a set of divisions, thus:

> *league* : $\mathbb{P}$*division*
>
> *league* $=$ {*div1, div2, div3*}

Exercise 4.11

With *league* defined as above, what does $\bigcup league$ represent?

If S is a set of sets of elements from T, that is $S : \mathbb{P}(\mathbb{P}T)$, write a formal definition of $\bigcup S$.

Distributed intersection

The ***distributed intersection*** of a set of sets S is written $\bigcap S$ (Fig 4.6). It is the set of elements that are members of all the sets in S.

Fig 4.6. Distributed intersection.

For example, if S is $\{\{1, 2, 3, 4\}, \{2, 3, 4, 5\}, \{3, 4, 5, 6\}\}$ then $\bigcap S$ is $\{3, 4\}$.

Exercise 4.12 ────────────────────────────────────

With *league* defined as before, what does $\bigcap league$ represent? What might we say about it?

If S is a set of sets of elements from T, that is $S : \mathbb{P}(\mathbb{P}T)$, write a formal definition of $\bigcap S$.

This operation is often called *generalized intersection*.

TYPES

This section describes what a type is. By use of the notion of type, Z can distinguish between well-formed and badly-formed expressions and can also simplify the use of generally defined functions.

Basic types

When we introduce a *given set*, we introduce a new ***basic type*** into the document. A given set represents a homogenous collection of objects, and this collection is quite distinct from any other. Usually we choose names that make this obvious, such as

$[NAME, ACCNUM]$

Then, if we declare

$nm : NAME; \; act : ACCNUM$

we should expect nm and act to be completely different *types* of object. This is why in Z each given set is a distinct type.

Compound types

Starting from such given sets, let us consider how we can form more:

> We can form *subsets*, by enumeration or comprehension.
> We can form the *cartesian product* of two sets.
> We can form the *power set* of a set.

A subset forms no new type, it simply collects together elements from another set.

Cartesian product and power set each form a new type of object. For example, the tuple *(25,42)*, which is a member of $\mathbb{Z} \times \mathbb{Z}$, and the set *{25,42}*, which is a member of $\mathbb{P}\mathbb{Z}$, are different types of object from the number *17*, which is a member of $\mathbb{Z}$.

A type which is formed by cartesian product or power set is called a **compound type**.

We can apply the power set and cartesian product operators as often as we wish. For example, the type of *league*, which we declared as a set of sets (see page 48), is $\mathbb{P}(\mathbb{P}\textit{TEAM})$.

By starting with the basic types of a specification and using power set and cartesian product, we generate nearly all the types of that specification. In fact, the only other types come from *schemas* and we will see how schemas are used as types in Chapter 6.

Types as maximal sets

Any value is a member of a set. The largest set, in Z, which contains this value is the **type** of that value, so the type of a value always contains the value as an element, and each type is a **maximal set**. Another way to say this is that no proper subset of a type is a type (there is no notion of sub-type). For example, if we introduce the basic types:

> *[MAN, WOMAN]*

we are saying that we will treat men and women as different types of thing. So if we declare:

> *m : MAN*
> *w : WOMAN*

then we cannot write a predicate such as *m≠w*: it would be meaningless since *m* and *w* are of different types. Neither can there be a type, larger than both *MAN* and *WOMAN*, which contains them both. If we wish to make such comparisons, then we must introduce sets *man* and *woman* as subsets of *the same* type. For instance:

[PERSON]
man : ℙPERSON
woman : ℙPERSON
m : man
w : woman

Now we *can* write a predicate such as $m \neq w$ since they are of the same type. Here also, *man* and *woman* are of the same type. Assuming that *man* is a *proper* subset of *PERSON*, it is not a type, even though we declared *m* using it.

Exercise 4.13

With the above definitions of *man*, *woman* and *PERSON*, write a predicate that states that a *PERSON* is either a *man* or a *woman* and that men and women are different.

In the basic library, the set of *integers*, $\mathbb{Z}$, is introduced as a given set and the set of **natural numbers**, $\mathbb{N}$, and the set of **positive natural numbers**, $\mathbb{N}_1$, are defined as subsets of $\mathbb{Z}$, thus:

[$\mathbb{Z}$]

$\mathbb{N} : \mathbb{P}\mathbb{Z}$
$\mathbb{N}_1 : \mathbb{P}\mathbb{Z}$

$\mathbb{N} = \{n : \mathbb{Z} \mid n \geq 0\}$
$\mathbb{N}_1 = \{n : \mathbb{Z} \mid n > 0\}$

That is, $\mathbb{Z}$ is a type but $\mathbb{N}$ is *not* a type.

Underlying type

Each member of a set has the same type. We have mentioned this idea already, but with only an intuitive understanding of 'type'. Now we can see what it implies. For example, with

[CUSTOMER, ACCOUNT]
cust1, cust2 : CUSTOMER
acc1, acc2 : ACCOUNT

{*cust1,cust2*} is a set but the expression {*cust1,acc1*} is not meaningful because *cust1* and *acc1* are of different types.

We will call the common type of all the members of a set the **under-**

lying type of that set. For example, the underlying type of

someprimes == {5, 3, 7, 19, 13}

is $\mathbb{Z}$, and the underlying type of

somesets == {{2}, {3, 5}, {3, 5, 7}, $\mathbb{N}$}

is $\mathbb{P}\mathbb{Z}$.

Types in declarations

When we declare a variable such as

n : someprimes

it is easy (but wrong) to think of *someprimes* as the 'type' of *n* (as in Pascal). The type of *n* is the *underlying type* of *someprimes*, namely $\mathbb{Z}$. Less obvious, perhaps, is that the type of $x{:}\mathbb{N}$ is also $\mathbb{Z}$ (because $\mathbb{N}$ is a subset of $\mathbb{Z}$), which is why we can write expressions containing naturals and integers, such as $\{x, -2\}$.

Exercise 4.14

With a given set *MYSET*, what is the type of each of the variables *a* to *f* declared below?

$a : \mathbb{N}$	$d : c$
$b : \mathbb{P}a$	$e : \mathbb{P}MYSET$
$c : MYSET$	$f : e$

We cannot assume the type of a variable from its use. In particular, we cannot introduce a quantified variable without providing an explicit declaration. For example, it might seem reasonable to say that no value in *miniset* exceeds *1000* like this:

$\forall x \in miniset \bullet x < 1000$

However, this is syntactically wrong. We must *declare* x, for instance:

$\forall x : \mathbb{N} \mid x \in miniset \bullet x < 1000$

or

$\forall x : miniset \bullet x < 1000$

The type of a set

The type of a set is the power set of the type of its members. For example, the type of the set *someprimes* is $\mathbb{P}\mathbb{Z}$. (Contrast this with the *underlying type* of the set.)

The type of a tuple

The type of a tuple is the cartesian product of the types of its elements. For instance, with

$p : PERSON$
$s : SALARY$

the tuple (p, s) has type $PERSON \times SALARY$.

Exercise 4.15

With

[CHAR] $c : CHAR$
$code ::= c4 \mid c8 \mid c12$ $r : code$
$n : \mathbb{N}$

what is the type of each of the five following terms?

(n, c) $(n, (c, r))$
(c, r) $\{(n, c)\}$
(n, c, r)

The type of an expression

It must be possible to determine to which basic type or compound type a value belongs. Hence any expression that denotes a value must be unambiguously typed. Also, the expressions that appear in a predicate must have appropriate types. For instance, in the predicate $x \in y$, the type of y must be the power set of the type of x. Thus, if

$x, y : \mathbb{N}$

the predicate $x \in y$ is meaningless, as y is not even a set.

SUMMARY

Every value in Z belongs to some type set.

Beginning with *given sets*, which form the *basic types*, new *compound types* are formed from the *power set* and *cartesian product* operations. All sets are subsets of some type, and all tuples are elements of some cartesian product type. Apart from schema types (to be introduced in Chapter 6) all types and all values are formed in this way.

The type of the value of each variable is the *underlying type* of the set used in its declaration.

Every expression must be unambiguously typed, and the types in a predicate must agree appropriately.

Exercise 4.16

Given the following data-types:

  $add\_code ::= added\_ok \mid duplicate\_name \mid file\_full$
  $srch\_code ::= name\_found \mid not\_found \mid file\_empty$

which of the following are meaningful expressions or predicates?

  $\{added\_ok, file\_full\}$
  $\{added\_ok, file\_empty\}$
  $\{add\_code\}$
  $add\_code \neq srch\_code$
  $added\_ok \neq duplicate\_name$
  $\exists\, ac : add\_code \bullet ac = added\_ok$
  $\exists_1 sc : srch\_code \bullet sc \neq name\_found$
  $\forall\, ac : add\_code \bullet ac \neq name\_found$

ANSWERS TO EXERCISES

Answer 4.1

  $\{2, 4, 6, 8\} = \{n : \mathbb{N} \mid 1 < n < 9 \wedge (\exists\, m : \mathbb{N} \bullet n = 2*m)\}$

Some possible ways of describing the empty set of integers are:

  $\{i : \mathbb{Z} \mid i \neq i\}$
  $\{n : \mathbb{N} \mid n = n + 1\}$
  $7..5$

Beware, $\{\ \}$ does not denote an empty set of *integers* without some way of deducing its type.

Answer 4.2

  $\{2, 4, 6, 8\} = \{n : \mathbb{N} \mid 1 \leq n \leq 4 \bullet 2*n\}$

Some elements of *pythag_number* are:

  $5\ \ (25 = 9 + 16)$
  $13\ \ (169 = 25 + 144)$
  $17\ \ (289 = 225 + 64)$

Answer 4.3

$\{2, 4, 6, 8\} = \{n : 1..4 \bullet 2*n\}$

$\{x : \{-1..1\}; \ y : 1..3 \bullet 4*y + x\} = \{3, 5, 7, 9, 11, 13\}$

Answer 4.4

$\{a, b : \mathbb{Z} \mid a > b \bullet (a, b)\}$

This is the 'greater than' relation itself (see Chapter 5).

Answer 4.5

The set of points between $x=y$ and the x-axis could be represented by:

$pts == \{x, y : \mathbb{N} \mid x \geq y \bullet (x,y)\}$

Answer 4.6

$A \subseteq B \Leftrightarrow \forall a : A \bullet a \in B$

'for all a in A it is the case that a is a member of B'.

Answer 4.7

$A \subset B \Leftrightarrow (\forall a : A \bullet a \in B) \wedge (\exists b : B \mid b \notin A)$.

'for all a in A it is the case that a is a member of B' and 'there exists a b in B such that b is not a member of A'.

$A \subset B \Leftrightarrow A \subseteq B \wedge A \neq B$

Answer 4.8

$7 \in \mathbb{Z}$	is *True*
$-2 \notin \mathbb{N}$	is *True*
$\mathbb{N} \subseteq \mathbb{Z}$	is *True*
$\mathbb{N} \subset \mathbb{Z}$	is *True*
$\mathbb{N} \subset \mathbb{N}$	is *False*
$0 \in \{\}$	is *False*
$\{\} \subset \{1\}$	is *True*
$\{\} \subset \mathbb{N}$	is *True*
$\mathbb{N} \in \mathbb{Z}$	is meaningless, because the only way the types would be correct would be if $\mathbb{Z}$ were a set of objects of the type of $\mathbb{N}$.

Subsets of $\{2,4,6\}$ are

$\{\}$,
$\{2\}, \{4\}, \{6\}$,
$\{2, 4\}, \{2, 6\}, \{4, 6\}$,
$\{2, 4, 6\}$

There are 1024 subsets of $1..10$ (that is, 2 to the power 10).

Answer 4.9

retcode1×retcode2 contains 6 elements, namely:

(a, ok), (b, ok), (c, ok),
$(a, fail)$, $(b, fail)$, $(c, fail)$

Answer 4.10

$\mathbb{P}_1 S = \mathbb{P}S \setminus \{ \emptyset \}$
$\mathbb{F}_1 S = \mathbb{F}S \setminus \{ \emptyset \}$

Answer 4.11

$\bigcup league$ represents the set of all teams in the league.
    Given $S : \mathbb{P}(\mathbb{P}T)$, then

$$\bigcup S = \{x : T \mid (\exists p : S \bullet x \in p)\}$$

Answer 4.12

$\bigcap league$ represents the set of all the teams that are in every division. Usually the rules say that no team can be in more than one division, so certainly no team can be in all divisions (we are assuming here that there is more than one division in the *league*), so we might say:

$$\bigcap league = \emptyset$$

Given $S : \mathbb{P}(\mathbb{P}T)$, then

$$\bigcap S = \{x : T \mid (\forall p : S \bullet x \in p)\}$$

Answer 4.13

$(PERSON = man \cup woman) \wedge (man \cap woman = \{\})$

Answer 4.14

a   is of type $\mathbb{Z}$
b   is of type $\mathbb{P}\mathbb{Z}$
c   is of type *MYSET*
d   is meaningless
e   is of type $\mathbb{P}MYSET$
f   is of type *MYSET*

Answer 4.15

(n, c) is of type $\mathbb{Z}×CHAR$.
(c, r) is of type $CHAR×code$.
(n, c, r) is of type $\mathbb{Z}×CHAR×code$.
$(n, (c, r))$ is of type $\mathbb{Z}×(CHAR×code)$.
$\{(n, c)\}$ is of type $\mathbb{P}(\mathbb{Z}×CHAR)$.

Answer 4.16

{*added_ok, file_full*}	is meaningful.
{*added_ok, file_empty*}	is nonsense.
{*add_code*}	is meaningful.
add_code ≠ srch_code	is nonsense.
added_ok ≠ duplicate_name	is meaningful (and *True*).
∃ *ac : add_code • ac = added_ok*	is meaningful (and *True*).
∃₁ *sc : srch_code • sc ≠ name_found*	is meaningful (and *False*).
∀ *ac : add_code • ac ≠ name_found*	is nonsense.

SPECIFICATION PROBLEMS

4.1 CENTRAL HEATING STATE DESCRIPTION

A central heating system contains a *control box*, a *room thermostat* and a *pump*. The control box has a *switch* and a *timer*. The switch allows the mode of operation to be selected. It has four positions:

* off
* continuous (always 'on')
* once (see below)
* twice (see below)

The timer provides four time settings, which we call *t1*, *t2*, *t3* and *t4*. If the switch is set to once or to twice, then the timer controls the system as follows:

switch = once   On at *t1* and off at *t4*.
switch = twice   On at *t1* and off at *t2*, then on at *t3* and off at *t4*.

Each time interval must be at least 10 minutes.
Declare variables that characterize this system and write predicates that define the possible states.

4.2 CENTRAL HEATING STATE EXTENDED

Extend the answer to problem 4.1 to include the following controls:

* A *boiler thermostat* that causes the boiler to fire when the water flowing through it drops below the set temperature.
* A *two-way valve*, allowing water to flow to heat the hot water tank, the central heating or both or neither.
* A *tank thermostat* (see below).

The valve is controlled by the room thermostat and the tank thermostat. When the room thermostat cuts in, the valve will open to allow flow to the central heating system. When the tank thermostat cuts in, the valve will open to allow flow to the hot water system.

Chapter 5
Data Models

'When I make a word do a lot of work like that,' said Humpty Dumpty, 'I always pay it extra.'
Lewis Carroll, Through the Looking Glass.

We have seen how to model collections of data using *sets* and *tuples*. In this chapter we look at how we can express *relationships* between such collections. In the real world we often meet tables and lists of objects. Programming languages model these with arrays, stacks, queues and the like. In Z, the mathematical abstraction we use to model such objects is the *relation*. The relation does 'a lot of work like that'.

As we shall see, a relation is simply a set of ordered pairs. Furthermore, we can use relations to define *functions*, which in turn can be used to define *sequences*. Relations, functions and sequences are powerful aids to data abstraction and it is interesting to note that they rest on an essentially simple base: namely, sets and tuples.

RELATIONS

A *relation* is a correspondence between the elements of two sets: the *from-set* and the *to-set*.

For instance, the relation *SquareOf* is a correspondence between integers ($\mathbb{Z}$) and natural numbers ($\mathbb{N}$). To declare a relation, we use a double-headed arrow:

SquareOf : $\mathbb{Z} \leftrightarrow \mathbb{N}$

Each member of a relation is an ordered pair of elements where the first element of the pair is a member of the from-set and the second element of the pair is a member of the to-set. Thus the relation itself is actually a *set*: namely a set of *ordered pairs*. So $(5,25)$, $(-3,9)$ and $(2,4)$ are all members of *SquareOf*.

In fact, $A \leftrightarrow B$ is merely a shorthand for $\mathbb{P}(A \times B)$, that is, the set of subsets of $A \times B$, and *SquareOf* was declared above simply as a subset of $\mathbb{Z} \times \mathbb{N}$. Usually we describe properties of the relation by specifying constraints that its members must satisfy. For example, the members (i, n) of the *SquareOf* relation must satisfy the constraint $i^2 = n$.

Maplet notation

Because a relation is a set of ordered pairs, we can refer to one of its members using the normal tuple notation, such as (5, 25). However, this notation is often cumbersome and when there is a natural 'direction' to the relation we use the **maplet** notation $a \mapsto b$. Thus, for example, we could say that $5 \mapsto 25$, $-3 \mapsto 9$ and $2 \mapsto 4$ are members of the relation *SquareOf*. $a \mapsto b$ means exactly the same as (a,b).

Examples

Many data collections can be modelled as relations. For example:

'Is an anagram of' is a correspondence between *words*.
'Is greater than' is a correspondence between *numbers*.
'Has a road to' is a correspondence between *towns*.

In these examples, the from-set and to-set are the same. This need not be the case:

'Is phone number of' is a correspondence between *phone numbers* and *names*.
'Is studying' is a correspondence between *students* and *subjects*.
'Is author of' is a correspondence between *writers* and *books*.

Given a particular relation, we can draw a diagram showing the correspondence. For instance, consider the map in Figure 5.1.

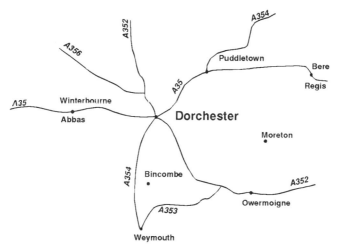

Fig 5.1. Map of (part of) Dorset.

The *Aroad* relation could be used to record the towns in the map that are connected by 'A' roads.

   Aroad : TOWN ⟷ TOWN

The relation is illustrated in Figure 5.2.

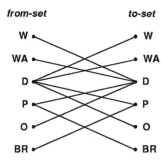

Fig 5.2. The *Aroad* relation.

The same information can be presented in a table, as in Table 5.1 (here we have also indicated *which* A roads are involved).

Table 5.1. The *Aroad* table.

	WA	*D*	*W*	*P*	*B*	*BR*	*O*	*M*
WA	.	A35	.	.	.	.	.	.
D	A35	.	A354	A35	.	.	A352	.
W	.	A354	.	.	.	.	.	.
P	.	A35	.	.	.	A35	.	.
B	.	.	.	.	.	.	.	.
BR	.	.	.	A35	.	.	.	.
O	.	A352	.	.	.	.	.	.
M	.	.	.	.	.	.	.	.

The *Aroad* relation exhibits many of the characteristics of a general relation:

- One element of the from-set may correspond to several elements of the to-set.
- One element of the to-set may correspond to several elements of the from-set.
- There may be members of the from-set that do not correspond to any member of the to-set.
- There may be members of the to-set that do not correspond to any member of the from-set.

Exercise 5.1

Draw a diagram to illustrate the relation *IsOn* : *TOWN↔ROAD* where

$TOWN = \{WA, D, W, M, P, BR, O\}$
$ROAD = \{A35, A354, A352\}$

as in the map above.

We could describe a small relation by enumerating all the pairs in the set.

Exercise 5.2

Given the following definitions:

writer ::= *Dickens* | *Lee* | *Grahame*
book ::=
  A_Tale_of_Two_Cities | *The_Wind_in_the_Willows* | *To_Kill_a_Mockingbird*

declare an *author* relation. Describe it by enumerating its members.

Exercise 5.3

Students can select any program of study from the following subjects: Maths, History, English, Art, Science and Geography. We are interested in only three students: Bill, Mary and Sue. Bill has selected History, Art and Science. Mary has selected Maths, History and Science. Sue has selected Maths, History, English and Science.

Express these facts by defining suitable sets and a relation *studies* that shows who is studying what. Draw a diagram to illustrate this relation.

Exercise 5.4

Using the answer to the last exercise, write a predicate that restricts each student to just three subjects.

Large relations

When a relation is a large or infinite set of pairs, it is more practical to describe it axiomatically. For instance, to describe a relation *GreaterThan* over the natural numbers, we could write:

$GreaterThan : \mathbb{N} \leftrightarrow \mathbb{N}$

$\forall a, b : \mathbb{N} \bullet (a, b) \in GreaterThan \Leftrightarrow a > b$

which describes *GreaterThan* as the set of all natural number pairs for which the first element is strictly greater than the second.

> **Exercise 5.5**
> Describe a relation *RootOf* which relates numbers to their square roots.

Infix notation

Often it is more natural to use the **_infix_** notation for relations, in which the relation name appears between the elements it relates. Relations that can be written in this way are declared with a specially formed name using the underscore symbol, for example,

   IsStudying : student ⟷ ℙsubject

allows us to write

   Bill IsStudying {History, Art, Science}

as an exact equivalent of

   *(Bill, {History, Art, Science}) ∈ _IsStudying_*

The built-in comparison operators, such as **<, >** and **≠**, are really the short names for infix relations, thus *x>y* is simply an abbreviation for *(x,y) ∈ _>_.*

The name *_IsStudying_* does not start with a letter, but with an underscore. This is an exception to the identifier rules that normally apply (see Appendix A for a summary) and is designed specifically to allow infix notations. We shall see later that this notation also applies to functions such as *_+_*, allowing us to write *a+b*.

The domain of a relation

The **_domain_** of a relation *R* is written **dom R**. It is the set of all the elements of the from-set of *R* that have corresponding members in the to-set. For example, the domain of *studies* (or of *_IsStudying_*) is *{Bill, Mary, Sue}*.

We can define the domain of *R : X⟷Y* thus:

   dom $R = \{x : X;\ y : Y \mid (x, y) \in R \bullet x\}$

which can be read: 'take an *x* in *X* and a *y* in *Y* such that *(x, y)* is in *R* and form the set of *x*'s'.

> **Exercise 5.6**
> Define the domain of a relation *R* even more succinctly with a set comprehension that looks like $\{p : R \bullet\ ...\ \}$. (Hint: see page 42.)

The range of a relation

The **range** of a relation *R* is written ran *R*. It is the set of all the elements of the to-set of *R* that have corresponding members in the from-set. For example, the range of *studies* is

{*Maths, History, English, Art, Science*}

Notice that *Geography* is *not* in the range.

Exercise 5.7

Write a definition of ran *R*.

Set operators

Because a relation is a set, we can use the set operators (union, intersection and difference) on relations. In particular, to add a new element pair to a relation, we can use the union operator. For example

studies : *student* ⟷ *subject*
name : *student*
sub : *subject*
newstudies : *student* ⟷ *subject*
newstudies = *studies* ∪ {(*name, sub*)}

The predicate states that *newstudies* is *studies* with the addition of one more pair (of course if (*name, sub*) is already in *studies* then *newstudies* is the same as *studies*).

As well as the normal set operators, there are a number that depend on the fact that a relation is a set of ordered pairs. These will be explained in Chapter 8.

The type of a relation

If *R* is a relation from set *A* to set *B*, then the members of *R* are ordered pairs of the form (*a, b*), where *a* is a member of *A* and *b* is a member of *B*. Thus, if the underlying type of set *A* is T_A and the underlying type of set *B* is T_B, then the type of an element of *R* is $T_A \times T_B$. Therefore, as *R* is a set of such elements, the type of *R* is $\mathbb{P}(T_A \times T_B)$.

FUNCTIONS

A ***function*** is a relation in which each member of the from-set corresponds to *at most one* member of the to-set. Thus, given a member of the domain, we can determine the single member of the range to which it is related. The *SquareOf* relation described earlier is actually a *function* because, given any integer, *i*, there is just *one* natural number, *n*, to which it corresponds (namely $n = i^2$). In contrast, *RootOf* is *not* a function since both (n, i) and $(n, -i)$ are members of *RootOf*.

Many data collections can be modelled as functions. For example:

A *sales catalogue* is a correspondence between the *name of an item* and its *price*.

A *symbol table* is a correspondence between the *name of a variable* and its set of *attributes*.

A *telephone directory* is a correspondence between the *name of a person* and their *telephone number* (we assume one number per person).

For each of these objects, each 'name' corresponds to just one 'value'. Thus it is helpful to declare such an object as a *function* (rather than simply a relation) to express this constraint. To declare a function, we use a single-headed arrow, for example:

salescat : *item* → *price*

This is equivalent to defining *salescat* as a *relation* and at the same time constraining it to be a function.

In general, in a function, several members of the domain can map to the same member of the range. For example, several different items could have the same price. The arrow reminds us that we can go unambiguously one way only. We say that each member of the domain (the left end of the arrow) *maps to* just one member of the range. Figure 5.3 illustrates the *salescat* function.

Exercise 5.8

symtab : *varname* ↔ *attrset* is declared as a relation. Write a *predicate* to constrain it to be a function.

Exercise 5.9

Previously we suggested a number of examples of *relations*, such as *Anagram*, *RoadTo*, *GreaterThan*, *PhoneNumber*, *Studying* and *Author*. Which of these relations do you think might also be *functions*?

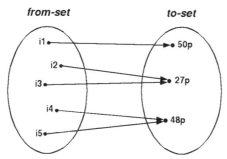

Fig 5.3. The *salescat* function.

Function application

If *f* is a function from set *A* to set *B*, and *a* is a member of set *A*, then the notation *f a* denotes the result of *applying* the function *f* to the element *a*. That is, it is the single element of set *B* that corresponds to *a*. For example, with

   salescat : *item* → *price*
   i : *item*

then *salescat i* is the *price* of item *i*.

In mathematics it is common to write function application with parentheses, as in f(x). This is permitted in Z also, and the parentheses would be simply interpreted in the usual way as grouping a sub-expression. However, the expression f(x,y) in mathematics usually denotes application of a function f to two arguments. In Z the expression *f(x,y)* would denote the application of a function *f* to a *single* argument consisting of the pair (*x,y*).

If *a* is not in **dom** *f*, we cannot determine the meaning of *f a*. For instance, if *i* ∉ **dom** *salescat*, we can write a predicate such as *salescat i* < *100*, but we cannot determine whether it is *True* or *False*.

Exercise 5.10

The symbols in a programming language each have two attributes: type and length. An INT is 2 bytes, a LONGINT is 4 bytes, a CHAR is 1 byte and a STRING is variable up to 255 bytes. Given

   [*SYMBOL*]
   intsy, strsy : *SYMBOL*

write an axiomatic definition for the attribute set (type and length).

┌─ **Exercise 5.11** ──┐
  Declare a symbol table that maps symbols to attributes. Write predicates that state that *intsy* is of type INT, and *strsy* is of type STRING.
└──┘

Defining a function

As with other relations, we usually do not specify the content of a
function that is part of the state data of a system. We may need to
define other functions, like the 'mathematical functions' in programming languages, where we *do* want to define their content. We can do
this by enumeration or, more usually, by axiomatic definition.

Here are two functions:

$SmallDouble == \{1 \mapsto 2, 2 \mapsto 4, 3 \mapsto 6, 4 \mapsto 8\}$

$$LargeDouble : \mathbb{N} \rightarrow \mathbb{N}$$
$$\forall n : \mathbb{N} \bullet LargeDouble\ n = 2*n$$

┌─ **Exercise 5.12** ──┐
  Write a definition of a *halve* function for the even numbers *2* to *10*.
└──┘

Recursive definitions

Sometimes it is useful to appeal to recursion to define a function. For
example, we could define the *factorial* function (*factorial n* is
$1*2*3*...*n$) thus:

$$fact : \mathbb{N} \rightarrow \mathbb{N}$$
$$fact\ 0 = 1$$
$$\forall n : \mathbb{N} \mid n > 0 \bullet fact\ n = n * fact\ (n-1)$$

┌─ **Exercise 5.13** ──┐
  Define the *sigma* function (*sigma n* is $1+2+3+...+n$).
└──┘

┌─ **Exercise 5.14** ──┐
  The number of combinations of *r* things selected from *n* is given by the
  formula:

  $(fact\ n) \div (fact(n-r) * fact\ r)$

  Define a combination function in two ways: firstly using *fact* as defined
  previously; secondly without using *fact*.
└──┘

Partial and total functions

Often, when we declare a function, it is useful to state whether or not all members of the from-set have a corresponding member in the to-set. For example, 'Does every item in the catalogue have a price?'. If the answer is Yes, then the function can be declared to be *total*.

A ***total function*** is a function in which the domain is the whole of the from-set. For example, the function *square* is a function from integers to natural numbers. As every integer has a square, we can define *square* to be a total function. In general, the from-set of a function may contain members that are not in the domain. For example, a *halve* function, mapping integers to integers, is not a total function as it maps only the *even* numbers.

The single-headed arrow we have been using so far actually declares the function to be total. Thus, if we declare a function

   passport : *person* → *passport_number*

then we are saying that everyone in the set *person* has a passport number. If this is not the case, that is, some people may *not* have a passport number, then we must declare the function to be *partial*, by using an arrow with a bar across it:

   passport : *person* ↛ *passport_number*

You could think of the bar as an obstacle that some members of the from-set may be unable to jump.

The ↛ symbol does not say that the set *person* actually *does* contain members that are not in dom *passport*, merely that it *might* do so.

In most cases we will find that the functions we meet in specifications are *not* total. This is because it is difficult to define a real-life set of values: it is easier to define a set that must include such values. For example, it is easier to say that 'names are made of letters' rather than enumerating all particular names.

Exercise 5.15

Given the declaration $f : A \nrightarrow B$ write a predicate that says that f is total.

Finite functions

If we know that the domain of a function is finite, we can use the symbol ⇸ to declare it, for example

   phonedir : *name* ⇸ *number*

This declares a partial **finite function**. A total function is finite if and only if its from-set is finite.

Though the implementation of a software system is virtually certain to involve only *finite* functions, most specification authors seem to prefer to use the ⇸ and → symbols. Usually, this is because the finite nature of a function seldom has any bearing on the specification, whereas its totality often does.

Override

As a function is a relation, we can add a new pair by using the *union* operator. For example,

> *salescat* : *item* ⇸ *price*
> *it* : *item*
> *pr* : *price*
> *newsalescat* : *item* ⇸ *price*
> *newsalescat* = *salescat* ∪ {(*it*, *pr*)}

However, if item *it* already exists in *salescat*, then *newsalescat* will *not* be a function, because it would contain conflicting prices for the item *it* (unless, by chance, *pr* = *salescat it*). Thus our specification is inconsistent. We need to 'guard' the predicate, thus:

> *it* ∉ dom *salescat* ∧
> *newsalescat* = *salescat* ∪ {(*it*, *pr*)}

But what if item *it* is already in *salescat*? Well, if we want to *replace* *it*, we need to say 'out with the old and in with the new', thus:

> *it* ∈ dom *salescat* ∧
> *newsalescat* = (*salescat* \ {(*it*, *salescat it*)}) ∪ {(*it*, *pr*)}

The **override** operator, ⊕, gives us a shorthand for the two expressions above, so we can write:

> *newsalescat* = *salescat* ⊕ {(*it*, *pr*)}

This says, 'if it's there, replace it, otherwise add it'. In fact, the override operator can deal with more than one pair at a time, replacing all simultaneously. So we might see an expression for the full catalogue for the next season, *salescat* ⊕ *newseason*, where *newseason* contained only the new or changed entries.

The type of a function

The type of a function is the same as the type of its underlying relation, that is, $\mathbb{P}(T_A \times T_B)$, where T_A is the type of the from-set and T_B is the type of the to-set.

> **Exercise 5.16**
> What is the type of the symbol table declared in Exercise 5.10?

> **Exercise 5.17**
> The given set [TEAM] contains all teams in a football league.
> Declare a relation *Fixture* to represent the fixtures (matches).
> Declare a function *Result* to represent the results of these matches.
> Declare *Home* and *Away* winners (sets of teams) and the set of winning teams, *Winners*.
> Write statements (predicates) relating these data constructs.

NUMBERS

There are a number of built-in numeric relations and functions in Z. We will take their definitions as axiomatic and simply show their signatures.

Relations between numbers

less than	$\_<\_$	$: \mathbb{Z} \times \mathbb{Z}$
greater than	$\_>\_$	$: \mathbb{Z} \times \mathbb{Z}$
less than or equal to	$\_\leq\_$	$: \mathbb{Z} \times \mathbb{Z}$
greater than or equal to	$\_\geq\_$	$: \mathbb{Z} \times \mathbb{Z}$
equal to	$\_=\_$	$: \mathbb{Z} \times \mathbb{Z}$
not equal to	$\_\neq\_$	$: \mathbb{Z} \times \mathbb{Z}$

These are all uses of the *infix* notation for relations (see page 62), for instance, $(a, b) \in \_\neq\_$ is equivalent to $a \neq b$.

Functions on numbers

addition	$\_+\_$	$: \mathbb{Z} \times \mathbb{Z} \to \mathbb{Z}$
subtraction	$\_-\_$	$: \mathbb{Z} \times \mathbb{Z} \to \mathbb{Z}$
multiplication	$\_*\_$	$: \mathbb{Z} \times \mathbb{Z} \to \mathbb{Z}$
prefix minus	$-$	$: \mathbb{Z} \to \mathbb{Z}$

Where, for example, $a+b$ is defined to mean $(\_+\_)(a, b)$. This is similar to the infix notation for relations, except that it is shorthand for a *value*, not a predicate.

We can use these to define other functions:

minimum   min
maximum   max
division   _div_ (or _÷_)
remainder   _mod_

All finite non-empty sets have a maximum and a minimum. This is not so for infinite sets; some have a minimum, some have a maximum, some have both and some have neither. Thus we declare min and max as *partial* functions

$$\mid \quad \text{min} : \mathbb{P}_1\mathbb{Z} \nrightarrow \mathbb{Z}$$

$$\mid \quad \forall S : \mathbb{P}_1\mathbb{Z};\ m : \mathbb{Z} \mid m \in S \wedge (\forall n : S \bullet m \leq n) \bullet \text{min}\, S = m$$

Exercise 5.18

Define the max function.

We can use max to define div:

$$\mid \quad \_\text{div}\_ : \mathbb{Z} \times \mathbb{Z} \nrightarrow \mathbb{Z}$$

$$\mid \quad \forall n, m : \mathbb{N} \mid m \neq 0 \bullet n \text{ div } m = \text{max}\{q : \mathbb{N} \mid q*m \leq n\}$$
$$\mid \quad \forall n, m : \mathbb{Z} \mid m \neq 0 \bullet (-n)\text{div}\, m = n \text{ div}(-m) = -(n \text{ div } m)$$

The symbol ÷ is just a synonym for div:

_÷_ == _div_

Exercise 5.19

Define mod.

SEQUENCES

It is often helpful to discuss collections of data arranged in a particular *order*, for example:

A bank statement containing a list of transactions ordered by date.
A phone directory containing a list of names ordered alphabetically.
A diary containing activities ordered by date and time.
An interrupt queue containing events in the order in which they occurred.

The mathematical structure that represents an ordered collection of data is a **sequence**. A sequence is a finite ordered collection of objects, each of the same type. We can declare a sequence by using the operator **seq**, so s:**seq** *A* declares s to be a sequence of elements from the set *A*, and the number of elements in s is written #s. To refer to an element in this sequence, we write *s n* where *n* is a natural number in *1..#s*.

We can define a small sequence by listing its elements, separated by commas, inside **sequence brackets**. For example, the sequence of vowels in the word 'phenobarbitone' is ⟨*e, o, a, i, o, e*⟩. Notice that some elements occur more than once; contrast this with a *set*.

More usually, we are dealing with large sequences and we use an axiomatic definition. For instance, we could describe an ordered array of numbers like this:

$$array : \text{seq } \mathbb{N}$$

$$\forall\, i, j : 1..\#array \mid i < j \bullet array\; i < array\; j$$

Notice this definition also says the numbers are all distinct.

A sequence is a function

Mathematically, a sequence is a function in which the domain is a set of consecutive natural numbers, starting at 1. Thus the sequence of vowels in 'phenobarbitone' could be written:

$$\{1 \mapsto e, 2 \mapsto o, 3 \mapsto a, 4 \mapsto i, 5 \mapsto o, 6 \mapsto e\}$$

or

$$\{4 \mapsto i, 3 \mapsto a, 5 \mapsto o, 6 \mapsto e, 2 \mapsto o, 1 \mapsto e\}$$

or any other set expression with the same meaning.

The members of a sequence

Each member of the set defined by a sequence is an ordered pair of the form (*n, a*), where *n* is a natural number and *a* is a member of the to-set. The *domain* of a sequence, s, is simply the contiguous set of natural numbers, *1..#s*, and ran s is the set of all elements that appear in the sequence s. We normally reserve the phrase 'members of a sequence' for the elements in ran s.

We can now see that a reference to a particular member of a sequence is just the ordinary notation for function application.

An empty sequence

An *empty sequence* can be written ⟨ ⟩.

If we know that a sequence is not empty, we can introduce it using the seq₁ operator. Thus:

seq *A* is the set of all sequences of elements of set *A* (including the empty sequence).

seq₁ *A* is the set of all non-empty sequences of elements of set *A*.

Sequence operators

Because a sequence is a function, all the functional operators can be applied to sequences (but note that the resulting function need not be a sequence). In addition, there are several operators that depend on the fact that the domain of a sequence is a set of consecutive natural numbers. Some simple sequence operators are explained here: others will be found in Chapter 8.

The *head* of a non-empty sequence, *s*, is written head *s*. It is the first element of the sequence. That is, head *s* is the same as *s*(1). If *s* is empty, head *s* has no meaning.

The *last* of a non-empty sequence, *s*, is written last *s*. It is the last element of the sequence. That is, last *s* is the same as *s*(#*s*). If *s* is empty, last *s* has no meaning.

The *tail* of a sequence, *s*, is written tail *s*. It is the sequence consisting of all elements of *s* except the first. If *s* contains only one element, then tail *s* is empty. If *s* is empty, then tail *s* has no meaning.

The *front* of a sequence, *s*, is written front *s*. It is the sequence consisting of all elements of *s* except the last. If *s* contains only one element, then front *s* is empty. If *s* is empty, then front *s* has no meaning.

The *concatenation* of two sequences, *s1* and *s2*, is written *s1*^*s2*. It is a sequence consisting of the elements of *s1* followed by the elements of *s2*.

For example, ⟨9, 7, 14⟩ ^ ⟨8, 2, 4, 3⟩ = ⟨9, 7, 14, 8, 2, 4, 3⟩.

We may notice that, if *s* is a non-empty sequence,

s = ⟨head *s*⟩ ^ tail *s* = front *s* ^ ⟨last *s*⟩

Exercise 5.20

Write definitions for head, last, tail and front for sequences of natural numbers.

The type of a sequence

Because a sequence is a function it is a set of pairs. The type of each such pair is $(\mathbb{Z} \times T_A)$, where T_A is the underlying type of set A. Thus the type of the sequence $s : \text{seq } A$ is $\mathbb{P}(\mathbb{Z} \times T_A)$.

In the basic library, the definitions of head, last, tail and front are given *generically* so that they can be applied to sequences of any type of element. We will introduce generic definitions in Chapter 9.

ANSWERS TO EXERCISES

Answer 5.1

The *IsOn* relation can be illustrated by a diagram or by a table as shown in Figure 5.4.

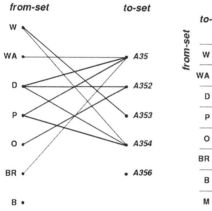

from-set \ to-set	A35	A352	A353	A354	A356
W			✓	✓	
WA	✓				
D	✓	✓		✓	
P	✓			✓	
O		✓			
BR	✓				
B					
M					

Fig 5.4. The *IsOn* relation and table.

Answer 5.2

author : *book* ↔ *writer*
author = {(*A_Tale_of_Two_Cities*, *Dickens*), (*To_Kill_a_Mockingbird*, *Lee*),
　　　　　(*The_Wind_in_the_Willows*, *Grahame*)}

Answer 5.3

student ::= *Bill* | *Mary* | *Sue*

subject ::= *Maths* | *History* | *English* | *Art* | *Science* | *Geography*

$BillSub = \{Bill\} \times \{History, Art, Science\}$
$MarySub = \{Mary\} \times \{Maths, History, Science\}$
$SueSub = \{Sue\} \times \{Maths, History, English, Science\}$

$studies : student \leftrightarrow \mathbb{P}\,subject$

$studies = BillSub \cup MarySub \cup SueSub$

Table 5.2. The *studies* table.

	Maths	*History*	*English*	*Art*	*Science*	*Geography*
Bill		X		X	X	
Mary	X	X			X	
Sue	X	X	X	X	X	

Answer 5.4
Each student is restricted to 3 subjects:

$\forall\, stu : student;\ setsub : \mathbb{P}\,subject \mid (stu, setsub) \in studies \bullet \#setsub \leq 3$

Later, we will see how 'domain restrict' can be used to express this more succinctly.

Answer 5.5

$RootOf : \mathbb{N} \leftrightarrow \mathbb{Z}$

$\forall\, n : \mathbb{N};\ i : \mathbb{Z} \bullet (n, i) \in RootOf \Leftrightarrow n = i * i$

Notice that this is an *implicit* specification of the relation. Unlike *SquareOf*, it does not tell us *how* to calculate the result, only a property of it. Moreover, this property may (or may not) be sufficient to define a range value uniquely. In the case of the *RootOf* definition shown here, there may be two range elements related to a domain element (+3 and −3 are each possible roots of 9) or none (23 has no integer root). *RootOf* is a perfectly well-defined relation but if it had been declared as $RootOf : \mathbb{N} \to \mathbb{Z}$ then there would be no *function* that could satisfy the given constraint. It would also fail if it were declared as a partial function.

Answer 5.6

$dom\,R = \{p : R \bullet first\,p\}$

Answer 5.7

$ran\,R = \{x : X;\ y : Y \mid (x, y) \in R \bullet y\}$

is one possible solution, and another is

$$ran\,R = \{p : R \bullet second\,p\}$$

Answer 5.8

$symtab : varname \leftrightarrow attrset$

$\forall\,v : dom\,symtab \bullet (\exists_1\,a : attrset \bullet (v, a) \in symtab)$

Answer 5.9

Possibly *PhoneNumber* (if each person is allowed only one number). None of the others! In each case, there might be several members of the range that correspond to one member of the domain (not unnaturally we assume joint authorship is possible).

Answer 5.10

$symtype ::= INT \mid LONGINT \mid CHAR \mid STRING$
$attr == \{STRING\} \times 0..255\ \cup\ \{(INT, 2), (LONGINT, 4), (CHAR, 1)\}$

Answer 5.11

$symtab : SYMBOL \rightarrow attr$
$symtab\,intsy = (INT, 2)$
$\exists\,n : \mathbb{N} \bullet symtab\,strsy = (STRING, n)$

Answer 5.12

$halve : \{2, 4, 6, 8, 10\} \rightarrow \mathbb{N}$

$\forall\,n : dom\,halve \bullet 2*(halve\,n) = n$

Answer 5.13

$sigma : \mathbb{N} \rightarrow \mathbb{N}$

$sigma\,0 = 0$
$\forall\,n : \mathbb{N} \mid n > 0 \bullet sigma\,n = n + sigma(n-1)$

Answer 5.14

$comb : (\mathbb{N} \times \mathbb{N}) \nrightarrow \mathbb{N}$

$\forall\,n, r : \mathbb{N} \mid n \geq r \bullet comb(n,r) = (fact\,n) \div (fact(n-r) * fact\,r)$

$comb : \mathbb{N} \times \mathbb{N} \nrightarrow \mathbb{N}$

$\forall n : \mathbb{N} \bullet comb(n,0)=1$
$\forall n,r : \mathbb{N} \mid n{\geq}r \wedge r{>}0 \bullet comb(n,r) = (comb(n,r{-}1)*(n{+}r{-}1)) \div r$

Answer 5.15

$f : A \nrightarrow B$

$\mathrm{dom}\, f = A$

Answer 5.16

$\mathbb{P}(SYMBOL \times \mathbb{P}(symtype \times \mathbb{Z}))$

Answer 5.17

$[TEAM]$
$Score == \mathbb{N} \times \mathbb{N}$

$Fixture : TEAM \leftrightarrow TEAM$
$Result : (TEAM \times TEAM) \nrightarrow Score$
$Home, Away, Winners : \mathbb{P}\,TEAM$

$\mathrm{dom}\, Result = Fixture$
$\mathrm{dom}\, Fixture \cap \mathrm{ran}\, Fixture = \{\,\}$
$Home = \{a,b : TEAM; x,y : \mathbb{N} \mid ((a,b),(x,y)) \in Result \wedge x{>}y \bullet a\}$
$Away = \{a,b : TEAM; x,y : \mathbb{N} \mid ((a,b),(x,y)) \in Result \wedge x{>}y \bullet b\}$

$Winners = Home \cup Away$
$Home \cap Away = \{\,\}$

Answer 5.18

$max : (\mathbb{P}_1\mathbb{Z}) \nrightarrow \mathbb{Z}$

$\forall S : \mathbb{P}_1\mathbb{Z}; \; m : \mathbb{Z} \mid m \in S \wedge (\forall n : S \bullet m{\geq}n) \bullet max\, S = m$

The crucial observation to make here is that there is *at most* one m that satisfies this constraint, and there need not be one at all. This justifies the use of the partial function arrow in the declaration part.

Answer 5.19

$\_mod\_ : (\mathbb{Z} \times \mathbb{Z}) \nrightarrow \mathbb{Z}$

$\forall n,m : \mathbb{Z} \mid m{\neq}0 \bullet n = m*(n \div m) + (n \bmod m)$

Answer 5.20

$\text{head} : (\text{seq}_1 \, \mathbb{N}) \rightarrowtail \mathbb{N}$

$\forall \, s : \text{seq}_1 \, \mathbb{N} \; \bullet \; \text{head} \, s = (s \, 1)$

$\text{last} : (\text{seq}_1 \, \mathbb{N}) \rightarrowtail \mathbb{N}$

$\forall \, s : \text{seq}_1 \, \mathbb{N} \; \bullet \; \text{last} \, s = (s \, \#s)$

$\text{tail} : (\text{seq}_1 \, \mathbb{N}) \rightarrowtail (\text{seq} \, \mathbb{N})$

$\forall \, s : \text{seq}_1 \, \mathbb{N} \; \bullet \; \langle \text{head} \, s \rangle \, ^\frown \text{tail} \, s = s$

$\text{front} : (\text{seq}_1 \, \mathbb{N}) \rightarrowtail (\text{seq} \, \mathbb{N})$

$\forall \, s : \text{seq}_1 \, \mathbb{N} \; \bullet \; \text{front} \, s \, ^\frown \langle \text{last} \, s \rangle = s$

SPECIFICATION PROBLEMS

5.1 SUBSTRINGS

$[CHAR]$
$string \; == \; \text{seq} \, CHAR$

Define a function *substr* that returns a substring of a specified string. For instance, *substr*("abcdef", 2, 3) is "bcd".

What does your definition say should be the value of:

substr("abc", 0, 1)
substr("", 0, 1)
substr("abc", 1, 0)
substr("abc", 2, 4)

Are these answers accidental? Is there anything wrong with the question? How many possible definitions do you think there might be? How would you decide which one should be chosen? Does the formal specification help to decide these questions? Should it?

Define a relation _*IsIn*_ so that *a IsIn b* means that the string *a* is a substring of the string *b*. Try to avoid some of the special cases that the substring function had.

5.2 PERMUTE AND SORT

Define a relation _IsPermOf_ : seq ℕ ↔ seq ℕ whose members are those sequences that are permutations (rearrangements) one of the other. For example,

   listA IsPermOf listB

means that *listA* is a permutation of *listB*.

Declare *listA* and *listB* each to be a sequence of numbers, and write predicates that state that *listB* is *listA* arranged in ascending order.

5.3 RIGHT ADJUSTED LINE

   [*CHAR*]
   blank : *CHAR*
   string == seq *CHAR*
   wid : ℕ

Define

- *words* to be the set of strings that consist of non-blank characters only.
- *blanks* to be the set of strings that consist of blank characters only.
- *full_lines* to be the set of strings formed from sequences of words, each separated by one blank, and with no leading or trailing blanks.
- *right_adjusted_lines* to be the set of sequences of words, each separated by one blank, preceded by as many blanks as necessary to make a line of length *wid* (use the *IsIn* relation if you wish).

According to your definitions, determine if the empty string (the sequence of characters of length zero) is in each of these sets.

5.4 CROSS REFERENCE TABLE

Here is a fragment of a BASIC program:

```
100 A = B * C - D
110 C = D + E
200 A = C - B
```

in which only assignment statements are permitted. Each statement is identified by a *statement number*. The body of a statement contains a number of *variables*.

Define a simple data model for such a program.

The 'cross-reference table' shows where each variable is referenced. Each line in the cross-reference table consists of a variable name and a list of statement numbers.

For the fragment above, the table contains:

```
A 100, 200
B 100, 200
C 100, 110, 200
D 100, 110
E 110
```

Define a model for the cross reference table and express constraints to relate it to the program.

Chapter 6
Schemas as State

'I see you're admiring my little box,' the Knight said in a
friendly tone. 'It's my own invention –'
Lewis Carroll, Through the Looking-Glass

At any moment a system can be regarded as having a 'state', that is, a
particular configuration. The possible states that a system may have
can be described by modelling the state with *state data* together with
some constraints. A combination of data and constraints is called a
schema. A large state can be built out of smaller parts by combining
the schemas that model them.

The 'E-shaped little box', which we first saw in Chapter 2, houses
the central concept of Z.

WHAT IS A SCHEMA?

A *schema* is a named collection of variables and predicates. To be
useful to the reader, it should be an abstraction of some real world
object or action. For instance, we might describe the characteristics of
a student thus:

┌─*Student*─────────────────────────────
│ *name* : seq *CHAR*
│ *number* : $\mathbb{N}$
│ *studying* : $\mathbb{P}$*SUBJECT*
├───────────────────────────────────────
│ *3 ≤ #studying ≤ 6*
└───────────────────────────────────────

Whenever we use the identifier *Student*, it stands for the named
values *name*, *number* and *studying*. The predicates express constraints
on the values or relationships between them. Our students each study
between 3 and 6 subjects.

This means that only *name*, *number* and *studying*, where
$3 \leq \#studying \leq 6$, describe a student. If *#studying=1* then these three
values, even though they are the correct type, would *not* describe a
Student, they would describe something else – a graduate, perhaps.

We often use schemas to describe such data aggregates (rather like
Pascal records). In this chapter we illustrate this use of schemas. In

the next chapter we will see how schemas can be used to represent operations or actions on the data.

SCHEMA SYNTAX

A schema definition consists of a **schema-name**, a **declaration-part** and a **predicate-part**.

A **schema-name** is a base-name with an optional prefix and an optional suffix. In this book, we will use the convention that each schema base-name starts with an upper case letter.

The **declaration-part** consists of a single declaration or a declaration list. Many writers write one declaration per line (a semi-colon is assumed at the end of each line) and this is the style we adopt. Unlike Pascal records, it doesn't matter what order the declarations are written in — it only matters what variables are declared.

The **predicate-part** consists of a single predicate or a number of predicates conjoined ('anded' together). We usually write each such predicate on a separate line (an *and* symbol is assumed to join them together), and thus it doesn't matter what order these predicates are written in.

A schema definition can be written vertically:

```
┌─schema-name──────────────────────────────
│  declaration-part
│  ────────────────
│  predicate-part
└──────────────────────────────────────────
```

or horizontally, using **schema brackets**, like this:

schema-name $\hat{=}$ [declaration-part | predicate-part]

These two forms are equivalent. For example,

```
┌─Student────────────────────      ─────────
│  name : seq CHAR
│  number : ℕ
│  studying : ℙSUBJECT
│  ─────────────────
│  3 ≤ #studying ≤ 6
└──────────────────────────────────────────
```

and

Student $\hat{=}$ [name : seq CHAR; number : ℕ; studying : ℙSUBJECT |
          $3 \leq \#studying \leq 6$]

mean the same thing. The choice of which to use is a question of style: if the schema definition would spill onto a second line, most writers prefer to use the vertical form. This does not mean the 'horizontal' form is constrained to one line — it can occupy as many lines as we wish — but the larger it gets the harder it is to read.

OMITTING THE PREDICATE PART

The predicate-part of a schema definition can be omitted, giving us the form:

schema-name ≙ [declaration-part]

or:

```
┌schema-name──────────────────────────────
│ declaration-part
└─────────────────────────────────────────
```

This form can be used to group together common data to be used in several places. Omitting the predicate part is equivalent to using the single predicate *True*, which is to say that there are no further constraints on the declared data.

COMPONENTS

The variables in the declaration part of a schema are called its ***components***. For instance, the components of *Student* are *name*, *number* and *studying*. We can use a schema as a type and can define variables of that type, for instance:

stu1, stu2 : *Student*
class : $\mathbb{P}$*Student*

stu1 and *stu2* are variables that have components *name*, *number* and *studying*. These components can be referred to by using the ***selection*** operator (dot). Thus *stu1.name* is the name of *stu1*, *stu2.studying* is the set of subjects being studied by *stu2* and so on. We might say:

stu1.name ≠ *stu2.name*

Indeed, we can probably say:

∀ *s1, s2* : *class* | *s1.name* ≠ *s2.name* • *stu1.number* ≠ *stu2.number*

to assert that students with different names also have different numbers. We could also say:

$\forall \; s1, s2 : class \mid s1 \neq s2 \; \bullet$
    stu1.name $\neq$ *stu2.name* $\land$ *stu1.number* $\neq$ *stu2.number*

if we wished to say that any two students who differ in any way, certainly have different names and different numbers.

The expression $s1 \neq s2$ means that same as

$(s1.name \neq s2.name) \; \lor$
$(s1.number \neq s2.number) \; \lor$
$(s1.studying \neq s2.studying)$

because a variable of schema type is completely determined by the values selected by its components.

Exercise 6.1

Write a schema to represent a piece on a draughts (checkers) board. Ask yourself 'What are the essential characteristics of a checkers piece?' Try to capture these in your definition.

Declare a variable *stone* to represent a black checkers piece in the first row.

STYLE

When we first start to write schemas, we are tempted to put too much into each one. To counteract this we should try to remember the '7 plus or minus 2' principle. Normally we aim for three or four declarations and no more than seven predicates. If we wish to express separate situations that are *disjoint*, for instance:

$(studying = \{Maths, Physics, Chemistry\}) \; \lor$
$(studying = \{English, French, German\})$

it is unwise to combine them in one schema. It is better to name such situations – perhaps *Science_Student* and **Language_Student** would be helpful in the example above. We can then write a schema for *each* situation and use *schema disjunction* to combine them. This will become clearer in the next chapter.

The formal text of a schema is only part of the story; to relate it to the real world we need explanatory text around it. We can divide such text into two parts: the text that describes the declaration part and the text that describes the predicate part. A common style is to precede the schema by an explanation of the declarations and follow it by an explanation of the predicates. These explanations can, and should, use the identifiers of the schema. In some cases, it is helpful to list the predicate explanation in lines that match the predicate part. We often use this style. For example, we might explain the *Student* schema like this:

> A *Student* is identified by a *name* (which is a sequence of characters), and a *number*. The set of subjects the student is studying is *studying*.

$$\begin{array}{|l}
\hline
\text{Student} \\
\hline
name : \text{seq } CHAR \\
number : \mathbb{N} \\
studying : \mathbb{P}\,SUBJECT \\
\hline
3 \leq \#studying \leq 6 \\
\hline
\end{array}$$

A *Student* must be studying at least three and no more than six subjects.

SCOPE

Each schema name has *global scope*, that is, it is known throughout the document in which the schema definition is written (except where the identifier is redeclared). Moreover, once an identifier has been used for a schema name, the decorated forms of that name mean something special (we will see this in Chapter 7) and they cannot be used for anything else.

The components of a schema S have *local scope*: they are known only in the predicate part of S and in the predicate part of any schema in which S is included. The box surrounding a schema has a 'closed' top and bottom to graphically suggest this closed scope. We can contrast this with an axiomatic definition, such as:

$$\begin{array}{|l}
x, y : \mathbb{N} \\
\hline
x < y \\
\end{array}$$

which is an 'open' box and declares variables *x* and *y* with global scope.

Note that the schema components are not known in the *declaration part* of that schema. This means that we are *not* allowed to write:

$$\begin{array}{|l}
\hline
S \\
\hline
numbset : \mathbb{P}\,\mathbb{N} \\
n : numbset \\
\hline
\end{array}$$

if we intend to declare *n* to be a member of the other component *numbset*. This is because the scope of the component *numbset* does not include the expressions that define the other components. *numbset* cannot be used to define *n*. There are theoretical reasons for this to do with recursion, but a good practical reason is that this makes definitions hard to read.

(In fact, if there were a *global* variable called *numbset*, the schema *S* would be valid, but the component called *n* would be declared as a member of the global set called *numbset* and *not* of the other component with the same name. Since this is obfuscation of a very high order, we are not even going to *consider* using it in this book!)

Holes in scope

Within one specification we can use the same name for two different variables. Of course, these two variables cannot then be known at the same place. For instance, the following phrases cannot validly occur in the same Z document:

[*NAME*]
x : *NAME*
x : $\mathbb{Z}$

for then the name *x* would be ambiguous. This would be an error.

However, we can use the same name for two different *local* variables, as with the identifier *surname* below:

```
┌─ Student ─────────────────────────────
│ surname : seq CHAR
│ number : ℕ
│ ─────────────────────────
│ #surname ≤ 30
└─────────────────────────────────────
```

```
┌─ Teacher ─────────────────────────────
│ surname : NAME
│ class : CLASSID
│ ─────────────────────────
│ surname ∉ BlackList
└─────────────────────────────────────
```

Here there are two different variables both called *surname*, one declared inside *Student* and one declared inside *Teacher*, and there is no *logical* conflict, even though they are of different types. (There can be a slight conflict in the mind of the reader, however, which can become acute as the schemas are used in other parts of the specification.)

Also, we can use the same name for a global and a local variable.

This creates a 'hole' in the scope of the global variable. For instance, if we further declared **surname** in an axiomatic definition, we would have *three* different variables each called **surname**. The global **surname** introduced by the axiomatic definition would be known everywhere except in the predicate parts of the schemas **Student** and **Teacher**.

SCHEMA SEMANTICS

Underneath, a schema consists of a *signature* and a *property*. Wherever the schema name is used, it stands for this signature and property, and nothing else. The signature and property of a schema determine everything about the schema, including how it combines with other schemas – this will be explained in Chapter 10.

We can think of the signature as coming from the declaration part and the property as coming from the predicate part. But this is not the whole story. The signature is *not* the same as the declaration part and the property is *not* the same as the predicate part. We will make this clear.

Schema signature

The *signature* of a schema is the (unordered) collection of names introduced in the schema, together with their corresponding *types*. For example, the **Student** schema has a signature that can be written:

$$number : \mathbb{Z}; \; name : \mathbb{P}(\mathbb{Z} \times CHAR); \; studying : \mathbb{P}SUBJECT$$

Although we tend to think of the declaration part of a schema as its signature, the two are not the same since the signature only contains the *types* of the components, not the *sets* which were used to declare them.

In a signature, the *order* of the names is irrelevant. Thus the previous signature could equally well be written:

$$name : \mathbb{P}(\mathbb{Z} \times CHAR); \; number : \mathbb{Z}; \; studying : \mathbb{P}SUBJECT$$

(There is no need to write signatures in a Z document, hence there is no Z notation for a signature: we have depicted it here in a natural way as a particularly simple sort of declaration list.)

Schema property

The *property* of a schema is the combined constraints introduced by the declarations and the predicates (the combination can be described by a single predicate). Although we tend to think of the *predicate part* as expressing these constraints, in fact constraints are often introduced by the *declaration part* too. For example, the declaration of *number* in the *Student* schema introduces the constraint *number*≥0 because, although its type is $\mathbb{Z}$, it is declared as being in $\mathbb{N}$. The complete property of *Student* can be written:

$3 \leq studying \leq 6$
$number \geq 0$
$name \in seq\ CHAR$

There are, of course, many equivalent ways of writing this.

Exercise 6.2

What are the signatures and properties of the schemas A, B and C below?

$A \triangleq [x, y : \mathbb{N};\ f : \mathbb{N} \nrightarrow \mathbb{Z}]$
$B \triangleq [a, b : seq\ CHAR \mid \#a = \#b]$
$String == seq\ CHAR$
$C \triangleq [i, j : \mathbb{N};\ t : \mathbb{N} \nrightarrow String \mid i < j]$

BINDING

A collection of variable names, $n_1, n_2, ...,$ each with an associated value, $v_1, v_2, ...,$ is called a ***binding***. We will write this:

$n_1 \text{->} v_1;\ n_2 \text{->} v_2;\ ...$

For example, given a collection of variables

$a : \mathbb{N};\ b : CHAR;\ c : \mathbb{Z} \nrightarrow \mathbb{N}$

we might have a binding

$a \text{->} 79;\ b \text{->} 'x';\ c \text{->} (-6,2)$

The signature of a schema is just such a collection of typed variables. Thus a schema can be regarded as the collection of all the bindings which satisfy its property, and a binding is like an example of a schema value.

For example, the schema $[a, b : \mathbb{N} \mid a < b < 3]$ has just three bindings:

$a \text{->} 0;\ b \text{->} 1$
$a \text{->} 0;\ b \text{->} 2$
$a \text{->} 1;\ b \text{->} 2$

> ── **Exercise 6.3** ────────────────────────────────────
> How many bindings are there of the *Checker* schema in the answer to
> Exercise 6.1? Enumerate them.
>   How many bindings are there of the schema *Little* $\hat{=} [a : \mathbb{N} \mid a*a = 3]$?

The type of a binding

A binding is a value, and thus has a type. Its *type* is just a collection
of typed variables, written in any order, so its type is a *signature*. We
will write the type of the binding

n_1->v_1; n_2->v_2; ...

as

n_1 : T_1; n_2 : T_2; ...

where T_i is the type of the value v_i.
    For instance, the type of the binding

a->*79*; *b*->*'x'*; *c*->*(-6,2)*

can be written:

a : $\mathbb{Z}$; *b* : *CHAR*; *c* : $\mathbb{Z}\times\mathbb{Z}$

The type of a schema

A schema can be regarded as a collection of bindings and its *under-lying type* is the type of these bindings. We can draw an analogy here
with sets. A set is a collection of elements and the type of each
element is the underlying type of the set.
    Two schemas have the same underlying type if and only if they have
the same signature. For example:

$[r:S1\leftrightarrow S2;\ x:\mathbb{N};\ c:CHAR]$

and

$[r:S1\nrightarrow S2;\ c:CHAR;\ x:\mathbb{Z}]$

have the same underlying type, which could be written:

$r:\mathbb{P}(S1\times S2);\ x:\mathbb{Z};\ c:CHAR$

When we declare a schema variable such as *stu1* : *Student*, we are
saying that *stu1* is one of the bindings of *Student*.

SCHEMA INCLUSION

A schema S can be included by name in the definition of another schema T. This technique is called **schema inclusion**. The definition of T can be written in vertical form

```
┌─ T ────────────────────────────────────
│  S
│  declaration-part
│  ───────────────────
│  predicate part
└─────────────────────────────────────────
```

or in horizontal form:

$T \; \hat{=} \; [S; \text{declaration-part} \mid \text{predicate-part}]$

The effect is as if the declaration and predicate parts of S had been copied into the corresponding parts of T.

Inclusion is a technique that is used widely in specifications. Since T can be viewed as an extension of S, this technique is also called **schema extension**.

For example, we might have described our *Student* schema like this:

$Course \; \hat{=} \; [studying : \mathbb{P}SUBJECT \mid 3 \leq \#studying \leq 6]$

```
┌─ Student ──────────────────────────────
│  name : NAME
│  number : ℕ
│  Course
│
└─────────────────────────────────────────
```

We see here how *inclusion* can be used to build a definition out of named parts and each part can have its own constraints. This is a way of localising explanations. If a constraint (such as $3 \leq \#studying \leq 6$) applies to only some of the components then these might form a simpler schema, and inclusion can bring them together.

```
┌── Exercise 6.4 ─────────────────────────────────────────
│  Split the Checker schema, described in the answer to Exercise 6.1, into
│  simpler named schemas and then use inclusion to describe Checker.
└──────────────────────────────────────────────────────────
```

The rules for combining schemas will be explained in Chapter 7. Here, it is worth noting that, to be combined, the schema signatures must be 'type compatible'. That is, the same variable may be declared in both schemas as long as it has the same *type*. The repeated declaration has no effect. For example, in:

$S \triangleq [a, b, c : \mathbb{N}]$
$T \triangleq [b, c, d : \mathbb{Z}]$
$U \triangleq [S; T]$

the signature of U is:

$a : \mathbb{Z}; \; b : \mathbb{Z}; \; c : \mathbb{Z}; \; d : \mathbb{Z}$

Two schemas which have the same component declared to have different types *cannot* be combined. For example, in:

$V \triangleq [a, b, c : \mathbb{N}]$
$W \triangleq [c, d : CHAR]$
$X \triangleq [S; T]$

X is not well-formed, that is, it is not meaningful.

Used as predicates

We may use a schema, S, as a predicate, standing for its property. For instance, it may appear as a predicate in the predicate part of another schema:

$$
\begin{array}{|l}
\hline
\multicolumn{1}{l}{\llcorner T} \\
\hline
x, y : \mathbb{Z} \\
\hline
S \\
x > y \\
\hline
\end{array}
$$

Here the variables of the signature of S are *not* re-introduced: the definition of T will only make sense if all the variables of S are already in scope where S is used. For instance, if S is defined as

$S \triangleq [x : \mathbb{N} \mid x^3 > 100]$

then the definition of T is perfectly valid. It is equivalent to

$$
\begin{array}{|l}
\hline
\multicolumn{1}{l}{\llcorner T} \\
\hline
x, y : \mathbb{Z} \\
\hline
x^3 > 100 \; \wedge \; x \geq 0 \\
x > y \\
\hline
\end{array}
$$

However, if S were defined so:

$S \triangleq [x, z : \mathbb{N} \mid x^2 + z^2 < 100]$

then the definition of *T* above would be *invalid* unless *z* were already declared as a global variable of the correct type.

In general, we can use *S* as a predicate provided all the variables of S are *in scope* (and have the correct types) where *S* is used. In this case the use of *S* is equivalent to using the property of *S*.

Although this technique is not often used, we might include *S* in the predicate part of another schema when we wish to emphasise that it is the *property* of *S* that we are interested in rather than its *signature*. For example, in describing *Checkers* (see the answer to Exercise 6.1) we might introduce the idea of 'white squares', thus:

```
┌WhiteSquare────────────────────────
  row, col : 1..8
 ├──────────────────────────────────
  (row + col) mod 2 = 1
└───────────────────────────────────
```

Now, if we wish to ensure that a *Checker* sits on a white square, we could describe it like this:

```
┌Checker─────────────────────────────
  row, col : 1..8
  colour : BW
  queen : YN
 ├──────────────────────────────────
  WhiteSquare
└───────────────────────────────────
```

emphasising that no new components are introduced by *WhiteSquare*, only an extra condition.

```
┌─── Exercise 6.5 ──────────────────────────────────────────
 Write down the signature and property of each of the following
 schemas.

   $A \; \hat{=} \; [a, b : \mathbb{N} \mid a < b]$
   $B \; \hat{=} \; [A; \; c, d : \mathbb{N} \mid c + d < 50]$
   $C \; \hat{=} \; [A; \; c, e : \mathbb{Z} \mid c > 100]$
   $D \; \hat{=} \; [B; \; f : \mathbb{N} \rightarrowtail \mathbb{N}]$
   $E \; \hat{=} \; [B; C]$
   $F \; \hat{=} \; [A; \; a : CHAR]$
   $G \; \hat{=} \; [a, b, c : \mathbb{Z} \mid A; b < c]$
   $H \; \hat{=} \; [a, c : \mathbb{Z} \mid A; b > c]$
└────────────────────────────────────────────────────────────
```

SCHEMA INCLUSION EXAMPLE

The most important reason for using schema inclusion is to allow us to separate helpful concepts in our specification and to label and describe them. A secondary reason is that inclusion permits schema 're-use', but really the fact that it is being re-used suggests that the schema represents a useful abstraction.

Suppose we are describing a banking application in which we deal with customer accounts. The bank keeps information about each customer, such as

```
┌─Customer──────────────────────────────
  name : String
  accno : ACCOUNTNUM
  addr : String
  date_of_birth : Date
  sex : MorF
  phone_num : PHONENUM
  balance : ℤ
  loanlimit : ℕ
  marital_status : MorS
└───────────────────────────────────────
```

(We will ignore the predicate part for the moment.)

We see that the schema is rather large (7+2 items) and contains a variety of information. Part is to do with money in the account, namely *balance* and *loanlimit*, and part is concerned with personal details. We can envisage transactions on the account that are interested only in the financial data. We might also imagine that certain types of personal data (perhaps used for checking a phone caller's identity) is private and restricted to certain bank employees. We might like to begin to express these ideas by separating the parts, for instance:

```
┌─AccInfo───────────────────────────────
  accno : ACCOUNTNUM
  balance : ℤ
  loanlimit : ℕ
├───────────────────────────────────────
  loanlimit < 10000
  balance + loanlimit > 0
└───────────────────────────────────────
```

```
┌─OpenInfo──────────────────────────────────
│ name : String
│ addr : String
│ phone_num : PHONENUM
└──────────────────────────
```

```
┌─ConfInfo──────────────────────────────────
│ date_of_birth : Date
│ sex : MorF
│ marital_status : MorS
└──────────────────────────
```

and combine them thus:

```
┌─PersInfo──────────────────────────────────
│ OpenInfo
│ ConfInfo
└──────────────────────────
```

```
┌─Customer──────────────────────────────────
│ PersInfo
│ AccInfo
└──────────────────────────
```

In this model, *Customer* is a schema with components *name*, *addr*, *accno* and so on. That is, *PersInfo* and *AccInfo* are not components of *Customer*. If we wish to refer to the 'personal information' part of *Customer*, we might define it thus:

```
┌─Customer──────────────────────────────────
│ pers : PersInfo
│ acc : AccInfo
└──────────────────────────
```

so that we can now refer to *pers* and *acc*.

Choosing the 'right' model for complex data collections is not easy. Generally, we cannot make decisions about the model without also considering the operations or transactions we wish to describe. This will be discussed further in the next chapter. We put the word 'right' in quotes, because, of course, there is no such thing as the right model. We seek a description that is clear and succinct, and which allows us to identify the important abstractions and to hide irrelevant detail. For example, we made no attempt to explain what we meant by a *Date*, *PHONENUM* or *ACCOUNTNUM*. If we discussed deposit and withdrawal transactions, these details would be irrelevant and are best suppressed.

Exercise 6.6

Describe a file of customer accounts based on the *Customer* schema. Discuss.

ANSWERS TO EXERCISES

Answer 6.1

The essential characteristics are:

- A position (row and column), which must be a 'white square'.
- A colour (black or white).
- An indication of whether or not it has been 'queened' (reached the furthest rank).

We might represent this thus:

$BW ::= black \mid white$
$YN ::= yes \mid no$

Checker ───────────────────────────
$row, col : 1..8$
$colour : BW$
$queen : YN$

───
$(row + col) \bmod 2 = 1$

The predicate constrains each piece to be on a white square.

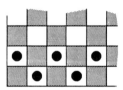

Fig 6.1. Part of a checkers board.

Here is a variable representing a black piece in row one:

$stone : Checker$
───
$stone.colour = black$
$stone.row = 1$

Answer 6.2

The signature of A is $x : \mathbb{Z}; \; y : \mathbb{Z}; f : \mathbb{P}(\mathbb{Z} \times \mathbb{Z})$ and its property is

$x \geq 0 \; \wedge \; y \geq 0 \; \wedge \; \text{dom} f \subseteq \mathbb{N}$

The signature of B is $a : \mathbb{P}(\mathbb{Z} \times CHAR)$; $b : \mathbb{P}(\mathbb{Z} \times CHAR)$ and its property is

$\#a = \#b \ \wedge \ a \in \text{seq } CHAR \ \wedge \ b \in \text{seq } CHAR$

The signature of C is $i : \mathbb{Z}$; $j : \mathbb{Z}$; $t : \mathbb{P}(\mathbb{Z} \times (\mathbb{Z} \times CHAR))$ and its property is

$i \geq 0 \ \wedge \ j \geq 0 \ \wedge \ i < j \ \wedge \ t \in \mathbb{N} \nrightarrow String$

Answer 6.3

For *Checker*, there are 32 x 2 x 2 = 128 bindings; 32 for the *row* and *col* combinations and 2 each for the values of *colour* and *queen*. Here are a few:

```
row->2; col->1; colour->black; queen->no
row->2; col->1; colour->black; queen->yes
row->2; col->1; colour->white; queen->no
row->2; col->1; colour->white; queen->yes
row->1; col->2; colour->black; queen->no
row->1; col->2; colour->black; queen->yes
```

and so on. It is the necessity of satisfying the predicate that restricts the combinations involving *row* and *col*.

For *Little* there are no bindings at all! The schema expression is still valid – though we must beware that we do not rely on it *having* a binding when we reason about the specification.

Answer 6.4

Here is one way to do it:

$Place \ \hat{=} \ [row, col : 1..8 \mid (row + col) \bmod 2 = 1]$
$PieceType \ \hat{=} \ [colour : BW; \ queen : YN]$
$Checker \ \hat{=} \ [Place; PieceType]$

Answer 6.5

The signature of A is $a : \mathbb{Z}$; $b : \mathbb{Z}$ and its property is $0 \leq a < b$.

The signature of B is $a : \mathbb{Z}$; $b : \mathbb{Z}$; $c : \mathbb{Z}$; $d : \mathbb{Z}$ and its property is

$0 \leq a < b \ \wedge \ 0 \leq c \ \wedge \ 0 \leq d \ \wedge \ c + d < 50$

The signature of C is $a : \mathbb{Z}$; $b : \mathbb{Z}$; $c : \mathbb{Z}$; $e : \mathbb{Z}$ and its property is

$0 \leq a < b \ \wedge \ c > 100$

The signature of D is $a : \mathbb{Z}$; $b : \mathbb{Z}$; $c : \mathbb{Z}$; $d : \mathbb{Z}$; $f : \mathbb{P}(\mathbb{Z} \times \mathbb{Z})$ and its property is

$0 \leq a < b \ \wedge \ 0 \leq c \ \wedge \ 0 \leq d \ \wedge \ c + d < 50 \ \wedge \ f \in \mathbb{N} \nrightarrow \mathbb{N}$

The signature of E is $a : \mathbb{Z}$; $b : \mathbb{Z}$; $c : \mathbb{Z}$; $d : \mathbb{Z}$; $e : \mathbb{Z}$ and its property is

$0 \leq a < b \ \wedge \ 0 \leq c \ \wedge \ 0 \leq d \ \wedge \ c + d < 50 \ \wedge \ c > 100$

Since the property of E is always *False*, E has no bindings.

The declaration of *F* is erroneous, because the declarations of *a* conflict. The signature of *G* is $a:\mathbb{Z}$; $b:\mathbb{Z}$; $c:\mathbb{Z}$ and its property is

$$0 \leq a < b \ \wedge \ b < c$$

The declaration of *H* is erroneous unless *b* is a global variable: for *A* to be included in the predicate part requires *b* to be in scope, for instance in the declaration part of *H*.

Answer 6.6
A set of *Customer* records is a *file*:

$$file : \mathbb{P}\,Customer$$
$$\forall f1, f2 : file \mid f1 \neq f2 \bullet f1.accno \neq f2.accno$$

in which no two distinct records have the same account number.

This suggests that a better model might be a function from account numbers to customers:

$$file : ACCOUNT \nrightarrow Customer$$
$$\forall n : \mathrm{dom}\ file \bullet (file\ n).accno = n$$

For each record in the file, the account number in the record itself (*accno*) is the same as the account number in the corresponding domain element.

We might now decide that the *accno* variable in *Customer* is redundant and just gets in the way, so we could redefine *AccInfo* without *accno*, like this:

```
┌─ AccInfo ─────────────────────────────
│ balance : ℤ
│ loanlimit : ℕ
├───────────────────────────────────────
│ loanlimit < 10000
│ balance + loanlimit > 0
└───────────────────────────────────────
```

Even in this small example we find that expressing requirements precisely allows us to detect redundancies and inelegancies and later remove them. During specification it is simpler to recast our definitions than it would be later to rewrite our design.

SPECIFICATION PROBLEMS

6.1 CROSS REFERENCE

Extend the definition of the cross-reference table introduced in Problem 5.4 to distinguish between 'where set' and 'where used' variables. For the following program fragment:

```
100 A = B * C - D
110 C = D + E
200 A = C - B
```

the table will look like this:

```
    SET             USED
A 100, 200
B                   100, 200
C 110               100, 200
D                   100, 110
E                   110
```

6.2 CHECKERS

Write a schema *Board* that describes the pieces on a checkers board. Use the *Checker*, *Place* and *PieceType* schemas from Exercise 6.4. Write two schemas, *WhitePieces* and *BlackPieces* and use them to describe the *Board* schema.

The initial state of a checkers board is shown in Fig. 6.2. Write a schema *InitBoard* that describes this initial state.

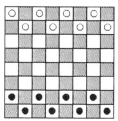

Fig 6.2. A checkers (draughts) board.

6.3 FILENAMES

A 'filename' is a string of *CHAR*, where *CHAR* consists of alphabetics (A to Z), numerics (0 to 9) and the dot symbol (.). The general format is:

name   or   *name.extn*

where *name* is a 1 to 8 character name, of which the first character is alphabetic and the remainder are alphanumeric, and *extn* is an extension of 1 to 3 alphanumeric characters. Describe the format of a filename (1) using schemas, and (2) using axiomatic definitions of sets.

Chapter 7
Schemas for Operations

'Where do you come from?' said the Red Queen, 'And
where are you going? Look up, speak nicely, and don't
twiddle your fingers all the time.'
Lewis Carroll, Through the Looking-Glass

By the simple expedient of recording 'where we come from' (the state
beforehand) and 'where we are going' (the state afterwards) we can
describe an operation on the state of a system. Since, in most cases,
we 'come from' and 'go to' bindings of the schema which describes the
state, this is a good candidate for reuse of that schema.

There is a conventional notation in Z that facilitates this form of
description and allows us to distinguish the 'before' and 'after' states
nicely – and without having to twiddle our notation all the time.

In this chapter we will illustrate this notation by means of an
example – a telephone directory. The exercises and their answers form
a vital part of this explanation.

THE PHONE DIRECTORY

Our simple phone directory contains names, phone numbers and
addresses:

$[NAME, NUMBER, ADDRESS]$

Each subscriber is identified by a *NAME* and has an *ADDRESS* and a
phone *NUMBER*. We will model the directory, *PhoneDir*, as an *addr*
function from *NAME* to *ADDRESS* and a *phone* function from *NAME* to
NUMBER:

$$
\begin{array}{|l}
\hline
PhoneDir \\\\
\hline
addr : NAME \nrightarrow ADDRESS \\\\
phone : NAME \nrightarrow NUMBER \\\\
\hline
dom\ addr = dom\ phone \\\\
\hline
\end{array}
$$

The same names occur in both *addr* and *phone*.

Notice that by declaring *phone* as a *function* we are saying that each
subscriber can have only *one* phone number. However, two subscribers

can share a number in this model. This is illustrated in Figure 7.1.

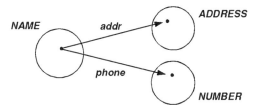

Fig 7.1. Phone directory model I.

Exercise 7.1

The predicate might suggest a different model based on the idea of a 'subscriber record'. Write down such an alternative model. Discuss.

Exercise 7.2

Describe a directory that allows only one name for each phone number.

Exercise 7.3

Describe a directory that allows several phone numbers for each subscriber. Discuss this exercise and the previous one. Which model do you think is 'better'? Why?

Operations

Given the first *PhoneDir* described on page 99 we will describe three operations on the directory:

- *Add* to add a new entry to the directory. We supply a name, an address and a phone number.
- *Delete* to delete an entry from the directory. We supply a name.
- *QueryPhoneNumber* to query a phone number. We supply a name and *QueryPhoneNumber* returns a phone number.

We describe each operation by a schema. In the declaration part we describe the **input** and **output** data and we need to refer to the directory state both *before* and *after* the operation.

We use a 'decorated' name to indicate the purpose of a variable in an operation schema. A **decoration** is a suffix to an identifier:

? for a variable which is an input to an operation.

! for a variable which is an output from an operation.

′ (dash or 'prime') for the value of a state variable after an operation.

These decorations are illustrated in Figure 7.2.

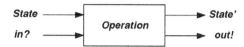

Fig 7.2. Decoration.

One way of remembering these decorations is to note that input data is often submitted to a computer with an element of doubt, and output sometimes causes a certain amount of surprise! For instance, *Add* has three inputs which we will call *name?, addr?* and *phone?*. Notice that a decorated name is distinct from the same name undecorated (the decoration is part of the name). Thus *addr?* (an input variable to *Add*) and *addr* (in the directory) are different variables.

The *Add* and *Delete* operations both change the directory content. We represent the content of the directory *before* an operation by the undecorated schema name, *PhoneDir*, and its content *after* the operation by *PhoneDir'*. This is a different schema from *PhoneDir*: it is constructed by decorating each variable in the signature of *PhoneDir* with a dash. So *PhoneDir'* is a shorthand for:

```
┌─PhoneDir──────────────────────────
│  addr' : NAME ⇸ ADDRESS
│  phone' : NAME ⇸ NUMBER
│ ─────────────────────────
│  dom addr' = dom phone'
└────────────────────────────────────
```

The Add operation

To keep this description simple we will ignore the possibility of errors for now; we will assume the addition is successful.

The input values are *name?, addr?* and *phone?*. The *Add* operation will add a new element *name? ↦ addr?* to the *addr* function, and a new element *name? ↦ phone?* to the *phone* function. Thus

$$addr' = addr \cup \{name? \mapsto addr?\}$$
$$phone' = phone \cup \{name? \mapsto phone?\}$$

records how the before values are related to the after values by an *Add*.

We can now write a schema to describe the operation:

```
┌─ Add ──────────────────────────────────────────┐
│ PhoneDir                                         │
│ PhoneDir'                                        │
│ name? : NAME                                     │
│ addr? : ADDRESS                                  │
│ phone? : NUMBER                                  │
├──────────────────────────────────────────────── │
│ addr' = addr ∪ {name? ↦ addr?}                   │
│ phone' = phone ∪ {name? ↦ phone?}                │
└──────────────────────────────────────────────────┘
```

where we have *included PhoneDir* and *PhoneDir'* so as to refer to the before and after states.

If we expand the *Add* schema to avoid schema inclusion we see:

```
┌─ Add ──────────────────────────────────────────┐
│ addr : NAME↦ADDRESS                              │
│ phone : NAME↦NUMBER                              │
│ addr' : NAME↦ADDRESS                             │
│ phone' : NAME↦NUMBER                             │
│ name? : NAME                                     │
│ addr? : ADDRESS                                  │
│ phone? : NUMBER                                  │
├──────────────────────────────────────────────── │
│ dom addr = dom phone                             │
│ dom addr' = dom phone'                           │
│ addr' = addr ∪ {name? ↦ addr?}                   │
│ phone' = phone ∪ {name? ↦ phone?}                │
└──────────────────────────────────────────────────┘
```

and notice that the state conditions (dom *addr* = dom *phone*) are automatically included. This means that we do not normally need to repeat that the operation changes a valid *PhoneDir* to another valid *PhoneDir*; the declaration part of *Add* implies that only this sort of operation is described.

```
┌─ Exercise 7.4 ─────────────────────────────────┐
│ Describe the *Delete* operation (ignore errors). │
└──────────────────────────────────────────────────┘
```

DECORATION

Let us summarize what we have said about decorating a schema name. Suffixes can be applied to a schema name to produce new, decorated, variables. The most common use of schema decoration is the dash suffix to decorate a collection of state variables.

If *S* is the name of a schema that denotes a system state before an operation, then *S'* denotes the system state after that operation. Thus *S'* is a shorthand for a new schema created from the schema *S* by adding a dash suffix to each of the variables in the *signature* of *S*. The *property* of *S'* is the same as the *property* of *S*, except that it refers to the dashed variables in place of the undashed ones.

The *?* and *!* decorations can also be applied to a schema name to to create collections of input or output variables (an example can be found in the answer to specification problem 7.1). In fact, as we shall see later, *schema decoration* is an example of a more general technique called *renaming* (which will be explained in Chapter 10).

Program variables

In Z, we deal with mathematical variables, that is, named *values*, and there is no concept of the location of the values. This is why we need to use different names for values before and after an operation. An assignment statement in a computer program, such as

    X = X + 1;

has no place in Z. We could express what should happen when the above assignment is executed by

$$x' = x + 1$$

(which is equally well expressed as $x'-1=x$ or $x+1=x'$) but this is a predicate about *values* x and x', not an assignment statement about some variable called x.

In some programming languages, a variable can be given the attribute INOUT. This indicates that the same location will be used both for storing the value at the beginning of a function and for storing the result at the end. In Z, there is no need for an INOUT attribute (it would make no sense). However, if an INOUT variable appears in an interface, a technique for reflecting this fact in the specification is to identify it by two variables such as *fred?* and *fred!* whose names differ only in their decoration. (And we would write informal text to relate these values to an actual interface.)

The Delta notation (Δ)

Because we often need to define operations that change the state data, it is useful to have a notation for the collection of 'before' and 'after' variables together. The Greek capital letter Delta, Δ, is used as a prefix to a schema name as a shorthand for such a collection. (In mathematics and physics, delta is traditionally associated with change.)

For example

ΔPhoneDir

is the same as

[*PhoneDir*; *PhoneDir'*]

So we could write *Add* as

```
┌─ Add ─────────────────────────────────────
│ ΔPhoneDir
│ name? : NAME
│ addr? : ADDRESS
│ phone? : NUMBER
│ ───────────────────────────────────
│ addr' = addr ∪ {name? ↦ addr?}
│ phone' = phone ∪ {name? ↦ phone?}
└────────────────────────────────────────────
```

The Δ notation suppresses irrelevant detail and captures an important concept, that is, a change to the state variables with invariants preserved. If the state description is complex, Δ is a very powerful shorthand.

The QueryPhoneNumber operation

QueryPhoneNumber has an *output* (a phone number) but does not change the directory content.

```
┌─ QueryPhoneNumber ─────────────────────────
│ ΔPhoneDir
│ name? : NAME
│ phone! : NUMBER
│ ───────────────────────────────────
│ phone! = phone name?
│ addr' = addr
│ phone' = phone
└────────────────────────────────────────────
```

The result, *phone!*, is simply the *NUMBER* corresponding to *name?*.

Notice that we need to state that the values in the directory are unchanged: it is *not* assumed. If we say nothing about them, then the reader can deduce nothing (and an implementation could change the directory all it liked and still satisfy the specification).

The Xi notation (Ξ)

For those operations that use the state data, but leave it unchanged, it is useful to have a shorthand that captures the same idea as Δ, and adds the notion that the state variables do not change. The Greek capital letter Xi, Ξ, is used as a prefix to a schema name as a shorthand for this notion. (Ξ is chosen because it looks like an equivalence symbol.)

To be more precise, if S is a schema, whose signature contains variables $v1, v2, v3, ...$, then ΞS stands for the schema:

$[\Delta S \mid v1' = v1 \ \wedge \ v2' = v2 \ \wedge \ v3' = v3 \ \wedge ...]$

For example,

$\Xi PhoneDir$

means the same as

$[PhoneDir;\ PhoneDir' \mid addr' = addr \ \wedge \ phone' = phone]$

and *QueryPhoneNumber* could be written

```
┌─QueryPhoneNumber──────────────────────
│ ΞPhoneDir
│ name? : NAME
│ phone! : NUMBER
│─────────────────────────────────────
│ phone! = phone name?
└─────────────────────────────────────
```

Like Δ, Ξ captures an important concept and suppresses irrelevant detail.

> **Exercise 7.5**
>
> Write a specification for a *QueryName* operation. The input is a *NUMBER* and the output is a *NAME*.

The Add operation revisited

So far, we have considered the 'normal' case for each of the operations. We will now consider some of the 'abnormal' possibilities. In the *Add* operation we assumed that it was possible to add the specified name and still retain *addr* and *phone* as *functions*. However, if *name?* is already in *addr* then the expression *addr* $\cup$ {*name?* $\mapsto$ *addr?*} does not denote a function as there would be two entries for the same name (unless, of course, by pure chance *addr?=addr name?*). So there is a *pre-condition* of *Add*, viz:

(*name?* ∉ dom *addr*) ∨ ((*name?, addr?*) ∈ *addr*)

Adding a pair that exists already seems pointless, so we might like to strengthen the specification by writing an explicit pre-condition in the predicates, thus:

```
┌─Add────────────────────────────────────
│ ΔPhoneDir
│ name? : NAME
│ addr? : ADDRESS
│ phone? : NUMBER
│────────────────────────────────────────
│ name? ∉ dom addr
│ addr' = addr ∪ {name? ↦ addr?}
│ phone' = phone ∪ {name? ↦ phone?}
└────────────────────────────────────────
```

But what if *name?* *is* already in the directory? We could just ignore this case. There is nothing 'wrong' in this, but when the name is already present, it leaves the implementer free to do whatever he likes. He could for instance, implement:

name? ∈ dom *addr*
addr' = {}
phone' = {}

We probably do not intend this freedom, and perhaps we meant to say 'if the name is already there, do not change the directory'.

So *Add* becomes:

```
┌─Add────────────────────────────────────
│ ΔPhoneDir
│ name? : NAME
│ addr? : ADDRESS
│ phone? : NUMBER
│────────────────────────────────────────
│ (name? ∉ dom addr
│  addr' = addr ∪ {name? ↦ addr?}
│  phone' = phone ∪ {name? ↦ phone?})
│  ∨
│ (name? ∈ dom addr
│  addr' = addr
│  phone' = phone)
└────────────────────────────────────────
```

This is valid Z and bad style. Even with careful layout, it is difficult for the reader to perceive what is being said. We have identified
two distinct situations and it is better to name them and describe each
separately. As we would like to distinguish these two cases at the
interface (so that the user of the interface knows which one occurred),
we will add a 'return code' value, called *rc!* (an output), taken from the
set:

$RetCode ::= OK \mid duplicate$

thus we arrive at:

```
┌─ AddOK ──────────────────────────────────
│ ΔPhoneDir
│ name? : NAME
│ addr? : ADDRESS
│ phone? : NUMBER
│ rc! : RetCode
├───────────────────────────────────────────
│ name? ∉ dom addr
│ addr' = addr ∪ {name? ↦ addr?}
│ phone' = phone ∪ {name? ↦ phone?}
│ rc! = OK
└───────────────────────────────────────────
```

```
┌─ AddDuplicate ───────────────────────────
│ ΞPhoneDir
│ name? : NAME
│ addr? : ADDRESS
│ phone? : NUMBER
│ rc! : RetCode
├───────────────────────────────────────────
│ name? ∈ dom addr
│ rc! = duplicate
└───────────────────────────────────────────
```

(Notice the use of Ξ to simplify the description.)

Now we want to say '*Add* is either *AddOK* or *AddDuplicate*' which we
can do by using schema disjunction, thus:

$Add \ \hat{=}\ AddOK \lor AddDuplicate$

```
┌─ Exercise 7.6 ────────────────────────────
│ Describe a *Replace* operation to replace an existing phone number by a
│ new one. Consider all possibilities.
└───────────────────────────────────────────
```

The pre-condition of an operation

On page 105, we mentioned that the 'pre-condition' for the *Add* operation was

$$(name? \notin \text{dom } addr) \ \vee \ ((name?, addr?) \in addr)$$

The **pre-condition** is a predicate that describes constraints on the *inputs* and *state* (*before* the operation) that must be satisfied for the operation to be performed. We can derive the pre-condition by formalizing the phrase *'there exist* suitable output and dashed variables'. For instance, the pre-condition of *AddDuplicate* is

$$\exists\, PhoneDir';\ rc!: RetCode \ \bullet \ (name? \in \text{dom } addr \ \wedge \ rc! = duplicate)$$

The predicate *name?* $\in$ dom *addr* places no constraint on *PhoneDir'*, so *any PhoneDir'* would satisfy this, for instance *addr'*={} and *phone'*={}. We can also see that a suitable *rc!* exists, because *duplicate*$\in$*RetCode*. Thus the pre-condition reduces to *name?* $\in$ dom *addr*. A more formal treatment of pre-condition will be presented in Chapter 10.

The initial state

So far, we have described various operations on a phone directory without saying anything about what it looks like when first created. That is, we have not described the *initial state*. We could describe an operation called 'Create' or 'SetUp' or some such. Generally, we use some name like *Init* meaning 'initial state'.

If we think of this as an operation, we see that there is no 'before' state — the directory didn't exist before being initialised — but there is an 'after' state. We will describe

```
┌─InitPD ─────────────────────────────
│  PhoneDir'
│ ────────────────────────────────────
│  addr' = {}
│  phone' = {}
└──────────────────────────────────────
```

The directory is initially empty.

Notes about decorations and prefixes

Some Z specifiers use *subscripts* as part of a schema name. For instance, different aspects of an *Add* operation might be called Add_0, Add_1 and so on. It is not clear whether the subscript is a *decoration* (in which case Add_0 should be derived from *Add*) or part of the base name (in which case Add_0 has its own, separate, definition). In this book we avoid subscripts and we advise you to do the same.

Some writers treat the Δ and Ξ prefixes as *pure conventions* rather than as part of Z proper. They allow a schema such as Δ*State* to be defined in any way the writer may choose, for instance:

Δ*State* $\triangleq$ [*State* ; *State'* | #*someset* < 24]

This differs from the usual meaning of Δ*State*. Similarly, Ξ*State* might be re-defined.

Until an agreed Z standard emerges, it is not clear whether the usual meanings as we have given them should be regarded as sacrosanct. We will stick to these and recommend that you do like-wise. It is better to introduce a new name (e.g. *DelState*) if we intro-duce a new meaning.

Some writers like to extend the notation by using their own prefixes. In general, such prefixes must be defined in terms of only the *signature* and *property* of the schema they apply to. In practice, these are often contrived and are better avoided.

SCHEMA AND AND OR

On page 106 we used *schema disjunction* ('or') and in Chapter 6 we introduced 'schema inclusion', which is actually a way of writing *schema conjunction* ('and').

There are several operators that we can use to combine schemas. In this chapter we will look at *and* and *or*; in Chapter 10 we will describe more schema operators.

When two schemas are combined the effect is to *merge* their signa-tures and *combine* their properties.

Merging signatures

In order that two signatures can be merged, they must be **type com-patible**. This means that, if any variable occurs in both schemas, it must have the same type in each of them. For example, if schemas *S1* and *S2* are defined as follows:

S1 $\triangleq$ [$x, y : \mathbb{Z}$; $c1 : CHAR$]
S2 $\triangleq$ [$y, z : \mathbb{Z}$; $c2 : CHAR$]

then they *can* be combined, because the common variable, y, has the same type in each. The result would be the schema [$x,y,z:\mathbb{Z};c1,c2:CHAR$] in which the common variable, y, appears just once in the signature.

In contrast, the schemas *T1* and *T2* defined below cannot be combined (and any attempt to do so is erroneous) because the common variable, *y*, has conflicting declarations.

$T1 \triangleq [x, y : \mathbb{Z};\ c1 : CHAR]$
$T2 \triangleq [z : \mathbb{Z};\ c2, y : CHAR]$

Notice that the common variable declarations need not be *identical*: the requirement is that they have the same *type*. Thus, for example, schemas *U1* and *U2* shown below *can* be combined, because the variable *y* is of type $\mathbb{Z}$ in each:

$U1 \triangleq [x, y : \mathbb{N};\ c1 : CHAR]$
$U2 \triangleq [y, z : \mathbb{Z};\ c2 : CHAR]$

However, the schema *U1* includes a property about *y*, namely that $y \geq 0$. The next sections explain how properties are combined.

Schema And (conjunction)

The **conjunction** of two schemas *S* and *T* is written $S \land T$, read '*S* and *T*'. It is a schema consisting of the signatures of *S* and *T* merged and the properties of *S* and *T* conjoined. For example, given

$Sab \triangleq [a,b:\mathbb{N} \mid a=b]$
$Sac \triangleq [a,c:\mathbb{N} \mid a=c]$

then $S \triangleq Sab \land Sac$ is the schema:

```
┌─ S ──────────────────────────────────
│ a,b,c : ℤ
│ ─────────────
│ a ≥ 0 ∧ b ≥ 0 ∧ c ≥ 0
│ a = b ∧ a = c
└───────────────────────────────────────
```

Often, we allow the declarations to remain intact in a simple case like this, so we might write

$Sab \land Sac = [a, b, c : \mathbb{N} \mid (a = b) \land (a = c)]$

Exercise 7.7

Using the schemas declared previously, write a vertical definition for

$S \triangleq \Xi PhoneDir \land$
$[PhoneDir;\ name? : NAME;\ phone! : NUMBER \mid phone! = phone\ name?]$

Schema Or (disjunction)

The ***disjunction*** of two schemas S and T is written S∨T, read 'S or T'. It is a schema consisting of the signatures of S and T merged and the properties of S and T disjoined. For example, given

$$Sab \;\hat{=}\; [a, b : \mathbb{N} \mid a = b]$$
$$Sac \;\hat{=}\; [a, c : \mathbb{N} \mid a = c]$$

then

$$Sab \vee Sac \;=\; [a, b, c : \mathbb{Z} \mid (a = b \geq 0) \vee (a = c \geq 0)]$$

Schema disjunction is often used as a way of breaking down a complex operation into more manageable pieces. We saw this technique used in the description of *Add*. The operation is divided into a number of separate cases and, for each case, a schema is defined to describe the effect of the operation. These schemas are then disjoined to give the overall definition of the operation.

In *Add*, the two cases did not 'overlap' and together accounted for all possibilities allowed by the state and inputs.

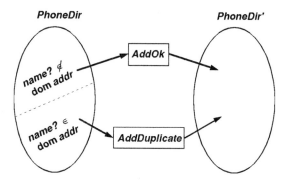

Fig 7.3. Schema disjunction (or).

Exercise 7.8

Consider an additional constraint on phone numbers, namely that they must be members of a global set called *ValidNumbers*. Write a new description of *PhoneDir*.

Exercise 7.9 illustrates the fact that, in general, cases may 'overlap' and not all possibilities need be covered. We strongly recommend that you attempt this exercise and read the answer supplied.

Exercise 7.9

Using *PhoneDir* from the previous exercise redefine the *Add* operation, assuming input variables:

name? : *NAME*
phone? : *NUMBER*

You may want to extend *RetCode*.

Is your specification *non-deterministic*? That is, given the before state and input values, does the specification admit more than one possible after state and output combination? Or is the result *determined*?

ANSWERS TO EXERCISES

Answer 7.1

Each subscriber has an address and a phone number:

```
┌─Subscriber────────────────────────────────
│ addr : ADDRESS
│ phone : NUMBER
│
└────────────────────────────────
```

The phone directory, *PhoneDir*, consists of a set of subscribers each identified by *NAME*, which we model as a function from *NAME* to *Subscriber*:

```
┌─PhoneDir────────────────────────────────
│ dir : NAME↦Subscriber
└────────────────────────────────
```

This is illustrated in Figure 7.4.

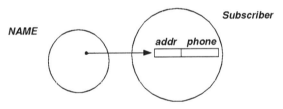

Fig 7.4. Phone directory model II.

At this stage, we cannot tell whether this model is 'better' or 'worse' than the one we first thought of. If there were many items of data associated with each subscriber, then this new model would be worth adopting. As there are only two, it is a moot point. We shall continue the description of the system based on the first model. When we investigate the operations on the directory, we might decide that our second model would be simpler.

Answer 7.2

We use our original model here and add a predicate to say that different subscribers have different numbers.

```
┌─PhoneDir ─────────────────────────────────────
│ addr : NAME⇸ADDRESS
│ phone : NAME⇸NUMBER
│─────────────────────────────────────────────
│ dom addr = dom phone
│ ∀ nm1, nm2 : NAME | nm1 ≠ nm2 • phone nm1 ≠ phone nm2
└─────────────────────────────────────────────
```

Answer 7.3

This directory contains addresses and phone numbers. Each subscriber has one address and one or more phone numbers. We choose to describe this as a mapping from name to address and a mapping from name to a *set* of numbers:

```
┌─PhoneDir ─────────────────────────────────────
│ addr : NAME⇸ADDRESS
│ phone : NAME⇸ℙNUMBER
│─────────────────────────────────────────────
│ dom addr = dom phone
│ ∀ pn : dom phone • phone pn ≠ ∅
└─────────────────────────────────────────────
```

All entries in the directory have at least one phone number. We might ask 'Can two people with different names have the same phone number?' There is no constraint that prevents this, so we deduce that shared numbers could exist. (How would you write such a constraint?)

We should try to describe all the 'constraints' we can think of that apply to the state data. These will be 'invariants' of the operations on the data, that is the operations must ensure that these constraints remain true. If an operation does not do so, then the specification is inconsistent.

In a large specification, it is impossible to think of all the constraints on the state data in the first description. As we describe the operations, other constraints may occur to us, so we revisit the state description and add them. When we do this, we must check again that the operations described so far still preserve the invariants.

Answer 7.4

The *Delete* operation has one input, *name?*, and changes the directory:

```
┌─Delete ───────────────────────────────────────
│ PhoneDir
│ PhoneDir'
│ name? : NAME
│─────────────────────────────────────────────
│ addr' = addr \ {name? ↦ (addr name?)}
│ phone' = phone \ {name? ↦ (phone name?)}
└─────────────────────────────────────────────
```

The entries corresponding to *name?* are removed from both *addr* and *phone*.

Answer 7.5

The *QueryName* operation has one input, *phone?*, and one output, *name!*. It does not change the directory:

```
┌─ QueryName ─────────────────────────────────────
│ ΞPhoneDir
│ phone? : NUMBER
│ name? : NAME
├──────────────────────────
│ phone? = phone name!
│
└────────────────────────────────────────
```

The output value, *name!*, is a *NAME* corresponding to *phone?*.

You may be surprised to see how similar this answer is to the *QueryPhoneNumber* schema. It is an illustration of an 'implicit' specification of a result. The predicate may or may not uniquely determine the value of the output variable. If many people can have the same phone number then this specification does *not* determine a unique value – this is not 'wrong', merely non-deterministic. See also the answer to Exercise 7.8.

Answer 7.6

First we describe the situation when the specified name *is* in the directory. We call this *ReplaceOK*. There are three inputs, *name?*, *addr?* and *phone?*, and a return code, *rc!*. The directory is changed:

```
┌─ ReplaceOK ─────────────────────────────────────
│ ΔPhoneDir
│ name? : NAME
│ addr? : ADDRESS
│ phone? : NUMBER
│ rc! : RetCode
├──────────────────────────
│ name? ∈ dom addr
│ addr' = addr ⊕ {name? ↦ addr?}
│ phone' = phone ⊕ {name? ↦ phone?}
│ rc! = OK
│
└────────────────────────────────────────
```

The *name?* is in *addr*, and the corresponding entries in *addr'* and *phone'* are replaced by the new values. The return code shows that the operation was *OK*.

Now we describe what happens when the specified name is *not* in the directory. We call this *ReplaceNoName*. The inputs and output are the same as before, but the directory is not changed:

```
┌─ ReplaceNoName ──────────────────────────────────
│ ΞPhoneDir
│ name? : NAME
│ addr? : ADDRESS
│ phone? : NUMBER
│ rc! : RetCode
├──────────────
│ name? ∉ dom addr
│ rc! = noname
└───────────────────────────────────────────────────
```

The *name?* is not in *addr* and the return code shows us that this is so.

We can now describe the complete *Replace* operation:

Replace ≙ *ReplaceOK* ∨ *ReplaceNoName*

In the foregoing we omitted to define *RetCode*. We do so now:

RetCode ::= *OK* | *noname*

(Though most writers use a 'declaration before use' style, it is not mandatory.)

We might notice that *ReplaceOK* and *ReplaceNoName* each have the same input/output variables. We might choose to 'factor out' this data, thus:

```
┌─ Rdata ──────────────────────────────────────────
│ name? : NAME
│ addr? : ADDRESS
│ phone? : NUMBER
│ rc! : RetCode
└───────────────────────────────────────────────────
```

This collection of data can be thought of as the interface parameters to the *Replace* operation.

Now we can write shorter descriptions of *ReplaceOK* and *ReplaceNoName*:

```
┌─ ReplaceOK ──────────────────────────────────────
│ ΔPhoneDir
│ Rdata
├──────────────
│ name? ∈ dom addr
│ addr' = addr ⊕ {name? ↦ addr?}
│ phone' = phone ⊕ {name? ↦ phone?}
│ rc! = OK
└───────────────────────────────────────────────────
```

```
┌─ReplaceNoName ──────────────────────────
│ ΞPhoneDir
│ Rdata
├──────────
│ name? ∉ dom addr
│ rc! = noname
└──────────────────────────────────────────
```

Answer 7.7

```
┌─S ──────────────────────────────────────
│ ΞPhoneDir
│ name? : NAME
│ phone! : NUMBER
├──────────
│ phone! = phone name?
└──────────────────────────────────────────
```

We see that this is just the same as the *QueryPhoneNumber* operation. That is, 'schema inclusion' and 'schema conjunction' are the same thing. Schema conjunction is a useful technique when there are many items of state data. It is often convenient to divide the state into a number of separate pieces, and write a schema to describe the effect of the operation on each piece (perhaps several pieces are unchanged, for example). We can then conjoin ('and') these schemas to describe the operation.

Answer 7.8

First we introduce the set of *ValidNumbers*:

ValidNumbers : ℙ*NUMBER*

Now the *PhoneDir* has an additional invariant

```
┌─PhoneDir ───────────────────────────────
│ addr : NAME↦ADDRESS
│ phone : NAME↦NUMBER
├──────────
│ dom addr = dom phone
│ ran phone ⊆ ValidNumbers
└──────────────────────────────────────────
```

which says that all the numbers should be valid ones.

Answer 7.9

We can foresee a third situation when we try to add a new entry to the directory, namely that the *NUMBER* we specify is invalid. So we extend *RetCode*:

RetCode ::= *OK* | *duplicate_name* | *invalid_number*

The *Add* operation has three input parameters and a return code, collected together in *ParmsToAdd*.

```
┌─ParmsToAdd──────────────────────────────────
│ name? : NAME
│ addr? : ADDRESS
│ phone? : NUMBER
│ rc! : RetCode
└
```

First we consider the 'OK' situation:

```
┌─AddOK──────────────────────────────────────
│ ΔPhoneDir
│ ParmsToAdd
├──────────────────────────────────────────
│ name? ∉ dom addr
│ phone? ∈ ValidNumbers
│ addr' = addr ∪ {name? ↦ addr?}
│ phone' = phone ∪ {name? ↦ phone?}
│ rc! = OK
└
```

If the specified name is not in the directory and the specified number is valid, then new entries are added to *addr* and *phone*, and the return code shows the result is *OK*.

Next we consider what happens if the name is already there:

```
┌─AddDuplicate───────────────────────────────
│ ParmsToAdd
│ ΞPhoneDir
├──────────────────────────────────────────
│ name? ∈ dom addr
│ rc! = duplicate_name
└
```

If the specified name is already in the directory, then the directory is not changed. The return code shows that there was duplication.

Finally we consider an invalid number:

```
┌─AddInvalidNumber───────────────────────────
│ ParmsToAdd
│ ΞPhoneDir
├──────────────────────────────────────────
│ phone? ∉ ValidNumbers
│ rc! = invalid_number
└
```

If the specified number is not valid, then the directory is not changed and the return code indicates the reason.

Now we can describe the *Add* operation:

Add ≙ *AddOK* ∨ *AddDuplicate* ∨ *AddInvalidName*

This is (deliberately) non-deterministic. If the input values consist of both an invalid number and an existing name, the specification does not say which return code to set: either *invalid_number* or *duplicate_name* would be a valid thing to do; either would *satisfy* the specification. Non-deterministic specifications are more common than deterministic ones and are a form of abstraction. By refusing to specify which result to give, the specification states that either will be satisfactory and that the user of the interface should not rely upon whichever is actually chosen.

SPECIFICATION PROBLEMS

7.1 CASH DISPENSER

The Thrifty Bank Corp. offers its customers a cash dispenser service. Each account holder can have up to three cash cards, each identified by a separate 4-digit PIN (Personal Identification Number) the first digit of which cannot be zero. To operate a cash dispenser, the customer inserts his card, enters the corresponding PIN and selects a transaction.

The machines provide the following transactions:

• Withdraw cash.
• Query balance.
• Request a cheque book.
• Request a statement.

For withdrawals, there is a limit of £100 per transaction and the balance may not be overdrawn.

Account details, including customer name, address and current balance, are held centrally. The dispensers are all on-line, and account balances are updated when the transaction occurs.

On each cash card, a magnetic stripe contains the account number and card number (1 to 3), but not the PIN (this is held centrally).

Write a formal specification of the account management system modelling each of the cash dispenser transactions. If you wish to extend the problem, you could consider how to model cheque book and statement issue, and how to handle 'locking' (two users could try to access the same account at the same time).

7.2 CALL AND RETURN

In an hypothetical microprocessor, a CALL instruction is 5 bytes long:

```
byte 1    OpCode (X'76')
byte 2-5  Branch Address
```

A RETURN instruction is 1 byte long:

```
byte 1    OpCode (X'77')
```

Model these instructions for a simple machine that has:

• A 'program counter' (address of next instruction – addresses identify a particular byte).

• A 'boot address' (the address at which the machine starts).
• A 'call stack' (for saving where to return).

First, write the specification as if the call stack were unlimited in size and then adapt your answer to cope with a stack which is bounded.

7.3 NIM

The game of NIM is played by two people. The game starts with three piles containing five, six and seven sticks respectively. Each player plays alternately. On each turn, the player removes some sticks from *one* pile. The loser is the player who removes the last stick (the other player is the winner).

Write a formal specification of the game state and a *Play* schema. Distinguish between:

• Game ended.
• Game continues.
• Illegal play.

7.4 TEXT EDITOR

Write a formal specification for the simple text editor, described below.

A document consists of a sequence of lines of characters. The user can edit one line at a time, (the 'current line') and a cursor shows the user the current position within the current line. This cursor can be moved anywhere within the current line and one character beyond the last.

When the user types a character, it is inserted at the current position in the current line.

There are six control keys, that provide the following functions:

• LEFT moves the cursor left one position.
• RIGHT moves the cursor right one position.
• UP makes the line preceding the current one become current (and resets the cursor to the start of the line).
• DOWN makes the line succeeding the current one become current (and resets the cursor to the start of the line).
• DELETE deletes the current character.
• CR (carriage return) inserts an empty line after the current line.

Write a formal description of these control keys and of the 'Insert Character' action.

7.5 EVENT HANDLER

Write a formal specification for the event handlers for a workstation containing:

• A two-button mouse.

- A keyboard.
- A screen.
- A system unit.

The mouse can be moved around the table. Movement in either the x-direction or the y-direction by more than 2mm causes an interrupt, and the amount of movement since the last mouse interrupt is provided with the event.

The two mouse buttons each cause an interrupt when they are pressed ('mouse down') and when they are released ('mouse up').

Each key on the keyboard (except CTL) causes an interrupt when it is pressed (but not when it is released). If the operator presses two (or more) keys simultaneously, only one interrupt will be generated.

The CTL key is a dead key. Pressing it does not cause an interrupt until another key is pressed too. It acts as a 'modifier' of this other key.

The system unit contains a number of 16-bit registers:

- The Xreg and Yreg control the position of a cross-hair on the screen. The screen is 1024 by 1024 pels, addressed from the top left, which is (0,0). So both X and Y coordinates range from 0 to 1023 (only the low order 10 bits of the registers are used).
- The Creg (control) and Dreg (data) are used by interrupt routines.
- The Preg (program) contains the address of the next instruction to be executed.

There are also a number of 'interrupt vectors' (addresses) two of which are relevant:

- V1 contains the address of the button event handler.
- V2 contains the address of the key event handler.

The data available with these input events and the required handling is explained below.

Mouse event (movement)

```
byte 1   01
byte 2   X-delta (8 bit signed value)
byte 3   Y-delta (8 bit signed value)
```

Increment the Xreg and Yreg with these deltas. The cross-hair is *not* to wrap: do not increment beyond 1023 or decrement below zero.

Mouse button event

```
byte 1   02
byte 2   button
         X'01' = button 1 down
         X'02' = button 2 down
         X'81' = button 1 up
         X'82' = button 2 up
```

Load the button value into the Dreg and branch to the address in V1.

Key event

```
byte 1  03
byte 2  01 = data / 02 = CTL
byte 3  key value (00-8F)
```

For a CTL key event, load the key value into the Creg, zero into the Dreg and branch to the address in V2. For any other event, load the key value into the Dreg, zero into the Creg and branch to the address in V2.

Chapter 8
More about Data Models

> And thick and fast they came at last
> And more, and more, and more –
>
> *Lewis Carroll, Through the Looking-Glass*

In this chapter, we develop the ideas introduced in Chapter 5. We introduce more *relational operators, sequence operators* and *constrained functions* namely *injections, surjections* and *bijections*.

The intention of this chapter is to expand the mathematical toolbox so as to model behaviour more readily. All of this chapter is devoted to standard functions and facilities that come in the basic library. We break no new notational ground.

RELATIONS

The rich and expressive language of relations is available to Z specifiers by virtue of many definitions that come in the basic library.

Inverse relation

The *inverse* R^{-1} is a relation in which the order of all pairs in R is reversed. If R is of type $A \leftrightarrow B$, then

$$R^{-1} == \{a : A; \; b : B; \; | \; (a,b) \in R \bullet (b,a)\}$$

Exercise 8.1

Write a predicate that states that *Aroad* (see page 60) is a symmetric relation.

Domain restriction

The relation $S \lhd R$ is the subset of R where the domain is restricted to set S (S must be the same type as $\mathrm{dom}\ R$). We take only those pairs (a,b) of R where $a \in S$. If R is of type $A \leftrightarrow B$ and S is of type $\mathbb{P}A$, then

$$S \lhd R == R \cap (S \times B)$$

Domain restriction is illustrated in Figure 8.1, where the solid lines show the relation $S \lhd R$.

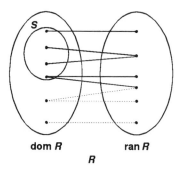

Fig 8.1. Domain restriction.

On page 74 we gave a predicate for restricting a student to three subjects:

∀ *stu* : dom *studies*; *setsub* : ℙ*subjects*
   | (*stu*,*setsub*) ∈ *studies* • #*setsub* ≤ 3

We can now see how this might be shortened.

∀ *stu* : dom *studies* • # ran({*stu*}◁*studies*) ≤ 3

Exercise 8.2

Refer to the sample answer for the Text Editor Specification Problem 7.4. Use ◁ to express the *InsertLine* operation more succinctly.

Domain subtraction

The relation *S*◁*R* is the subset of *R* where set *S* is subtracted from the domain (*S* must be the same type as dom *R*). We take only those pairs (*a*,*b*) of *R* where *a*∉*S*. If *R* is of type *A*↔*B* and *S* is of type ℙ*A*, then

   S◁*R* == *R* \ (*S*×*B*)

Domain subtraction is illustrated in Figure 8.2, where the solid lines show the relation *S*◁*R*.

Exercise 8.3

Given

   A = {*a*,*b*,*c*,*d*,*e*,*f*}
   B = {*1*,*2*,*3*,*4*,*5*}
   R = {(*a*,2), (*b*,1), (*b*,4), (*d*,1), (*e*,4), (*f*,2), (*f*,5)}
   S = {*a*,*b*,*c*}

draw a table to illustrate that (*S*◁*R*) ∪ (*S*◁*R*) = *R*.

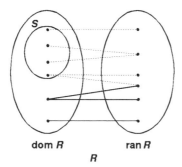

dom *R*   ran *R*

R

Fig 8.2. Domain subtraction.

Range restriction

The relation $R \triangleright S$ is the subset of R where the range is restricted to set S (S must be the same type as ran R). We take only those pairs (a,b) of R where $b \in S$. If R is of type $A \leftrightarrow B$ and S is of type $\mathbb{P}B$, then

$$R \triangleright S = R \cap (A \times S)$$

Range restriction is illustrated in Figure 8.3, where the solid lines show the relation $R \triangleright S$.

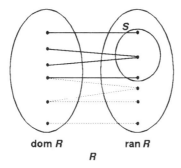

dom *R*   ran *R*

R

Fig 8.3. Range restriction.

Range subtraction

The relation $R \triangleright\!\!\!- S$ is the subset of R where set S is subtracted from the range (S must be the same type as ran R). We take only those pairs (a,b) of R where b∉S. If R is of type A⟷B and S is of type ℙB, then

$$R \rhd S = R \setminus (A \times S)$$

Range subtraction is illustrated in Figure 8.4, where the solid lines show the relation R⊳S.

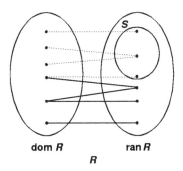

dom *R*   ran *R*

R

Fig 8.4. Range subtraction.

┌─ **Exercise 8.5** ───┐
│ Write a formal expression relating ▷ and ⊳ like that in Exercise 8.3. │
└──┘

Relational image

The **relational image** R(|S|) is the subset of ran R to which the elements of S are mapped (S must be the same type as dom R). If R is of type A⟷B and S is of type ℙA, then

$$R(\!|S|\!) == \operatorname{ran}(S \lhd R)$$

Relational composition

Two relations can be **composed** by the relational operators:

> **Forward relational composition**, written ;
> **Backward relational composition**, written ∘

These two operators provide alternative ways of writing the same thing.

R1;R2 can be read as 'apply R1 then R2', which is the natural left to right reading. If R1 is of type A⟷B and R2 is of type B⟷C, then

$$R1 \,;R2 \;==\; \{a:A; \; b:B; \; c:C \mid (a,b) \in R1 \;\wedge\; (b,c) \in R2 \bullet (a,c)\}$$

That is, R1;R2 is a relation A⟷C where members of the domain of R1 are mapped to elements of B and thence through the relation R2 to elements of C.

Relational composition is illustrated in Figure 8.5, where the solid lines show the relation *R1;R2*.

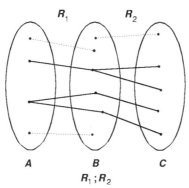

Fig 8.5. Relational composition.

R1○R2 can be read as '*R1* of *R2* of', which is the usual mathematical notation:

$R1 \circ R2 \ == \ R2 ; R1$

For example, suppose the relation

studies : *STUDENT↔SUBJECT*

shows which students study what subjects, and the relation

teaches : *SUBJECT↔TEACHER*

shows who teaches each subject. Then,

studies ; *teaches*

is a relation *STUDENT↔TEACHER* showing which teachers teach which students.

The identity relation

The *identity*, id *S*, is the relation that relates each member of set *S* to itself:

id $S == \{x : S \bullet x \mapsto x\}$

For example, if $S == 1..6$ then

id $S = \{(1,1), (2,2), (3,3), (4,4), (5,5), (6,6)\}$

which we can illustrate by a table (Table 8.1).

Table 8.1. An identity relation.

	1	2	3	4	5	6
1	X					
2		X				
3			X			
4				X		
5					X	
6						X

Transitive relations

A relation is called *transitive* if elements that are related to one another indirectly are, in fact, already related directly. If R is of type $S \leftrightarrow S$, then R is transitive if and only if:

$$\forall a, b, c : S \bullet ((a,b) \in R \land (b,c) \in R) \Rightarrow (a,c) \in R$$

We previously described the *Aroad* relation as the collection of towns *directly* linked by A-roads (see page 60). So (*Weymouth,Dorchester*) and (*Dorchester,Puddletown*) are in *Aroads*, but (*Weymouth,Puddleton*) is *not* (because the route goes via *Dorchester*). Thus we see that *Aroad* is *not* transitive. If we describe an *Aroute* relation as the collection of towns linked *directly* or *indirectly* by A-roads, then (*Weymouth,Puddletown*) *is* in *Aroute* and we can see that *Aroute* is *transitive*.

Exercise 8.6

Consider the following relations between people: *BrotherOf*, *OlderThan* and *NeighbourOf*. Which of these is transitive?

Another way to say that the relation R is transitive is to say that it satisfies the condition $R \,;\, R \subseteq R$. You should convince yourself that this is the same as the condition above.

Transitive closure

The *transitive closure* of a relation $R : S \leftrightarrow S$ is written R^+. It is the smallest transitive relation that contains R.

There are two ways to define R^+: one from the 'inside' (the constructive method) and one from the 'outside'. Outside first:

$$R^+ \;==\; \bigcap \{r : S \leftrightarrow S \mid r \,;\, r \subseteq r \land R \subseteq r\}$$

which is merely the formal expression of the phrase 'the smallest ($\cap$) transitive relation ($r \mathbin{;} r \subseteq r$) that contains R'. It is a simple exercise for mathematicians to verify that this is indeed a transitive relation itself, and that it contains R. It must also be contained in any other such relation. This is a concise and neat definition but it is a little terse and doesn't help us to understand what R^+ means. The 'insider' definition is better for this.

First we define a 'power' operation on relations:

$$\_^- : (S \leftrightarrow S) \times \mathbb{N} \to (S \leftrightarrow S)$$

$$\forall r : S \leftrightarrow S \bullet r^0 = \mathrm{id}\, S \wedge (\forall n : \mathbb{N} \bullet r^{n+1} = r \mathbin{;} r^n)$$

(Here we are taking a liberty with the notation, but one that is commonly taken in the Z literature. The notation is confusable with the usual notation for squares and cubes and with the inverse of a relation. The alternative is to invent a new notation, and few authors can live with this. The definition above has two underscores, one placed in the normal position and one in the superscript position, to indicate the two parameters to the 'power' operation.)

We have defined a whole series of relations with this operation. We have $R^1 = R$, $R^2 = R \mathbin{;} R$, $R^3 = R \mathbin{;} R \mathbin{;} R$, and so on.

Now, two elements directly related by R we can say are 'one step apart', and if $(a,b) \in R$ and $(b,c) \in R$ then a and c are 'two steps apart', and all elements exactly two steps apart are related by R^2. In general, elements n steps apart are related by R^n. Our definition of R^+ simply says that it relates elements that are 'any number of steps' apart. So, the 'inside' definition is:

$$R^+ \mathrel{==} \bigcup \{n : \mathbb{N} \mid n > 0 \bullet R^n\}$$

which is sometimes written informally as: $R \cup R^2 \cup R^3 \cup \ldots$

This turns out to mean the same as the outsider definition above.

Exercise 8.7

Write down the members of R^+ where $R = \{(1,2), (1,3), (2,4), (4,7)\}$

We can illustrate transitive closure using the the directed graph shown in Figure 8.6. This can be defined as a set of *links*, thus:

$$links \mathrel{==} \{a \mapsto c, b \mapsto d, c \mapsto e, c \mapsto g, d \mapsto f, f \mapsto g, f \mapsto h, g \mapsto i\}$$

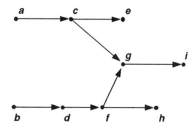

Fig 8.6. A directed graph.

Then the relation *links*$^+$ is the set of pairs showing the possible destinations from each node, thus:

links$^+$ =
$\{ a \mapsto c, a \mapsto e, a \mapsto g, a \mapsto i,$
$\quad c \mapsto e, c \mapsto g, c \mapsto i,$
$\quad d \mapsto f, d \mapsto g, d \mapsto h, d \mapsto i,$
$\quad f \mapsto g, f \mapsto h, f \mapsto i,$
$\quad g \mapsto i \}$

Relational image can be used to give an expression for the set of all destinations from specified nodes, for instance *links*$^+$ (|{c}|) is the set of all nodes that can be reached from c, namely $\{e, g, i\}$.

Reflexive relations

A relation is said to be ***reflexive*** if each element is related to itself. If R is of type S↔S, then R is reflexive if and only if:

$\forall x : S \bullet (x,x) \in R$

that is, if and only if id $S \subseteq R$. Thus, *Aroute* is a reflexive relation, and *Aroad* is not.

For any relation R:S↔S, the relation R ∪ id S is reflexive.

Exercise 8.8 ───
Prove that R ∪ id S is reflexive.
───

Reflexive transitive closure

The ***reflexive transitive closure*** of a relation R : S↔S is written R* . It is the smallest reflexive transitive relation that contains R:

$R^* == R^+ \cup$ id S

Exercise 8.9

Given

$R = \{(1,2), (1,3), (2,4), (4,7)\}$

write down R^* .

Exercise 8.10

Modify the insider definition for transitive closure so as to provide a direct definition of *reflexive* transitive closure. How might you modify the outsider definition to achieve this?

We could extend this discussion of relations to include symmetric relations (where $R^{-1}=R$), equivalence relations (which are reflexive, symmetric *and* transitive) and order relations (which satisfy different conditions again). There are no standard notations in the basic library for these, but it is not too difficult to introduce some for the purposes of a particular specification.

CONSTRAINED FUNCTIONS

By placing various constraints on the mapping, we can create a function that is an *injection*, a *surjection* or a *bijection*. Because these can be defined as functions with added constraints, we do not really need to use them, and many authors restrict themselves to the 'simple arrows', and add explicit constraints if necessary.

Injection

An ***injection*** is a one-to-one function, that is, distinct elements of the domain map to distinct elements of the range. This means that an element of the range identifies at most one element of the domain – the one from which it comes. This is like the definition of a function, with the roles of domain and range reversed. This inspires the definitions that follow. Arrows with a head and a tail are used to denote sets of injections: *partial* ($\rightarrowtail$), *total* ($\rightarrowtail\!\!\!\rightarrow$) and *finite* ($\rightarrowtail\!\!\!\!\!\rightarrow$).

$A \rightarrowtail B == \{f : A \rightarrow B \mid f^{-1} \in B \rightarrow A\}$

> The set of all (partial) functions from A to B whose inverse is also a (partial) function.

$A \rightarrowtail\!\!\!\rightarrow B == \{f : A \rightarrow B \mid f^{-1} \in B \rightarrow A\}$

> The set of all total functions from A to B whose inverse is also a function.

$A \rightarrowtail B == \{f : A \nrightarrow B \mid f^{-1} \in B \nrightarrow A\}$

The set of all finite functions from A to B whose inverse is also a (finite) function.

Figure 8.7 illustrates an injection.

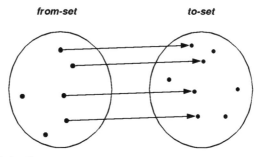

from-set   **to-set**

Fig 8.7. An injection.

Exercise 8.11

With the above definition, prove that distinct elements of the domain of $f : A \rightarrowtail B$ map to distinct elements of the range.

Surjection

A **surjection** is a function whose range is the whole of the to-set, that is, it 'fills' the to-set. A surjection is often called 'onto'. Arrows with two heads are used to denote sets of surjections: *partial* ($\nrightarrow\!\!\!\rightarrow$) and *total* ($\twoheadrightarrow$).

$A \nrightarrow\!\!\!\rightarrow B == \{f : A \nrightarrow B \mid \operatorname{ran} f = B\}$

The set of all (partial) functions from A to B whose range is the whole of B.

$A \twoheadrightarrow B == \{f : A \rightarrow B \mid \operatorname{ran} f = B\}$

The set of all total functions from A to B whose range is the whole of B.

Figure 8.8 illustrates a surjection.

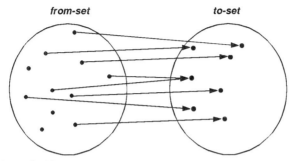

Fig 8.8. A surjection

Bijection

A **bijection** is a function that is a total one-to-one correspondence between the from-set and the to-set. An arrow with two heads and a tail is used to denote a set of bijections (>⤖):

A>⤖B == $\{f : A$>⤖$B \mid f \in A$—⤖$B\}$

> The set of all total injections from A to B which are also total surjections.

That is, each member of the from-set maps to one and only one member of the to-set, and each member of the to-set is associated with a member of the from-set.

Figure 8.9 illustrates a bijection.

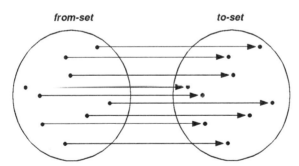

Fig 8.9. A bijection.

Exercise 8.12

Re-classify the following functions, keeping the same from-set and to-set for each, and giving suitable declarations for them as partial, total, surjective, injective or bijective.

$e : \mathbb{N} \nrightarrow \mathbb{N} \mid e = \{n : \mathbb{N} \bullet n \mapsto (n + 1)\}$

$f : \mathbb{Z} \nrightarrow \mathbb{N} \mid f = \{n : \mathbb{Z} \bullet n \mapsto n^2\}$

$g : \mathbb{N} \nrightarrow \mathbb{N} \mid g = \{n : \mathbb{N} \bullet n^2 \mapsto n\}$

$h : \mathbb{Z} \times \mathbb{Z} \nrightarrow \mathbb{N} \mid h = \{m, n : \mathbb{Z} \bullet (m,n) \mapsto (3*m + 2*n)\}$

$p : 1..n \twoheadrightarrow 1..n$

Data Types and constructor functions

Let us look again at the solution to Specification Problem 6.3 (Filenames), found on page 216. As part of that solution, we introduced a given set *CHAR*, and two subsets, *Alpha* and *Numeric*, and certain constraints on them.

Suppose, instead, we had started with the notion of two given sets *ALPHA* and *NUMERIC* and then wished to combine these to give *CHAR*. We cannot form the union *ALPHA∪NUMERIC* (because *ALPHA* and *NUMERIC* are different *types*). To form such a combination, we need to introduce:

- Another given set *CHAR*.
- A function that maps *ALPHA* onto a subset of *CHAR*.
- A function that maps *NUMERIC* onto another subset of *CHAR*.

Moreover these two subsets must be disjoint. This is shown in Figure 8.10.

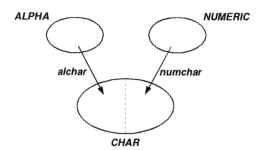

Fig 8.10. Combining *ALPHA* and *NUMERIC*.

So we could write:

[CHAR]
alchar : ALPHA→CHAR
numchar : NUMERIC→CHAR

We can say more than this, however. Clearly no character can be both *ALPHA* and *NUMERIC*, so we know that

ran alchar ∩ ran numchar = {}

Also, each element of *ALPHA* maps to a distinct element of *CHAR* (so that we can still distinguish different *ALPHA* characters), thus *alchar* is an *injection*:

alchar : ALPHA >↦ CHAR

but, in fact, *every* element of *ALPHA* maps to an element of *CHAR* so *alchar* is *total*, viz:

alchar : ALPHA>→CHAR

and similarly

numchar : NUMERIC>→CHAR

Finally, we wish to say that the set *CHAR* consists solely of the elements mapped from *ALPHA* and those mapped from *NUMERIC*:

CHAR = ran ALPHA ∪ ran NUMERIC

This method of combining two (or more) different types to produce a third is captured by the data type definition

CHAR ::= alchar≪ALPHA≫ | numchar≪NUMERIC≫

which introduces the set *CHAR* and injections *alchar* and *numchar* as just described. The symbols ≪ and ≫ are called **disjoint union brackets** and the functions *alchar* and *numchar* are called **constructor functions**.

The above data type definition is a shorthand for:

[CHAR]

alchar : ALPHA>→CHAR
numchar : NUMERIC>→CHAR

CHAR = ran ALPHA ∪ ran NUMERIC
ran ALPHA ∩ ran NUMERIC = ∅

In the solution to Problem 6.3 we also declared a character *dot* which we observed was neither *Alpha* nor *Numeric*.   We can extend our datatype definition to cope with this, thus

　　CHAR ::= alchar≪ALPHA≫ | numchar≪NUMERIC≫ | dot

This is equivalent to:

[*CHAR*]

> *alchar* : *ALPHA*>→*CHAR*
> *numchar* : *NUMERIC*>→*CHAR*
> *dot* : *CHAR*
> ───────────────
> *CHAR* = ran *ALPHA* ∪ ran *NUMERIC* ∪ {*dot*}
> ran *ALPHA* ∩ ran *NUMERIC* = {}
> *dot* ∉ (ran *ALPHA* ∪ ran *NUMERIC*)

Exercise 8.13

Extend the *CHAR* data-type to include two more special characters, *dash* and *colon*. Write the new data-type definition and show its equivalent expansion.

Exercise 8.14

Given a function, *CodePoint*, which maps each *CHAR* onto a distinct *code point* in the range 1 to 255,

　　CodePoint : CHAR>→*1..255*

write an expression representing the code point that corresponds to the *NUMERIC* value

　　n : NUMERIC

Lambda abstraction

In elementary textbooks on Algebra, a function definition is written like this:

　　$f(x,y) = x^2 + 5x + y^2$

To evaluate a particular use of the function, we substitute the parameter values in the right hand side expression, for instance:

　　$f(3,2) = 3^2 + 5*3 + 2^2 = 28$

In this example, the function f maps two values, x and y to another value. In Z we might declare it as:

$f : (\mathbb{Z} \times \mathbb{Z}) \to \mathbb{Z}$

and the evaluation rule can be written as a set expression, thus:

$f = \{x, y : \mathbb{Z} \bullet (x,y) \mapsto x^2 + 5*x + y^2\}$

Such an expression is rather cumbersome, and the **lambda abstraction** provides us with a shorthand for it. Thus, for example, the same function can be written as:

$\lambda x, y : \mathbb{Z} \bullet x^2 + 5*x + y^2$

We could name this function, thus:

$quad == \lambda x, y : \mathbb{Z} \bullet x^2 + 5*x + y^2$

and then use it like this: $quad(3,2)$ (an expression whose value is 28). Or we can use the lamda abstraction directly, for instance

$(\lambda x, y : \mathbb{Z} \bullet x^2 + 5*x + y^2)(3,2)$

which denotes an integer, value 28.

The general form of lambda abstraction is written thus:

λ declaration | constraint • term

(The constraint is optional – if it is omitted, so is the constraint bar.)

The declaration introduces bound variables which are identified as parameters of the function (and constrained by the constraint), and the term defines the rule for evaluating the function.

Lambda abstractions are quite useful for defining **projections** – functions that select a component of a pair or triple, or a component from a schema binding. For instance:

$COUPLE == MAN \times WOMAN$

$man == \lambda m : MAN; w : WOMAN \bullet m$
$woman == \lambda m : MAN; w : WOMAN \bullet m$

defines projections *man* and *woman* so that, given a couple *c:COUPLE*, the male component can be written *man c* and the female *woman c*. This is a useful notation if it is likely that complex expressions occur which result in values of type *COUPLE*.

The same thing works well for schema components. For instance, given *Part*, *partno* and *list* shown below

```
┌Part──────────────────────────────────────────
│ numb : ℕ
│ desc : STRING
└────────────────────────────────────────
```

partno == λ *Part* • *numb*
list : seq *Part*

then the corresponding list of part *numbers* is simply *partno* ∘ *list*. In this circumstance the selection operator (*p.numb*) is not so useful as a projection function.

Choice term (mu-expression)

The general form of a *choice term* is very similar to a lambda abstraction, namely

μ declaration | constraint • term

(The constraint is optional − if it is omitted, so is the constraint bar.)

The semantic difference is that a choice term defines a *value*, whereas lambda defines a *function*. Thus the choice term must constrain the bound variables so that term defines a *single* value, and the type of a choice term is the type of the term. Thus, usually, a choice term will contain a constraint.

An example of a choice term is shown below.

$$\mu\, x, y : \mathbb{N} \mid x = 3 \wedge y = 2 \; \bullet \; x^2 + 5{*}x + y^2$$

This has exactly the same effect as applying the function shown in the previous section to the arguments (*3,2*). That is, it denotes the value 28.

SEQUENCES

Reverse

The *reverse* of a sequence, s, is written rev s. It is a sequence consisting of the elements of s in reverse order. If s is empty, rev s is empty.

We can define the reverse of a sequence of elements of type *T* recursively as follows:

rev : seq $T \rightarrow$ seq T

$\forall s : \text{seq } T \bullet$
$(s = \langle \rangle \Rightarrow \text{rev } s = \langle \rangle$
$\quad s \neq \langle \rangle \Rightarrow \text{rev } s = \langle \text{last } s \rangle \cap \text{rev front } s)$

Exercise 8.15

Check this definition with some sample sequences.

Exercise 8.16

Write another definition of rev using head and tail instead of last and front. How would you prove that this is equivalent to the previous definition?

Squash

If f is a finite function whose domain is a set of integers, then squash f is the sequence formed by arranging the elements of ran f in ascending order of their corresponding domain values. For example, if f is the function (*not* a sequence, notice)

$\{7 \mapsto l, 5 \mapsto e, 13 \mapsto o, -4 \mapsto h, 9 \mapsto l\}$

then squash f is the sequence $\langle h, e, l, l, o \rangle$.

That is, we are 'squashing' the domain of f so that it becomes a set of consecutive natural numbers starting at 1, while maintaining the original order.

Exercise 8.17

Write a formal definition of squash for a sequence of elements of type T. (Hint: use recursion.)

Index restriction

If s is a sequence and X is a set of integers, then $X \upharpoonright s$ is the sequence s restricted to just those elements that have indexes in X:

$X \upharpoonright s == \text{squash}(X \lhd s)$

Exercise 8.18

What is $\{1,2,5,6,9\} \upharpoonright \langle p,a,r,e,n,t,h,e,s,i,s \rangle$?

Write down a simple definition of tail using index restriction.

Refer to the answer to Exercise 8.2 and use squash to simplify it as it suggests. Then simplify it still further by using index restriction.

Sequence restriction

If *s* is a sequence of elements from set *A*, and *B* is a set of the same type as *A*, then *s* ↾ *B* is the sequence *s* restricted to the elements that appear in set *B*:

  s ↾ *B* == squash(*s*▷*B*)

This is sometimes called *filtering*.

Exercise 8.19

What is ⟨*p,a,r,e,n,t,h,e,s,i,s*⟩ ↾ {*e,p,t*}?

Distributed concatenation

The ***distributed concatenation*** operator, ^/ , concatenates all the sequences in a sequence of sequences.

If *ss* is a sequence of sequences all of whose elements are of the same type, then ^/*ss* is a sequence consisting of all the elements within the sequences in *ss* taken in order.

For a sequence of elements of type *T* we can define ^/ thus:

$$^\/ : \text{seq (seq } T) \rightarrow \text{seq } T$$

$$^\/ \langle\rangle = \langle\rangle$$
$$\forall s : \text{seq } T \bullet\ ^\/ \langle s \rangle = s$$
$$\forall ss1, ss2 : \text{seq(seq } T) \bullet\ \ ^\/ (ss1\ ^\frown ss2) = (^\/ ss1)\ ^\frown (^\/ ss2)$$

For example, a certain text file is stored as a sequence of characters (*charfile*), but while being edited is regarded as a sequence of lines (*linefile*). The line ends are indicated by the *NEWLINE* character when stored, so this character does not appear in a line:

NEWLINE : *CHAR*
LINE == seq (*CHAR* \ {*NEWLINE*})

linefile : seq *LINE*
charfile : seq *CHAR*

The relationship between the two forms of the file can be recorded as an equation, as follows. We firstly define a function (*addNL*) that appends a *NEWLINE* character to a line, and then *charfile* is the concatenation of the *linefile* after applying *addNL* to each of its lines:

$addNL \ == \ \lambda \ ln : LINE \ \bullet \ ln \char94 \ \langle NEWLINE \rangle$

$charfile = \char94/ \ (addNL \circ linefile)$

Exercise 8.20

Given:

[CHAR]
word == seq CHAR
sentence == seq word

write an expression for the *set* of characters, *charset*, appearing in a sentence *sen : sentence*.

Sequences of relations

Distributed override and *distributed composition* are two operators provided for combining sequences of *relations*.

If *SR* is a sequence of relations then $\oplus/ SR$ is a relation consisting of the relations in *SR* taken in order and combined with the functional override operator. This is the operator **distributed override**. (Note that the relations in *SR* must all be of the same type.) If *R1* and *R2* are each relations of the same type then:

$\oplus/\langle R1,R2 \rangle == R1 \oplus R2$

and, for example, if

$A == \{John \mapsto 11111, Bill \mapsto 22222, Mary \mapsto 33333, Mary \mapsto 99999\}$
$B == \{Bill \mapsto 44444, Susi \mapsto 55555\}$
$C == \{Mary \mapsto 66666, Susi \mapsto 77777, Elly \mapsto 88888\}$
$S == \langle A, B, C \rangle$

then $\oplus/S$ is the relation $(A \oplus B) \oplus C$, that is

$\{John \mapsto 11111, Bill \mapsto 44444, Mary \mapsto 66666, Susi \mapsto 77777, Elly \mapsto 88888\}$

Notice that *all* the pairs involving *Mary* have been overridden.

If *SR* is a sequence of relations then $;/SR$ is a relation consisting of the relations in *SR* taken in order and combined with the relational composition operator. This is the operator **distributed composition**. (Note that the relations in *SR* must all be an *appropriate* type.) If *R1* is of type $A \leftrightarrow B$ and *R2* is of type $B \leftrightarrow C$ then:

$;/\langle R1,R2 \rangle == R1;R2$

For example, if

$Wives == \{John \mapsto Mary, Pete \mapsto Susan, Dave \mapsto Ann\}$
$Mums == \{Mary \mapsto Bill, Mary \mapsto Carol, Susan \mapsto Alice, Ann \mapsto Joe\}$
$Dads == \langle Wives, Mums \rangle$

then ;/*Dads* is the relation

$\{John \mapsto Bill, John \mapsto Carol, Pete \mapsto Alice, Dave \mapsto Joe\}$

ANSWERS TO EXERCISES

Answer 8.1

$Aroad^{-1} = Aroad$

is the simple condition for symmetry.

Answer 8.2

```
┌ InsertLine ─────────────────────────────────────────
│ ΔTextFile
├─────────────────────────────────────────────────────
│ row' = row + 1
│ text' = (1..row ⊲ text) ⁀ ⟨ ⟨⟩ ⟩ ⁀ {i : row + 1..#text • (i − row) ↦ (text i)}
```

Note that the new line is an empty one − an empty sequence of characters − and that the set comprehension is a sequence which is the remainder of the original file. We feel we would like to write (*row*+1..#*text*⊲*text*) for this part of the file, but this is not a sequence (the domain does not start at *1*), so instead we explicitly give the sequence function. When we meet squash we can simplify this further.

Answer 8.3

The elements of $S \triangleleft R$ and $S \trianglelefteq R$ are shown in Table 8.2, from which we can see that $(S \triangleleft R) \cup (S \trianglelefteq R) = R$.

Table 8.2. Domain restrict and subtract.

	1	2	3	4	5
a		◁			
b	◁			◁	
c					
d	◁				
e				◁	
f		◁			◁

Answer 8.4

The override operator can be defined as follows:

$f \oplus g = ((\text{dom } g) \lhd f) \cup g$

With this definition it should be clear that override applies equally well to relations as to functions.

Answer 8.5

$(R \rhd S) \cup (R \rhd\!\!\!\!\!\!- S) = R$

Answer 8.6

Consider a family of five children: Alan, Bill, Charley, Dora, Eve.
The _BrotherOf_ relation is (we use abbreviations):

{   (A,B), (A,C), (A,D), (A,E),
 (B,A),   (B,C), (B,D), (B,E),
 (C,A), (C,B),   (C,D), (C,E)}

We can see that if x *BrotherOf* y and y *BrotherOf* z then x *BrotherOf* z, thus *BrotherOf* is transitive.

Similarly, *OlderThan* is transitive.

Suppose Alan, Bill, Charley, Dora and Eve live in adjacent houses, as in Figure 8.11.

| Alan | Bill | Charley | Dora | Eve |

Fig 8.11. Neighbours.

The *NeighbourOf* relation is:

{(A,B), (B,C), (C,D), (D,E), (B,A), (C,B), (D,C), (E,D)}

and we can see that, for instance, A *NeighbourOf* B and B *NeighbourOf* C, but (A,C) $\notin$ _NeighbourOf_, so *NeighbourOf* is *not* transitive.

Answer 8.7

$R^+ = \{(1,2), (1,3), (2,4), (4,7), (1,4), (2,7), (1,7)\}$

Answer 8.8

dom $R \subseteq S$
So $\forall x : \text{dom } R \bullet x \in \text{dom id } S$
So $\forall x : \text{dom } R \bullet (x,x) \in \text{id } S$
So $\forall x : \text{dom } R \bullet (x,x) \in R \cup \text{id } S$

So $R \cup \text{id } S$ is reflexive.

Answer 8.9

$R^* = \{(1,2), (1,3), (2,4), (4,7), (1,4), (2,7), (1,7),$
$(1,1), (2,2), (3,3), (4,4), (5,5), (6,6), (7,7)\}$

Answer 8.10

Inside becomes, if anything, simpler:

$R^* \;==\; \bigcup \{n : \mathbb{N} \bullet R^n\}$

Outside becomes slightly more complicated:

$R^* \;==\; \bigcap \{r : S \leftrightarrow S \mid r \text{or} \subseteq r \wedge (R \cup \text{id } S) \subseteq r\}$

the extra complication being the need to insist that each r is reflexive (the id S term guarantees this).

Answer 8.11

If $f a = f b$ then this element is in the domain of f^{-1}, and so also:

$f^{-1}(f a) \;=\; f^{-1}(f b)$

which implies that $a = b$ (because $f^{-1} \circ f$ is an identity function).

Thus, if $a \neq b$ then $f a \neq f b$, at least for all elements in the domain of f, which expresses the condition we wished to prove.

Answer 8.12

$e : \mathbb{N} \rightarrowtail \mathbb{N}$

> e is total and injective, but not surjective (because 0 is not in the range).

$f : \mathbb{Z} \rightarrow \mathbb{N}$

> f is total but neither injective nor surjective (-3 and 3 both map to 9 and 2 is not in the range).

$g : \mathbb{N} \rightarrowtail \mathbb{N}$ or $g : \mathbb{N} \twoheadrightarrow \mathbb{N}$

> g is injective and surjective, but not total. There is no single arrow notation for the set of functions $(\mathbb{N} \rightarrowtail \mathbb{N}) \cap (\mathbb{N} \twoheadrightarrow \mathbb{N})$ although it would not be hard to invent one!

$h : \mathbb{Z} \times \mathbb{Z} \twoheadrightarrow \mathbb{N}$

> h is total, but not injective (since $(0,0)$ and $(-2,3)$ both map to 0), and it is surjective (because $(k,-k)$ maps to k for any $k : \mathbb{N}$).

$p : 1..n \twoheadrightarrow 1..n$

> p is given as a total surjection, but since the from- and to-sets are finite and the same size, this implies that p is a bijection. Bijections where the from- and to-sets are identical are often called *permutations*.

Answer 8.13

   $CHAR ::=$ *alchar*≪*ALPHA*≫ | *numchar*≪*NUMERIC*≫ | *dot* | *dash* | *colon*

This is equivalent to:

   [*CHAR*]

> *alchar* : *ALPHA* $\rightarrowtail$ *CHAR*
> *numchar* : *NUMERIC* $\rightarrowtail$ *CHAR*
> *dot* : *CHAR*
> ──────────────
> *CHAR* = ran *ALPHA* ∪ ran *NUMERIC* ∪ {*dot, dash, colon*}
> ran *ALPHA* ∩ ran *NUMERIC* = {}
> {*dot, dash, colon*} ∩ ran *ALPHA* = {}
> {*dot, dash, colon*} ∩ ran *NUMERIC* = {}
> *dot* ≠ *dash* ≠ *colon* ≠ *dot*

Answer 8.14

numchar n is the *CHAR* corresponding to the *NUMERIC* n, so the codepoint corresponding to n is *CodePoint(numchar n)*.

Answer 8.15

Empty sequences and those containing only one element are trivial.
   Consider a sequence of two elements $\langle a,b \rangle$:

rev s = $\langle$ last $s \rangle$ ^ rev front s
     = $\langle b \rangle$ ^ rev $\langle a \rangle$
     = $\langle b,a \rangle$

Now consider a sequence of three elements $\langle a,b,c \rangle$:

rev s = $\langle$ last $s \rangle$ ^ rev front s
     = $\langle c \rangle$ ^ rev $\langle a,b \rangle$
     = $\langle c \rangle$ ^ $\langle b,a \rangle$
     = $\langle c,b,a \rangle$

Answer 8.16

> rev : seq $T \rightarrow$ seq T
> ──────────────
> ∀ s : seq T •
> $(s = \langle \rangle \Rightarrow$ rev $s = \langle \rangle$
> $s \neq \langle \rangle \Rightarrow$ rev $s =$ rev tail s ^ head $s)$

As is usual with recursive definitions we use induction to prove things about them. As is also usual we have to prove something more general than the desired result in order to deduce the result. In our case it is prudent to prove the fact that:

$$s, t : seq\ T\ |\ rev(s \wedge t) = rev\ t \wedge rev\ s$$

for either of the definitions of rev. It then follows that they are both equivalent (they both satisfy each other's definition constraints).

We prove this by induction on the length of the sequence s and use the definition of rev above. If s is empty or a singleton list (say $\langle h \rangle$) then it is easy to see that the above condition is true. This is how the induction starts. Now, suppose that this property is true for a sequence s and suppose $h{:}T$ is another element and $s' == \langle h \rangle \wedge s$. We shall prove the statement true for s'.

the left-hand-side
$$= rev\ (s' \wedge t)$$
$$= rev\ ((\langle h \rangle \wedge s) \wedge t)$$

from the definition of s',

$$= rev\ (\langle h \rangle \wedge (s \wedge t))$$

by the associativity of $\wedge$,

$$= rev\ (s \wedge t) \wedge \langle h \rangle$$

from our definition of rev,

$$= rev\ t \wedge rev\ s \wedge \langle h \rangle$$

because it is true for s (by induction)

$$= rev\ t \wedge rev(\langle h \rangle \wedge s)$$

from our definition of rev,

$$= rev\ t \wedge rev\ s'$$
$$= \textit{the right-hand-side}$$

from the definition of s', so proving the property true for the larger sequence s'.

This is the induction completed, proving the property true for all sizes of sequence s. We leave it to the reader to prove the property assuming the *other* definition of rev.

Answer 8.17

Here is a possible definition:

$$squash : (\mathbb{Z} \nrightarrow T) \rightarrow seq\ T$$
$$squash\ \emptyset = \langle \rangle$$
$$\forall f : \mathbb{Z} \nrightarrow T \bullet squash\ f = \langle f\ min(dom\ f) \rangle \wedge squash(\{min\ (dom\ f)\} \lhd f)$$

where you should notice that only *finite* partial functions are in the domain of squash.

Answer 8.18

$\{1,2,5,6,9\} \upharpoonright \langle p,a,r,e,n,t,h,e,s,i,s \rangle = \{(1,p), (2,a), (3,n), (4,t), (5,s)\}$

or, in short: $\langle p,a,n,t,s \rangle$.

Given $s : seq_1 X$ the following short definition uses index restriction:

$tail\, s = 2..\#s \upharpoonright s$

In Exercise 8.2 we encountered an expression

$\{ i : row + 1..\#text \bullet (i - row) \mapsto (text\ i) \}$

and this could have been written as:

$squash(row + 1..\#text \lhd text)$

which is closer to our intuition. Closer still is $row + 1..\#text \upharpoonright text$.

Answer 8.19

$\langle p,a,r,e,n,t,h,e,s,i,s \rangle \upharpoonright \{e,p,t\} = \langle p,e,t,e \rangle$

Answer 8.20

$sen : sentence$
$charset : \mathbb{P}CHAR$
$charset = ran\ (^\wedge / \, sen)$

SPECIFICATION PROBLEMS

8.1 SUBSTRING

Define a *substr* function (see Chapter 5) using squash.

8.2 PERM

Use the data models introduced in this chapter to define the _IsPermOf_ relation from problem 5.2.

8.3 CAR RADIO

My digital car radio has 3 wave bands: medium, long and UHF. In each band, there is a set of stations (usable wavelengths) and the radio is designed so that it can be tuned only to these. (That is, it is impossible to select an arbitrary wavelength: I can select only transmitting stations.)

Initially, when the radio is delivered, the lowest station on the medium band is selected. The controls and indicators are shown in Figure 8.12.

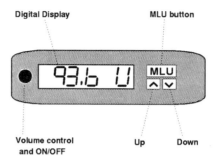

Fig 8.12. A simple car radio.

- MLU cycles round the medium, long and UHF bands.
- UP/DOWN changes the current station.
- VOL controls the volume and acts as an ON/OFF switch.

The MLU button will change to the next band (M-L-U-M) and select the lowest station on that band. The UP/DOWN buttons cause the radio to search for the next station in the current band (U, L or M) either 'up' or 'down' the band. When either end is reached, the search 'wraps' to the other end of the band. The MLU, UP and DOWN buttons have no effect when the radio is turned off.

Write a formal specification for this radio.

8.4 GO

The game of GO is played on a board that contains a square grid of lines, usually 19 by 19, but sometimes smaller, though never less than 11 by 11. Each player has a box of stones: one box contains white stones, the other black. The two players alternately place a stone on the board. Stones are placed at the line intersections, and a stone may be placed on any empty intersection.

The detailed rules are not important. Suffice it to say that the objective of the game is to make territory by surrounding it with stones of your colour. In this process, *connected groups* of stones are important. The purpose of this exercise is to formalize the conditions that define connected groups.

A collection of stones (of the same colour) forms a 'connected group' if you can 'walk' from any stone in the group to any other. You can step across adjacent stones in the same row or in the same column: diagonal steps are not allowed.

Some such groups are illustrated in a corner of a GO board in Figure 8.13.

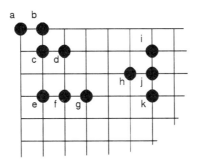

Fig 8.13. Part of a GO board.

There are three groups in this figure:

{a, b, c, d},
{e, f, g} and
{h, i, j, k}.

Write a schema *Stone* that describes the characteristics of a single stone placed on the board.

Write a relation *touching* that expresses the condition that two stones are touching.

Write a relation *joined* that expresses the condition that two stones are joined.

Write a schema *Group* that describes the characteristics of a group of connected stones.

Chapter 9
Abstract Data Types, Promotion and Generics

'But that must happen very often,' Alice remarked
thoughtfully.
'It always happens,' said the Gnat.
Lewis Carroll, Through the Looking-Glass

When describing operations that 'fit' around some particular data
abstraction (an *abstract data type*), particular idioms have been found
useful. Also, when embedding operations in larger contexts
(*promotion*) a certain use of schemas to capture the 'embedding'
abstraction saves repetition. Finally, when defining schemas or functions that have properties common to many underlying types we can
spare repeating ourselves by using *generic* constructions.

In general, when something 'happens very often', we look for a way
to capture the abstraction – the common thread – and to record its
essential character in a single description which we can then reuse.
This chapter looks at some of the ways of doing this in Z.

ABSTRACT DATA TYPES

The idea of an abstract data type (ADT) first appeared around 1972.
ADTs are now supported in some programming languages, such as
Modula-2, and they form a central concept in Object Oriented Program-
ming.

A well-designed system *encapsulates* its objects and controls the
user's access to them. That is, the system hides the implementation
details and provides a well-behaved set of *access functions* to its
objects. The system designer thereby keeps a measure of control over
the possible states of the system, and reduces the risk of error. Maintenance is simpler too, because the designer can change the details of
the implementation without affecting users, providing the interfaces to
the access functions are preserved.

An **abstract data type** is a class of objects together with a set of
operations which can be applied to them. We can describe an abstract
data type with a collection of schemas. Consider, for example, a stack
of natural numbers:

$Stack \;\hat{=}\; [stk : \text{seq } \mathbb{N}]$

The important characteristics of a stack are what *operations* we can perform on it (the same is true of any object, of course). What can we do with a stack? We can put things on it ('push'), take them off again ('pop'), ask if the stack is empty and so on. Whether the stack be implemented as an array, a linked list or whatever, doesn't affect the 'stackiness' of the stack. It is these three operations that characterize it. We often draw a 'doughnut', or wheel, to illustrate this idea, as shown in Figure 9.1.

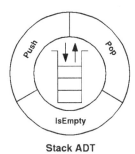

Stack ADT

Fig 9.1. A stack abstract data type.

The stack is protected by the operations that surround it: no-one 'gets in' except through these operations. We can write schemas to describe the initial state of a stack and these three operations:

$InitStack \; \hat{=} \; [Stack' \mid stk' = \emptyset]$

$$
\begin{array}{|l}
\hline
\;Push \rule{7cm}{0pt} \\
\;\Delta Stack \\
\;elem? : \mathbb{N} \\
\hline
\;stk' = \langle elem? \rangle \hat{\;} stk \\
\hline
\end{array}
$$

$$
\begin{array}{|l}
\hline
\;Pop \rule{7cm}{0pt} \\
\;\Delta Stack \\
\;elem! : \mathbb{N} \\
\hline
\;stk \neq \langle \rangle \\
\;stk' = tail\; stk \\
\;elem! = head\; stk \\
\hline
\end{array}
$$

(We do not specify what happens when the stack is empty.)

$YesNo ::= \; YES \mid NO$

```
┌─IsEmpty ──────────────────────────────────
│ ΞStack
│ empty! : YesNo
├──────────────────────────────────
│ (stk = ⟨⟩ ∧ empty! = YES) ∨
│ (stk ≠ ⟨⟩ ∧ empty! = NO)
└──────────────────────────────────
```

We can think of these five schemas (*Stack*, *InitStack*, *Push*, *Pop*, and *IsEmpty*) as defining an ADT and we could write explanatory text saying so. (There is no construct in Z that provides such a grouping.)

We can then use this ADT as part of a larger construct, say a family of stacks, one per *USER*, thus:

Family ≙ [*userstk* : *USER*↦*Stack*]

We will return to this simple ADT later.

PROMOTION: TEXT EDITOR EXAMPLE

To show a more substantial example and illustrate the technique called **promotion** we will use the Text Editor specification from Chapter 7 (described on page 226). The original solution described a family of operations on a *text file*, namely:

Left
Right
DeleteChar
InsertChar
Up
Down
InsertLine

The first four of these operations affect only *one line* (the current line) and we might find it easier to think about the specification if we consider a *Line* (and its operations) as a separate type of object, an ADT. We can then use this *Line* to describe a text file.

The line

We start by recalling the notion of a character string:

string == seq *CHAR*

A *Line* consists of text before the current position, *bef*, and the remainder, *aft*. The whole line is *txt*.

$$Line \; \widehat{=} \; [bef,aft,txt : string \; | \; txt = bef \; ^\frown aft]$$

The current position can be moved left

LeftOK ────────────────────────────
$\Delta Line$

$bef \neq \langle \rangle$
$bef' = $ front bef
$aft' = \langle$ last $bef \rangle \; ^\frown aft$
---

provided there is some text *before* the current position. In this case the last character is removed from *bef* and concatenated to *aft* (the value of *txt* does not change).

Left is either *LeftOK* or (if there is no text before the current position) has no effect:

$$Left \; \widehat{=} \; LeftOK \; \vee \; [\Xi Line \; | \; bef = \langle \rangle]$$

The current position can be moved right

RightOK ────────────────────────────
$\Delta Line$

$aft \neq \langle \rangle$
$bef' = bef \; ^\frown \langle$ head $aft \rangle$
$aft' = $ tail aft
---

provided there is some text after the current position. The **head** character is removed from *aft* and concatenated to *bef* (the value of *txt* does not change).

Right is either *RightOK* or (if there is no text after the current position) has no effect:

$$Right \; \widehat{=} \; RightOK \; \vee \; [\Xi Line \; | \; aft = \langle \rangle]$$

The *InsertChar* operation inserts a character, *chr?*, immediately before the current position:

$$InsertChar \; \widehat{=} \; [\Delta Line; chr? : CHAR \; | \; bef' = bef \wedge aft' = \langle chr? \rangle \; ^\frown aft]$$

bef does not change and the character *chr?* is prefixed to *aft*.

┌─── **Exercise 9.1** ────────────────────────────
What happens to *txt* according to the *InsertChar* schema?

The *DeleteChar* operation deletes the character immediately after the current position:

DeleteChar $\;\hat{=}\;$ [Δ*Line* | *aft* $\neq \langle\rangle \wedge$ *bef′* = *bef* $\wedge$ *aft′* = tail *aft*]

bef does not change and head *aft* is removed provided there is text after the current position.

Exercise 9.2

What exactly does *DeleteChar* say about a line with *aft* = $\langle\rangle$?

Finally, we should consider the initial state of a *Line*, which should be empty:

InitLine $\;\hat{=}\;$ [*Line* | *txt* = $\langle\rangle$]

The text file

Having got the behaviour of a *Line* clear in our minds we can describe a text file as a sequence of such lines:

TextFile ─────────────────────

text : seq *Line*
row : $\mathbb{N}$

---

row $\leq$ #*text*

The variable *row* identifies the current line, so its value must be no more than #*text*.

Exercise 9.3

Why didn't we use the declaration *row* : 0..#*text* and omit the predicate part altogether?

Consider *TextFile* carefully. Its model is a sequence of *Line* states and each *Line* has a current position (represented by split text in this case). This is not the same as our earlier specification model, where only the current line had a current position. For the moment, however, we can better illustrate promotion by leaving *Line* embedded wholly in the text sequence, and we will return to this slight anomaly later.

We can now describe the operations on a *text file*. All the *Line* operations apply, but, instead of changing any *Line* state they change the current line of the text file. We can capture this change of viewpoint with a promotion schema *PromoteLine*, and four promoted operations, *TFLeft*, *TFRight*, *TFInsertChar*, and *TFDeleteChar*.

Each of these operations changes the text file state and the content of one line

```
┌─PromoteLine ─────────────────────────────
│ ΔTextFile
│ ΔLine
├──────────
│ θLine = text row
│ text' = text ⊕ {row ↦ θLine'}
│ row' = row
└──────────────────────────────────────────
```

but which line? Well, the one corresponding to *row* of course, which is what the first predicate says!

The symbol *θ* ('theta') means 'the current binding of' (it will be explained more fully later in this chapter). So we read *θLine* as 'the *Line*', that is, the one introduced in the declarations.

Thus the predicate says 'the particular *Line* we are talking about here is the same as *text row*'. It identifies *which* line we are discussing. *θLine = text row* means the same as:

$$bef = (text\ row).bef$$
$$aft = (text\ row).aft$$
$$txt = (text\ row).txt$$

The second predicate in *PromoteLine* says that these operations change the value of *text* by overriding *text row* with the value of the *Line* after the line operation.

Finally the last predicate in *PromoteLine* says that the row number does not change for line operations. It is the 'same' current line.

We now 'promote' the *Line* operations to *TextFile* (*TF*) operations, thus:

$$TFLeft \triangleq Left \wedge PromoteLine$$
$$TFRight \triangleq Right \wedge PromoteLine$$
$$TFInsertChar \triangleq InsertChar \wedge PromoteLine$$
$$TFDeleteChar \triangleq DeleteChar \wedge PromoteLine$$

These operations apply only when there is a *Line* to operate upon, which we can see by examining the schema *PromoteLine*,

$$AtALine \triangleq [TextFile \mid row > 0]$$

and do not apply to cases when there is no current line, when we will decide that no action should be taken at all:

$NotAtALine \;\hat{=}\; [TextFile \mid row = 0]$
$NoLineNoAction \;\hat{=}\; \Xi TextFile \;\wedge\; NotAtALine$

So we can express the complete promoted operations as follows:

$TextFileLeft \;\hat{=}\; (TFLeft \wedge AtALine) \;\vee\; NoLineNoAction$
$TextFileRight \;\hat{=}\; (TFRight \wedge AtALine) \;\vee\; NoLineNoAction$
$TextFileInsertChar \;\hat{=}\; (TFInsertChar \wedge AtALine) \;\vee\; NoLineNoAction$
$TextFileDeleteChar \;\hat{=}\; (TFDeleteChar \wedge AtALine) \;\vee\; NoLineNoAction$

Finally, we can describe other operations on a text file that are not promotions of *Line* operations. The initial state of a *TextFile* is:

```
┌─ InitTextFile ──────────────────────────────────
│  TextFile′
│ ─────────────────────────────────────────────────
│  text′ = ⟨⟩
│  row′ = 0
└──────────────────────────────────────────────────
```

which is empty.

The operation of line insertion is:

```
┌─ InsertLine ────────────────────────────────────
│  ΔTextFile
│ ─────────────────────────────────────────────────
│  row′ = row + 1
│  text′ = (1..row ◁ text) ⌢ ⟨μ In : InitLine • In⟩ ⌢ (row + 1..#text ↾ text)
└──────────────────────────────────────────────────
```

This requires the notion of an empty line (the initial state of *Line* it so happens).

The *InsertLine* operation inserts an empty line after the current row and makes this new line current. That is, *text′* is the first *row* elements of *text*, concatenated with an empty line concatenated with the remaining elements of *text*. The μ expression here denotes the (single) binding of the schema *InitLine* – the empty *Line*.

UpOK describes the effect of a 'cursor up' key:

```
┌─ UpOK ──────────────────────────────────────────
│  ΔTextFile
│ ─────────────────────────────────────────────────
│  row > 0
│  row′ = row − 1
│  text′ = text
└──────────────────────────────────────────────────
```

when the current row is 1 or greater. The *row* number is decremented and the *text* is unchanged.

Notice that, due to our 'slight anomaly' about each *Line* having a 'current position', the effect of this schema is to 'restore the current position of the previous line' rather than either inheriting a position or resetting it to the 'left' end of the line. We will return to this below.

The full operation of *Up* is either *UpOK* or has no effect (if *row* is zero).

$$Up \; \hat{=} \; UpOK \; \vee \; NoLineNoAction$$

Similarly *DownOK* describes the effect of a 'cursor down' key

```
┌─DownOK ──────────────────────────────
│ ΔTextFile
│ ─────────────────
│ row < #text
│ row' = row + 1
│ text' = text
└──────────────────────────────────────
```

when the current row is not the last. The *row* number is incremented and the *text* is unchanged.

Down is either *DownOK* or has no effect (if *row* is already the last).

$$Down \; \hat{=} \; DownOK \; \vee \; [\Xi TextFile \mid row = \#text]$$

By tackling the specification in this way, we have separated two ideas:

What constitutes a line and what can be done to it.
What constitutes a text file and what can be done to it.

This separation allows us to concentrate on one idea at a time, with a better chance of getting each right.

```
┌── Exercise 9.4 ──────────────────────────────────
│ Promote the *Stack* operations introduced at the beginning of this
│ chapter to the *Family* of stacks.
└──────────────────────────────────────────────────
```

The text file anomaly

Now we briefly return to the 'slight anomaly' in *TextFile*. We would prefer not to specify each *Line* within *text* to have a current position of its own, although this forces the separation between the data types more strongly. We would like to represent matters more accurately, and still retain the ability to 'inherit' the operations from *Line*, if possible. Here are some exercises to indicate an approach.

We shall revert to defining a text file as a sequence of *string* values and a current *row*.

Exercise 9.5

Define the schema *TextFile2* by declaring *text* as seq *string* and embedding a current line description taken, as far as possible, from *Line*.

Consider promoting the *Line* operations again to the schema state *TextFile2*.

Exercise 9.6

Define the promotion schema *PromoteLine2* that would enable you to promote the *Line* operations to *TextFile2*.

With this modification we can promote the *Line* operations easily.

Exercise 9.7

Exhibit a *Line* operation promoted to *TextFile2*.

You may wish to read the answers and proceed to specify the other operations.

BINDING FORMATION (θ)

We will now explain the use of θ more formally.

The expression θS, where S is a schema name, is the **binding** of S that has component values equal to the current values of the variables in S.

When one schema, S, is included in the declaration part of another, T, then in the predicate part of T we can refer to the 'current instance' of S, using θ. θS can be read as 'the S' (in current scope). (In fact, θS can be used anywhere that S is known, but it transpires that the normal use is as described above.)

We can make this clearer by an example. Suppose the schema *Triangle* and the function *perimeter* are defined thus:

```
┌─ Triangle ──────────────────────────────
│  sidea, sideb, sidec : ℕ
├──────────────────────────────────────────
│  sidea ≥ sideb ≥ sidec
│  sidea < sideb + sidec
└──────────────────────────────────────────
```

$$\begin{array}{|l}
\hline
perimeter : Triangle \rightarrow \mathbb{N} \\
\hline
\forall\, t : Triangle \bullet perimeter\, t = t.sidea + t.sideb + t.sidec \\
\end{array}$$

Now suppose we want to define a schema to represent small triangles, namely those with a perimeter less than *100*. We could do it like this:

$$\begin{array}{|l}
\hline
\;SmallTriangle \text{——————————————} \\
\quad Triangle \\
\hline
\quad sidea + sideb + sidec < 100 \\
\hline
\end{array}$$

Alternatively, we could use the *perimeter* function, and the shorthand $\theta Triangle$ ('the Triangle') to produce the more appealing definition:

$$\begin{array}{|l}
\hline
\;SmallTriangle \text{——————————————} \\
\quad Triangle \\
\hline
\quad perimeter(\theta Triangle) < 100 \\
\hline
\end{array}$$

Decorated binding

$\theta S'$ is a binding of S, and is *not* a binding of S'. That is, the variable names of the binding are *not* decorated. The values of the components of $\theta S'$ are taken from the current components in S', but its type is the underlying type of S.

Thus the type of θS is the same as the type of $\theta S'$. This definition of θ allows well-typed expressions of the form $\theta S = \theta S'$ to be written.

We can, for instance, use θ to define the meaning of Ξ, thus

$$\Xi S \;\hat{=}\; [\Delta S \mid \theta S = \theta S']$$

Notice, however, if the schema S *contains* any decorated variables, such decoration *does* appear in the bindings of S and hence in its underlying type. For example, if

$$T \;\hat{=}\; [a, a' : \mathbb{N} \mid a' = a + 1]$$

and a is 79, then θT is $a\text{->}79$; $a'\text{->}80$, and the type of θT is $a:\mathbb{Z}$; $a':\mathbb{Z}$.

Moreover, if U is a schema and V is defined as $V \hat{=} U'$, then the type of θV is *not* the same as the type of $\theta U'$.

It is important to realise that the expression $\theta S'$ is *atomic*, that is, it cannot be split into its constituent parts. An expression such as $(\theta S)'$ is meaningless.

As another example of the use of θ, consider the *RequestCBOK* trans-action described in the answer to Specification Problem 7.1 cash dispenser). We wrote this as:

```
┌─ RequestCBOK ──────────────────────────────
│ ChangeStatus
│ rc! : RetCode
├────────────────────────────────────────────
│ (cust′ accno?).stat.CBreq = ON
│ ∀ n : dom AccountFile | n ≠ accno? •
│    ((cust′ n).stat.CBreq = (cust n).stat.CBreq)
│ ∀ n : dom AccountFile •
│    ((cust′ n).stat.stmtreq = (cust n).stat.stmtreq)
│ rc! = OK
└────────────────────────────────────────────
```

This might be made clearer by using θ, thus:

```
┌─ RequestCBOK ──────────────────────────────
│ ChangeStatus
│ ΔAccount
│ rc! : RetCode
├────────────────────────────────────────────
│ θAccount′.stat.CBreq = ON
│ θAccount′.stat.stmtreq = θAccount.stat.stmtreq
│ cust′ = cust ⊕ {accno? ↦ θAccount′}
│ rc! = OK
└────────────────────────────────────────────
```

We introduce $\Delta Account$ as a 'model' for an account, both before and after a change. The predicates say that

- The new *Account CBreq* is *ON*.
- The *Account stmtreq* is unchanged.
- The new *cust* function has the entry for the account identified by *accno?* replaced by 'the new Account' just described.

REDUCING THE INTERFACE – HIDING

Both in *RequestCBOK* and in the promotion examples we have been a little 'cavalier' with the signature of the operation schemas. It looks as though more and more components are appearing, which are not really part of the interface that the operation schema describes. They serve only to name parts so that the explanation (the predicates) are easier to frame.

If possible we would like to remove the inessential parts of the sig-

nature that are only introduced to explain transitions or support promotions. The *hiding* operation allows us to cleanly suppress components for this and other purposes.

Let us revisit the stack example (see the answer to Exercise 9.4).
We described the *FamilyPush* operation thus:

FamilyPush $\hat{=}$ *Push* $\wedge$ *PromoteStack*

Which can be expanded thus:

$$
\begin{array}{|l}
\hline
\Delta Stack\text{——————————————————} \\
\Delta Family \\
elem? : \mathbb{N} \\
usr? : USER \\
\hline
\theta Stack = userstk\ usr? \\
userstk' = userstk \oplus \{usr? \mapsto \theta Stack'\} \\
stk' = \langle elem? \rangle \,^\frown stk \\
\hline
\end{array}
$$

If we expand the declaration part we get:

userstk, userstk' : $USER \rightarrow\!\!\!\!+ Stack$
stk, stk' : seq $\mathbb{N}$
elem? : $\mathbb{N}$
usr? : *USER*

If we are interested in the *interface* to the *FamilyPush* operation, we
need Δ*Family* (the state), *user?* and *elem?*. We do not really need *stk*
and *stk'*. Actually any such stack values that satisfy the predicates
will do; the rest of the operation is determined if these *exist*. So we
'hide' the components *stk* and *stk'* in the interface, like this:

FamilyPushCall $\hat{=}$ *FamilyPush* \ (*stk,stk'*)

This is called **hiding**. In general, the expression $S \setminus (n_1, n_2, ...)$ is a
schema whose components are the same as the components of S except
that the variables named $n_1, n_2, ...$ are removed from the signature and
existentially quantified in the property. Thus, for example, the definition of *FamilyPushCall* is a shorthand for

```
┌─FamilyPushCall ──────────────────────────────────
│ ΔFamily
│ usr? : USER
│ elem? : ℕ
├──────────────────────────────────────────────
│ ∃ stk, stk' : seq ℕ •
│  (stk' = ⟨elem?⟩ ^ stk
│   stk  = userstk usr?
│   userstk' = userstk ⊕ {usr? ↦ stk'})
└──────────────────────────────────────────────
```

Of course, we could have hidden these variables when we defined *FamilyPush*: we didn't really need a separate schema. Thus we could define:

$$FamilyPush \;\hat{=}\; (Push \wedge PromoteStack) \setminus (stk, stk')$$

Generally accepted Z permits only a list of variables in the 'hiding list'. In this book, we extend the syntax to allow a *schema* to appear. Thus we could write, in this case:

$$FamilyPush \;\hat{=}\; (Push \wedge PromoteStack) \setminus \Delta Stack$$

```
┌─── Exercise 9.8 ────────────────────────────────
│ Modify the definitions of TFLeft and TFRight to hide those variables
│ that are not needed at the interface. Then show the expansion of the
│ predicate part of TFLeft.
└──────────────────────────────────────────────
```

A more exact definition of hiding will be given in Chapter 10.

INVARIANTS

We have seen that when we use an ADT, any *invariants* that were declared with that ADT hold for all instances. For example, all instances of *Line* have the invariant

$$txt = bef \;{}^\frown\; aft$$

Sometimes, when we use multiple instances, we introduce additional invariants. To illustrate this, let's return again to the *Stack*. Suppose when we originally described this we had thought of two other notions, namely a stack is of limited size and a stack has an 'owner'.

$[USER]$
$MaxStackSize : ℕ$

```
┌─Stack────────────────────────────────────
│ stk : seq ℕ
│ owner : USER
│───────────────────────────────────────────
│ #stk ≤ MaxStackSize
```

When we introduce a *MatchedFamily* of stacks, we decide to stipulate that the owner of a stack is recorded in the stack itself, and matches:

```
┌─MatchedFamily──────────────────────────────
│ userstk : USER⇸Stack
│───────────────────────────────────────────
│ ∀ u : dom userstk • (userstk u).owner = u
```

Now consider describing a family of stacks where the total space available for stack allocation can accomodate only *MaxElem* elements. We can reflect this new constraint in the *LimitedFamily* schema below.

MaxElem : ℕ

```
┌─LimitedFamily──────────────────────────────
│ MatchedFamily
│───────────────────────────────────────────
│ #{usr : USER; indx : ℕ
│   | usr ∈ dom userstk ∧ indx ∈ dom (userstk usr).stk • (usr,indx)}
│   ≤ MaxElem
```

The predicate needs some explanation. It says that the number of elements in a particular set does not exceed *MaxElem*. What are the elements of the set? They are pairs formed from *USER* values and stack element indexes.

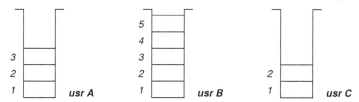

Fig 9.2. Stack space.

Each stack in the family is identified by its *USER* and each element in a stack is identified by its index. So if we count the pairs *(usr,indx)* there will be precisely one for each element in each stack of the family.

In this simple example we can see that there are invariants appropriate to the individual stack, and invariants appropriate to the *family* of stacks. As we build up large state descriptions from schemas, by including and combining them, one of the guiding principles is to place invariants as 'low down' in the description as possible. In fact the structure of a description can often be determined by the parts that are linked by predicates in an invariant.

GENERICS

We shall look at the stack abstract data type one more time. We described our *Stack* ADT with elements as numbers. Of course, the *Pop* and *Push* operations could apply to a stack containing any kind of element. It would be more useful, therefore, to describe a **generic** stack. We can do this by treating the element type as a **generic parameter** to the stack declaration and to each of the operations:

$Stack[T] \;\hat{=}\; [stk : seq\ T]$

```
┌─Push[T]──────────────────────────
│ ΔStack[T]
│ elem? : T
│─────────────────────────────────
│ stk' = ⟨elem?⟩ ^ stk
└─────────────────────────────────
```

```
┌─Pop[T]───────────────────────────
│ ΔStack[T]
│ elem! : T
│─────────────────────────────────
│ stk' = tail stk
│ elem! = head stk
└─────────────────────────────────
```

When we *instantiate* a stack, we supply a type that is an **actual generic parameter** to replace *T*, for example:

$IntegerStack \;\hat{=}\; Stack[\mathbb{Z}]$
$CharStack \;\hat{=}\; Stack[CHAR]$

Similarly, we can describe operations on such stacks by instantiating the generic *Push* and *Pop*, such as:

$PushInt \;\hat{=}\; Push[\mathbb{Z}]$
$PopInt \;\hat{=}\; Pop[\mathbb{Z}]$
$PushChar \;\hat{=}\; Push[CHAR]$
$PopChar \;\hat{=}\; Pop[CHAR]$

Many of the built-in functions we have been using throughout the book are actually defined as **generic functions** in the basic library, and we have implicitly been supplying actual generic parameters when we use them. To illustrate how this works, let's see how we might define a *union* function generically.

A generic function is written somewhat like a schema box but has a *double* bar at the top and *generic parameters* in place of the schema name, thus:

$$
\begin{array}{l}
\boxed{\begin{array}{l}
[T]\!=\!\!=\!\!=\!\!=\!\!=\!\!=\!\!=\!\!=\!\!=\!\!= \\
\ union : (\mathbb{P}\,T \times \mathbb{P}\,T) \rightarrowtail \mathbb{P}\,T \\
\hline
\ \forall\, a, b : \mathbb{P}\,T\ \bullet\ union(a,b) = \{x : T \mid x \in a \wedge x \in b\}
\end{array}}
\end{array}
$$

(Functionally, *union* is the same as the ∪ symbol, which has an infix syntax.)

Now, to use *union* we must supply an actual generic parameter for *T*. For instance, suppose we want to refer to the union of two sets of integers

S1, S2 : $\mathbb{P}\,\mathbb{Z}$

We can either supply the actual generic parameter explicitly:

union[$\mathbb{Z}$] (*S1, S2*)

or we can omit it:

union (*S1, S2*)

In the second case, the value of *T* is implied by the underlying type of both *S1* and *S2*. Usually, when we use the built-in generic functions, we omit the actual generic parameters.

(In general the underlying type of an expression can be complex, and the signature of a generic function or relation can be a complex function of its generic parameters. To enable them to be matched, and ensure that unambiguous actual generic parameters are implied, we rely upon the simple type-structure of Z. This is not a subject we will go into any further in this book.)

The sequence functions **head**, **tail**, **front** and **last** are examples of generic functions supplied in the basic library. In Chapter 5 we showed how to define these for sequences of numbers. We can now see how to define them generically.

┌─── **Exercise 9.9** ───────────────────────────────────┐
Write generic definitions for head and tail.
└──┘

┌─ **Exercise 9.10** ──┐
Write generic definitions for first and second (see page 42).
└──┘

ANSWERS TO EXERCISES

Answer 9.1
The value of *txt'* is determined by the constraint in *Line'*, which implies that *txt'=bef'^aft'*. Therefore it is like *txt* except that a new character has been 'inserted' in it.

Answer 9.2
DeleteChar says nothing about this case: there are no bindings for which *aft* is empty. This is just as well, for tail is not defined for an empty sequence. This means that the specification of *Line* operations is incomplete and we ought to explain what happens in this case. An extension can be safely left as an exercise, provided we decide exactly what *should* happen.

It is a subtle point in Z specifications that omitting the predicate *aft≠⟨⟩* would *not* be equivalent. Instead it would mean that the pre-condition of the *DeleteChar* schema would be undetermined because the expression tail *aft* would be undefined. It is good practice always to consider the domain of functions when they are applied.

Answer 9.3
Because *0..#text* would not be defined in the declaration part of the schema *TextFile*. We are not allowed to use *text* outside its scope.

Answer 9.4
Initially, the family of stacks is empty:

$InitFamily \triangleq [Family' \mid userstk' = \emptyset]$

The *AllocateStack* operation adds a new empty stack to the family:

┌─ *AllocateStack* ─────────────────────────────
│ ΔFamily
│ InitStack
│ usr? : USER
├───
│ usr? ∉ dom userstk
│ userstk' = userstk ∪ {usr? ↦ θStack'}
└───

We describe a promotion schema:

```
┌─ PromoteStack ─────────────────────────────
│ ΔFamily
│ ΔStack
│ usr? : USER
├────────────────────────────────────────────
│ θStack = userstk usr?
│ userstk' = userstk ⊕ {usr? ↦ θStack'}
└────────────────────────────────────────────
```

Now we can promote *Push* and *Pop*:

FamilyPush ≘ *Push* ∧ *PromoteStack*
FamilyPop ≘ *Pop* ∧ *PromoteStack*

Answer 9.5
The following schema is sufficient

```
┌─ TextFile2 ────────────────────────────────
│ text : seq string
│ row : ℕ
│ Line
├────────────────────────────────────────────
│ row > 0 ⇒ text row = txt
│ row ≤ #text
└────────────────────────────────────────────
```

where we have used *Line* directly in the state to represent the current line. Note that there is no constraint upon *Line* when *row* = 0.

Answer 9.6
The promotion schema has less work to do this time, since the *Line* schema components are already present in the state.

```
┌─ PromoteLine2 ─────────────────────────────
│ ΔTextFile2
├────────────────────────────────────────────
│ text' = text ⊕ {row ↦ txt'}
│ row' = row
└────────────────────────────────────────────
```

which simply says that *row* stays the same, and the *Line* operations just change the *row* numbered string, as before.

Answer 9.7
The *Left* operation can be 'lifted' as follows:

TF2Left ≘ *Left* ∧ *PromoteLine2*

and the others are similar. We can perform the same step as in *TextFile* to specify no action when there is no line. Indeed the same schema definition (except that it refers to *TextFile2*) can be used.

You might like to proceed and define the *Up* and *Down* operations on this state, which will actually be slightly different from before, allowing the possibility that the 'current position' be reset to the left margin (or some other definition – you choose).

Answer 9.8
Hiding variables:

$TFLeft \; \hat{=} \; (Left \wedge PromoteLine) \setminus \Delta Line$
$TFRight \; \hat{=} \; (Right \wedge PromoteLine) \setminus \Delta Line$

An elaboration of *TFLeft* gives:

TFLeft
$\Delta TextFile$

$\exists \; bef, bef', aft, aft', txt, txt' : seq \, CHAR \; \bullet$
$\quad (\; (txt = bef \,^\frown aft \; \wedge \; txt' = bef' \,^\frown aft')$
$\quad (\theta Line = text \, row \wedge text' = text \oplus \{row \mapsto \theta Line'\})$
$\quad (bef \neq \langle \rangle \; \wedge \; bef' = \text{front} \, bef \wedge aft' = \langle \text{last} \, bef \rangle \,^\frown aft)$
$\quad \vee$
$\quad (bef = \langle \rangle = bef' \; \wedge \; aft' = aft))$

---

which can be written (by substituting for *bef, aft* and so on):

TFLeft
$\Delta TextFile$

$\quad (\; (text \, row).txt = (text \, row).bef \,^\frown (text \, row).aft$
$\quad (text' \, row).txt = (text' \, row).bef \,^\frown (text' \, row).aft$
$\quad (text \, row).bef \neq \langle \rangle$
$\quad (text' \, row).bef = \text{front}((text \, row).bef)$
$\quad (text' \, row).aft = \langle \text{last}((text \, row).bef) \rangle \,^\frown (text \, row).aft \,)$
$\quad \vee \; (\; (text \, row).bef = \langle \rangle$
$\quad (text' \, row).bef = (text \, row).bef$
$\quad (text' \, row).aft = (text \, row).aft \,)$

Answer 9.9

$[T]$
$head : (seq_1 \, T) \rightarrow T$

$\forall s : seq_1 \, T \; \bullet \; head \, s = s \, 1$

$[T]$
$tail : (seq_1 \, T) \rightarrow (seq \, T)$

$\forall s : seq_1 \, T \; \bullet \; \langle head \, s \rangle \,^\frown tail \, s = s$

Answer 9.10

$$
\begin{array}{|l}
\hline
[T1,T2] \\
\text{first} : (T1 \times T2) \rightarrowtail T1 \\
\hline
\forall\, a : T1;\ b : T2\ \bullet\ \text{first}(a,b) = a \\
\hline
\end{array}
$$

$$
\begin{array}{|l}
\hline
[T1,T2] \\
\text{second} : (T1 \times T2) \rightarrowtail T2 \\
\hline
\forall\, a : T1;\ b : T2\ \bullet\ \text{second}(a,b) = b \\
\hline
\end{array}
$$

SPECIFICATION PROBLEMS

9.1 PHONE DIRECTORY SYSTEM

Describe a Phone Directory System (PDS) for a country, in which each *TOWN* has its own directory. Use the *PhoneDir* introduced in Chapter 7 and promote its operations into a PDS.

The following operations are required:

* *AddTown*, add a new (empty) directory to the PDS.
* *DeleteTown*, delete a directory from the PDS.
* *ListTowns*, list all town names.

Chapter 10
Operating with Schemas

'For although common Snarks do no manner of harm,
   Yet I feel it my duty to say,
Some are Boojums –' The Bellman broke off in alarm,
   For the Baker had fainted away.

Lewis Carroll, The Hunting of the Snark, Fit the Second

We are now familiar with 'common' schemas and many of their uses. We have learnt how to use them as types and to combine them with disjunction and conjunction. In some situations other ways of using schemas are useful and help us to express a description clearly. These other uses of schemas are explained in this chapter.

Many of the examples in this chapter make use of the game of NIM in Chapter 7. We reproduce the definitions here for easier reference.

Three piles are named *A, B, C,* and the game state consists of these piles, each with a number of sticks in it:

pileid ::= *A | B | C*
Game ≙ [*pile : pileid*→ℕ]

To make a play we need a pile identity, *p?,* and the number of sticks the player wishes to take, *take?.* A return code, *rc!,* shows the result:

code ::= *error | fin | ok*
Parameters ≙ [*p? : pileid; take? :* ℕ$_1$*; rc! : code*]

Play is permitted if there are enough sticks in the pile:

```
┌─PlayOK ──────────────────────────────────
│ ΔGame
│ Parameters
├───────────
│ pile p? ≥ take?
│ pile' = pile ⊕ {p? ↦ (pile p? − take?)}
└───────────────────────────────────────────
```

the set of piles being updated by decrementing the count for *p?* by *take?.*

Play is prohibited if there are too few sticks:

168

```
┌─PlayErr──────────────────────────────────
│  ΞGame
│  Parameters
├──────────────────────────
│  pile p? < take?
│  rc! = error
└──────────────────────────────────────────
```

Play is complete when all piles are empty, and can proceed if there are sticks remaining:

Ended ≙ [*Game* | ran *pile* = {0}]
Open ≙ [*Game* | ran *pile* ≠ {0}]

PlayMore is a play that leaves the game in an *Open* state, *PlayLast* is a play that ends the game, and the general play is either of these or *PlayErr*:

PlayMore ≙ [*PlayOK* | *Open'* ∧ *rc!=ok*]
PlayLast ≙ [*PlayOK* | *Ended'* ∧ *rc!=fin*]
Play ≙ *PlayMore* ∨ *PlayLast* ∨ *PlayErr*

SIGNATURE AND PROPERTY NOTATION

In Chapter 7 we introduced schema conjunction and disjunction with illustrations of their uses. Here we wish to be more precise and we introduce some extra notation. We shall write

sig *S*   for the *signature* of *S*, and
prop *S*   for the *property* of *S*.

The signature is a collection of variable names, each supplied with its *type*. The property is the constraint placed upon the components of *S*, including all the constraints implied by the declaration part of *S*.
    For example, if

$S \triangleq [a, b : \mathbb{N}; \ c : GIVEN; \ x : \mathbb{PN} \ | \ a \in x \wedge b < a]$

then

sig *S* is $a : \mathbb{Z}; \ b : \mathbb{Z}; \ c : GIVEN; \ x : \mathbb{PZ}$.
prop *S* is $a \in x \wedge b < a \wedge x \subseteq \mathbb{N} \wedge a \geq 0 \wedge b \geq 0$.

Notice that *all* the constraints are expressed in prop *S* so that the schema [sig *S* | prop *S*] is *identical* to the schema *S*.
    sig *S* can be thought of as a finite partial function from identifiers to types. However *it is not a Z notation* and *it does not denote a Z object*.

Why not? Because the set of all Z identifiers is not a value in Z, and nor is the set of all types. We cannot define either of these sets. We say this to prevent use of sig S or prop S in a Z specification – these have been invented for use only in this chapter.

In what follows we will make use of sig S as a partial function (a set of pairs). For instance, we will use set difference

sig S \ sig T

to denote the set of variables (with their types) that are in the signature of S and not in the signature of T. Furthermore, we shall implicitly assume that expressions like these (for signatures) only make sense when they behave like partial functions, so that it is not allowed for there to be a single variable name paired with two different types.

DECLARATIONS

We have described a schema as a collection of declarations and constraints. In set comprehension, predicate quantification, function abstraction (λ) and the choice operation (μ) a schema can be used in place of a declaration list and constraint.

SET COMPREHENSION

If S is the name of a schema then

{S • expression}

is equivalent to the expression

{sig S | prop S • expression}

and

{S | predicate • expression}

is equivalent to the expression

{sig S | predicate ∧ prop S • expression}

For example, given

```
┌─Fred───────────────────────────────
│ x, y : ℕ
├─────────────────────────────────────
│ −4 ≤ x + y ≤ 4
└─────────────────────────────────────
```

then the set {*Fred* • $x*y$} is the set of the products of the pairs of natural numbers whose sum is in the set $-4..4$. In full this is

$$\{x, y : \mathbb{Z} \mid y \geq 0 \ \wedge \ x \geq 0 \ \wedge \ -4 \leq x + y \leq 4 \ \bullet \ x*y\}$$

which in this case is simply the set $0..4$.

Exercise 10.1

In NIM, express the set $\{PlayOK \ \bullet \ pile\}$ without using schema names. Hint: do not substitute for the sig and prop of *PlayOK*; think about the *meaning* of the expression and deduce a simpler form.

In both forms of set comprehension using schemas the expression clause can be omitted, so we can write

$\{S\}$

In this case the typical element is defined to be θS, so that $\{S\}$ is equivalent to

$\{S \ \bullet \ \theta S\}$

which is the set of all bindings which satisfy the schema S. Here, θS takes the place of the 'characteristic tuple' which we described for ordinary declaration lists in Chapter 4.

Note that this introduces a possible ambiguity in the notation since $\{S\}$ could denote a set containing the single element S. This is resolved by the rule that if S is the name of a schema $\{S\}$ denotes a set of bindings, and if S is the name of a variable it denotes a singleton set.

QUANTIFIERS

If S is the name of a schema then

$\forall S \ \bullet \ predicate$

is equivalent to the predicate

$\forall \text{sig} \ S \mid \text{prop} \ S \ \bullet \ predicate$

and,

$\exists S \ \bullet \ predicate$

is equivalent to the predicate

$\exists \text{sig} \ S \mid \text{prop} \ S \ \bullet \ predicate$

For example, if we were convinced that there were games of NIM with piles of 1000 sticks in them we could assert that $\exists Game \ \bullet \ 1000 \in \text{ran} \ pile$.

If, on the contrary, we thought that no NIM game was allowed with piles of greater than 10 sticks we could assert ∀ *Game* • ran *pile* ⊆ *0..10*.

Just as in set comprehension, it is valid to apply further constraints so that, for instance,

∀ *Game* | ran *pile* ⊆ *0..10* • *pile A* + *pile B* + *pile C* ≤ *30*

says that games with piles restricted to a maximum of 10 sticks each have the sum of their piles no greater than 30. This happens to be *True*.

LAMBDA

If S is the name of a schema then

λS • expression

is equivalent to the expression

{S • θS ↦ expression}

that is, it is a function which maps each schema binding to the value of the expression.

As before, we can add another constraint to restrict the domain of the functi⌄n, so that

λS | predicate • expression

is equivalent to the expression

{S | predicate • θS ↦ expression}

For example, we can define a function called *NoOfSticks*:

NoOfSticks == λ*Game* • *pile A* + *pile B* + *pile C*

which gives, for each game of NIM, the number of sticks remaining in its piles. Now we could assert

∀ *Game* | ran *pile* ⊆ *0..10* • *NoOfSticks* θ*Game* ≤ *30*

An equivalent way to define *NoOfSticks* is

$$NoOfSticks : Game \rightarrow \mathbb{N}$$
$$\forall g : Game \bullet NoOfSticks\ g = g.pile\ A + g.pile\ B + g.pile\ C$$

Notice that the component of **Game** becomes a local variable of the lambda expression, and that the function defined has the schema type of **Game** as the type of its (only) parameter.

MU

If *S* is the name of a schema then

$\mu S \bullet$ expression

is equivalent to the expression

μ sig *S* | prop *S* • expression

and, just as for normal μ expressions, it is a requirement that there is only one possible value that satisfies the schema.

If **expression** is omitted then it is taken as the schema binding θS. It is quite common to find this form used in combination with further constraints in a predicate clause, so we might see:

$\mu Game$ | $pile = \{A \mapsto 5, B \mapsto 6, C \mapsto 7\}$

to denote the conventional starting *Game* for our game of NIM. (Notice that the starting *pile* value is *distinct* from the starting *Game*.) In this case $\mu Game$ would not be valid because there are many possible game states. However, since there is only one final position, we *can* denote it by

$\mu Game$ | ran *pile* = $\{0\}$

or, more briefly, by $\mu Ended$, since we have defined the schema *Ended* already.

Exercise 10.2

Using the definitions starting on page 150, which of the following are valid?

$\mu TextFile$ | #*text* = 0
$\mu Line$ | *txt* = $\langle\rangle$
$\mu TextFile$ | *text* = $\langle \mu Line \mid txt = \langle\rangle\rangle$

SCHEMA OPERATIONS

We will use the **sig** and **prop** notation to define the logical operations of conjunction, disjunction, negation, implication and equivalence, as well as universal and existential quantification as they apply to schemas. We will then define renaming and hiding and finally proceed to the more specialized operations of pre-condition, composition and overriding.

SCHEMA CONJUNCTION

If S and T are the names of schemas then

$$S \wedge T \triangleq [\text{sig } S; \text{sig } T \mid \text{prop } S \wedge \text{prop } T]$$

which is equivalent to the definition given in Chapter 7.

For the expression to denote a valid schema, the two signatures must combine to form another valid signature — which is just another way to say that the signatures are *compatible*.

In practice, schemas combined by conjunction often have some identical declarations in their declaration parts. In this case it is unnecessary to separate the declaration into a type and a constraint (for the signature and property), and the declaration can be taken intact into the resulting schema. This works because the constraint will appear in both properties (prop S and prop T) and so can be 'factored out' of the resulting property and re-combined with the signature to form the original declaration. In general, schemas that are *included* in the declaration part of both S and T can be left intact in the resulting conjunction, by the same reasoning. So, for example, in NIM we could define a schema

$$LastPlay \triangleq PlayOK \wedge Ended'$$

Here *Ended'* has *Game'* in its declaration part and *PlayOK* has $\Delta Game$ (i.e. *Game* and *Game'*) and *Parameters* in its declaration part. We can immediately write out an equivalent form

```
┌─ LastPlay ────────────────────────────
│ Game
│ Game'
│ Parameters
├────────────────
│ pile p? ≥ take?
│ pile' = pile ⊕ {p? ↦ (pile p? − take?)}
│ ran pile' = {0}
└────────────────────────────────────────
```

without the need to derive signatures.

<hr>
Exercise 10.3

In the Cash Dispenser sample specification of Chapter 7 we could have defined *ChangeNowt* as follows

$ChangeNowt \triangleq \Xi AccountFile \wedge ValidPin$

Write out a schema for *ChangeNowt* without deriving the signature and property completely. What logical rule do we rely upon to 'factor out' predicates from the property of a conjunction?
<hr>

SCHEMA DISJUNCTION

If S and T are the names of schemas then

$S \vee T \triangleq [\text{sig } S;\text{sig } T \mid \text{prop } S \vee \text{prop } T]$

which is equivalent to the definition given in Chapter 7.

Just as for conjunction the signatures must be *compatible*, otherwise the right hand side of this definition would not have a valid signature.

If the two schemas have identical declarations in their declaration parts then, as for conjunction, it is not necessary to separate the type information from the constraint. The common constraints will 'factor out' of the disjunction's property and can recombine with the declarations.

<hr>
Exercise 10.4

In NIM, *Play* is defined as *PlayMore*∨*PlayLast*∨*PlayErr*. Express this as a single schema without deriving the signatures and properties completely. What logical rule do we rely upon when we 'factor out' predicates from the property of a disjunction?
<hr>

SCHEMA NEGATION

If S is the name of a schema then

$\neg S \triangleq [\text{sig } S \mid \neg \text{prop } S]$

Note that it is the *property* that is negated, and that the *signatures* of S and $\neg S$ are identical.

We have not used negation before, but we could have done. In the NIM example we described two game states:

$Ended \triangleq [Game \mid \text{ran } pile = \{0\}]$
$Open \triangleq [Game \mid \text{ran } pile \neq \{0\}]$

We could have defined $Open \triangleq \neg Ended$ which would have directly indicated the *meaning* of *Open* and made the definition more readable.

It looks as though negation is simple to apply, but some caution is needed. To demonstrate this we shall expand the definition of ¬*Ended*.

sig *Ended*   is   *pile* : $\mathbb{P}$(*pileid*×$\mathbb{Z}$)
prop *Ended*   is   ran *pile* = {0} ∧ *pile* ∈ *pileid*→$\mathbb{N}$

where the declaration of *pile* in *Game* leads to the second constraint.

This means that, copying the definition of schema negation,

¬ *Ended* = [*pile* : $\mathbb{P}$(*pileid*×$\mathbb{Z}$) | ¬(ran *pile* = {0} ∧ *pile* ∈ *pileid*→$\mathbb{N}$)]

Is this the same as the *Open* schema? Using the fact that ¬(*p*∧*q*) is equivalent to ¬*p*∨¬*q* we can re-express the predicate part to get the schema

[*pile* : $\mathbb{P}$(*pileid*×$\mathbb{Z}$) | ran *pile* ≠ {0} ∨ *pile* ∉ *pileid*→$\mathbb{N}$]

and, using the fact that *p*∨*q* is equivalent to (*p*∧¬*q*)∨*q* we can write this as

[*pile* : $\mathbb{P}$(*pileid*×$\mathbb{Z}$) | (ran *pile* ≠ {0} ∧ *pile* ∈ *pileid*→$\mathbb{N}$) ∨ *pile* ∉ *pileid*→$\mathbb{N}$]

which 'conveniently' splits into

[*Game* | ran *pile* ≠ {0}] ∨ [*pile* : $\mathbb{P}$(*pileid*×$\mathbb{Z}$) | *pile* ∉ *pileid*→$\mathbb{N}$]

In other words

¬ *Ended* = *Open* ∨ ¬ *Game*

which is probably *not* what we expected. There are a lot more states that satisfy ¬*Ended* than just *Game*s that have not ended, namely all those things which are *not* games but have the same signature as *Game*.

This may not be what we expected but it *is* what we said: states that are not *Ended* include states that are of the same form (type) but are not *Game*s at all. In the NIM exercise we only ever used *Open* in schemas that included *Game*, so this was quite safe, since the non-*Game* states are then eliminated. In general a wise safeguard is always to use schema negation in conjunction with an appropriate state schema.

Exercise 10.5

In the sample solution to the Cash Dispenser specification problem of Chapter 7 there is an opportunity to use schema negation. Can you find it? Does it help to make the specification clearer?

SCHEMA IMPLICATION

If S and T are the names of schemas then

$S \Rightarrow T \; \hat{=} \; [\mathsf{sig}\, S; \mathsf{sig}\, T \; | \; \mathsf{prop}\, S \Rightarrow \mathsf{prop}\, T]$

Exercise 10.6

Show that, given schemas S and $T, S \Rightarrow T$ is the same as $\neg S \vee T$

When we explored the meaning of schema negation we discovered some unexpected results which could be traps for the unwary. As schema implication is equivalent to an expression involving schema negation we must take care. $S \Rightarrow T$ brings with it all states that are $\neg S$.

For example we can consider again the game of NIM. We shall suppose that we wish to change the rules of the game slightly: if a pile contains an even number of sticks then we will only allow half of its sticks to be removed, instead of any number.

First we define what we mean by an 'even pile' and a 'half take':

$EvenPile \; \hat{=} \; [Game; p?: pileid \; | \; (pile\, p?) \bmod 2 = 0]$
$HalfTake \; \hat{=} \; [Game; p?: pileid; take?: \mathbb{N}_1 \; | \; 2*take? = pile\, p?]$

which describe under what conditions the restriction applies and our condition on play if it does, respectively. Now, consider a new version of NIM, which we shall call EvenNIM, described by the following play:

$EvenPlayOK \; \hat{=} \; PlayOK \; \wedge \; (EvenPile \Rightarrow HalfTake)$

This allows normal NIM play as long as the condition described by *EvenPile* does not apply, and imposes the extra condition *HalfTake* when it does.

Exercise 10.7

Apply the definition of $\Rightarrow$ and expand the schema *EvenPlayOK*.

Notice that we do not have to fully specify the play in *HalfTake*, but only an extra condition. Also, the use of schema conjunction implies that the EvenNIM plays are also valid NIM plays. Of course it is a matter of opinion whether this enhances the presentation of the rules of EvenNIM.

SCHEMA EQUIVALENCE

If S and T are the names of schemas then

$S \Leftrightarrow T \; \hat{=} \; [\mathsf{sig}\, S; \mathsf{sig}\, T \; | \; \mathsf{prop}\, S \Leftrightarrow \mathsf{prop}\, T]$

> **Exercise 10.8**
>
> Show that $S\Leftrightarrow T$ is equivalent to $(\neg S \wedge \neg T) \vee (S \wedge T)$. How can we interpret this for schemas?

Since the schema equivalence operation involves schema negation we must use it with care.

SCHEMA UNIVERSAL QUANTIFICATION

If S and T are the names of schemas then

$$\forall S \bullet T \;\hat{=}\; [\text{sig } T \setminus \text{sig } S \mid \forall S \bullet \text{prop } T]$$

which is a schema formed from T which describes 'the T states for which all S are valid'. Notice that the signature of the resulting schema does not include components of S.

It is difficult to illustrate the use of schema universal quantification because, as for schema implication, there have been few applications. Here is a simple and rather contrived example involving point and line graphs. Figure 10.1 illustrates the sort of graph we mean.

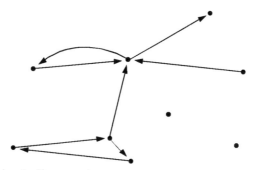

Fig 10.1. A simple line graph.

Given a basic set of points

[*POINT*]

and a fixed subset of these on which to construct a graph (a network of lines)

points : $\mathbb{P}$*POINT*

we can define a *Graph* as the set of interconnections of these *points*:

> ┌─*Graph*──────────────────────
> │ *join* : *points*$\leftrightarrow$*points*
> └──────────────────────────────

where each line (all of them represented by the single relation *join*) links two points. All the points linked in *join* must be **points** of the Graph, but there may be points not linked to any other.

A special point (*place*) of the fixed set is called a *Place*:

Place ≙ [*place : points*]

and two points connected (directly or indirectly) by lines of a *Graph* form a *Path*:

Path ≙ [*start, place : points*; *Graph* | *start join* place]

where we have used the reflexive transitive closure of *join* to indicate that a *chain* of links forms a path. (The chain may be of zero length since the transitive closure is reflexive.)

We can now define a connected graph as one that possesses a root (*start*) to which all other places are joined by a path:

ConnectedGraph ≙ ∀ *Place* • *Path*

or, in other words, a graph with a *start* point joined to each *place* by a *Path*.

Exercise 10.9

Write out the signature and property of *ConnectedGraph* using the definition of ∀.

Another form schema universal quantification may take is:

∀ declaration-list | predicate • *T*

with the obvious changes to the definition. The **predicate** is optional as usual.

SCHEMA EXISTENTIAL QUANTIFICATION

If *S* and *T* are the names of schemas then

∃ *S* • *T* ≙ [sig *T* \ sig *S* | ∃ *S* • prop *T*]

which is a schema formed from *T* which describes 'the *T* states for which there is a valid *S*'. Notice that the signature of the resulting schema does not include components of *S*.

As for universal quantification, it is possible to replace *S* by a declaration list and constraint, with evident meaning.

The principal use of this form is in describing states for which an operation has a defined result. For instance, consider the NIM game and ask which states can occur immediately before the final state? The final state is the one which was characterized as *Ended* and a valid move is characterized by the schema *PlayOK*. We can therefore immediately write down the schema that describes exactly which *Game* states precede *Ended* states as:

   Penultimate $\hat{=}$ $\exists$ *Ended'* $\bullet$ *PlayOK*

which we can read as 'those *PlayOK* states for which there can be *Ended* (after) states'.

Since the quantified states are removed from the signature of the result, *Penultimate* does not refer to *Game'* states (there are no dashed variables in the resulting schema). We decorated *Ended* to ensure that it was the state *before* a final state that was characterized.

┌─ **Exercise 10.10** ──────────────────────────────────┐
│ Write out the signature and property of *Penultimate* by using the defi-
│ nition of $\exists$ and simplify the property as much as you can.
└──┘

RENAMING

If *S* is the name of a schema, $new_1, new_2,...$ are names of variables *not* in the signature of *S* and $old_1, old_2,...$ are names of components of *S* then

   $S[new_1/old_1, new_2/old_2, ...]$

is a schema which is exactly like *S* except that the component named old_1 is renamed new_1, old_2 is renamed new_2, and so on.

For example, we might create another 'copy' of the NIM game state:

   OtherGame $\hat{=}$ *Game* [*otherpile/pile*]

which is equivalent to the definition

┌─*OtherGame*──
│ *otherpile* : *pileid*$\twoheadrightarrow\mathbb{N}$
└──

All the constraints apply in the new schema, expect that they refer to the new names instead of the old ones.

This is a useful operation for describing identically structured, but distinct, parts of a larger state. We could, for instance, define a larger game of NIM called SuperNIM, which has double the number of piles:

   SuperGame $\hat{=}$ *Game* $\wedge$ *OtherGame*

where *pile* and *otherpile* are two separate groups of piles in this game.

Valid play on the *OtherGame* part of this state is similar to that on the original *Game* state,

$$OtherPlayOK \; \hat{=} \; PlayOK[otherpile/pile, \, otherpile'/pile']$$

and uses the same parameters.

We could define play in SuperNIM to be play in one or other (but not both) of the games:

$$SuperPlayOK \; \hat{=} \; (PlayOK \wedge \Xi OtherGame) \vee (OtherPlayOK \wedge \Xi Game)$$

Exercise 10.11

Explain what happens to the *Parameters* part of the signature of *SuperPlayOK*.

SuperNIM is a slightly unpredictable game, since the inputs for this play operation are not sufficient to determine which of the two groups of sticks the pile identifier *p?* refers to. As it stands, therefore, the play allows either group of piles to satisfy the specification – not an entirely satisfactory arrangement for the player.

Exercise 10.12

Given the definitions

$groupid ::= this \mid that$
$This \; \hat{=} \; [group : groupid \mid group = this]$
$That \; \hat{=} \; [group : groupid \mid group = that]$

define a better play schema for *SuperGame* to give the player control over which group is meant.

Renaming is useful to avoid name clashes when composing a system from smaller parts. Decoration is a form of systematic renaming used for precisely this purpose.

HIDING

If *S* is the name of a schema then

$$S \setminus (n_1, n_2, \ldots)$$

is equivalent to

$$\exists \, n_1 : T_1; \; n_2 : T_2; \ldots \; \bullet \; S$$

where n_1 has type T_1, n_2 has type T_2, and so on, in the signature of *S*.

This is called **hiding** and is a useful operation to remove components from a schema (perhaps one formed from a schema operation) that are not part of the interface described by the schema (see Chapter

9). So, for instance, the variable *rc!* in the schema *SuperPlayOK* could be 'hidden' by

$$SuperPlayNorc \triangleq SuperPlayOK \setminus (rc!)$$

We permit hiding components identified by a schema, too. If *S* and *T* are the names of schemas then

$$S \setminus T \triangleq \exists T \bullet S$$

so that the two notations, hiding by schema and schema existential quantification, are interchangeable.

The hiding operation was used and explained in Chapter 9. It is re-expressed here since we now have a succinct definition in terms of schema existential quantification.

SCHEMA PRE-CONDITION

If *S* is the name of a schema describing an operation (state *State*, inputs *In?* and outputs *Out!*) then

$$pre\,S \triangleq \exists\,(State' \wedge Out!) \bullet S$$

which should have the same signature as *State*∧*In?* and which characterizes exactly those states and inputs that are related to states and outputs by the operation *S*. In short, this is the condition for *S* to 'work'. Pre-condition was used and explained in Chapter 7. Here we have a succinct definition.

In NIM we can ask what the conditions on valid play are. This is expressed as pre *PlayOK*. Using the definition this is

$$\exists\,Game';\ rc!:code \bullet PlayOK$$

which expands to

┌─ pre *PlayOK* ──────────────────────────────
│ *Game*
│ *p? : pileid*
│ *take?* : $\mathbb{N}_1$
├───
│ $\exists\,Game'; rc! : code \bullet$
│ $pile\,p? \geq take? \wedge pile' = pile \oplus \{p? \mapsto (pile\,p? - take?)\}$

┌─ **Exercise 10.13** ─────────────────────────
│ Calculate the pre-condition of *PlayLast*. Simplify the schema as much as possible.

SCHEMA COMPOSITION

If S and T are the names of schemas describing operations with the same state *State* then

$$S \, \mathring{,} \, T \, \hat{=} \, (S[-''/-'] \wedge T[-''/-]) \setminus State''$$

where, *for this definition only*, we have used $S[-''/-']$ as a shorthand for redecorating the dashed components of S to double dashes, and $T[-''/-]$ for decorating all the undecorated components to make them double dashed. The effect is that the output states of S are identified with the input states of T and both are hidden in the resulting schema (by hiding *State''*).

This operation is called **schema composition** because it behaves like function composition. $S \mathring{,} T$ relates starting states to the ending states which can be obtained by first performing operation S and then performing operation T.

SCHEMA OVERRIDING

If S and T are the names of schemas describing operations then

$$S \oplus T \, \hat{=} \, T \vee (\neg \, \text{pre} \, T \wedge S)$$

which describes an operation which is everywhere like S except where T can possibly apply (**pre** T) where it behaves like T instead. Thus the operation T 'overrides' that of S.

This can be useful in extending an operation by cases, forming a series of exceptions to what has been described before.

ANSWERS TO EXERCISES

Answer 10.1

This is the set of *pile* functions that appear in 'before' *Game* states of a *PlayOK* play. To appear here there must be at least one pile with sticks in it. One way of expressing this is

$\{pile : pileid \rightarrow \mathbb{N} \mid \exists \, p : pileid \bullet pile \, p > 0\}$

To obtain this from the original expression we have to observe that most of the declarations in *PlayOK* are irrelevant to the value of *pile* provided that we can find at least one *p?* and *take?* with *pile p? ≥ take?*. Since *take?>0* follows from its declaration we can deduce the constraint in the answer.

Answer 10.2

The first two are valid but $\mu TextFile \mid text = \langle \mu Line \mid txt = \langle \rangle \rangle$ is not valid because, although the *text* part of the *TextFile* state is uniquely defined by the embedded μ expression, there is another part of the state, *row*, which could either be 0 or 1. Each μ expression must have a unique interpretation.

Answer 10.3

An equivalent form would be

```
┌─ ChangeNowt ────────────────────────────────
│ ΞAccountFile
│ Card?
│ pin? : PIN
│ ────────────────────────────────────────────
│ pin? = (cust accno?).fxd.pinlist cardno?
└─
```

The logical rule we rely upon is that $(p \wedge q) \wedge (p \wedge r)$ is equivalent to $p \wedge (q \wedge r)$, where p is the constraint associated with the declaration that the two schemas have in common, and $p \wedge q$ and $p \wedge r$ are the properties of the schemas. After this rearrangement, p can be safely taken back into the declaration part to combine once more with its declaration.

Answer 10.4

PlayMore and *PlayLast* both include *PlayOK* but *PlayErr* does not. However, *PlayErr* includes *ΞGame* and *Parameters* and *PlayOK* includes *ΔGame* and *Parameters*, so the common parts can be identified as *ΔGame* and *Parameters*, provided we do not forget the constraint that comes with *ΞGame*. The schema can be expressed as

```
┌─ Play ───────────────────────────────────────
│ ΔGame
│ Parameters
│ ──────────────────────────────────────────────
│ (Open' ∧ rc! = OK)
│ ∨
│ (Ended' ∧ rc! = fin)
│ ∨
│ (θGame = θGame' ∧ (pile p?) < take? ∧ rc! = error)
└─
```

The logical rule that allows us to 'factor out' common predicates is that $(p \wedge q) \vee (p \wedge r)$ is equivalent to $p \wedge (q \vee r)$. This is one of the distributive laws we saw in Chapter 3.

Answer 10.5

The *InvalidPin* schema looks and feels like the negation of the *ValidPin* schema. It might make reading the description easier if we used ¬ *ValidPin* in place of *InvalidPin*. Note that this is only ever used in conjunction with the state *AccountFile* and so the possibility of allowing extra states (that for example have *cust* not a partial function) is avoided.

Answer 10.6

Because prop $S \Rightarrow$ prop T is equivalent to $(\neg \text{prop } S) \vee \text{prop } T$ (see Chapter 3) the property of $S \Rightarrow T$ is the same as that of $\neg S \vee T$. The signatures are the same from the simple signature rules of schema negation and schema disjunction.

Answer 10.7

EvenPile$\Rightarrow$*HalfTake* has signature *pile*:$\mathbb{P}$(*pileid*$\times\mathbb{Z}$); *p?:pileid*; *take?:$\mathbb{Z}$*, and property

$$((pile \in pileid \twoheadrightarrow \mathbb{N}_1) \wedge ((pile \, p?) \bmod 2 = 0))$$
$$\Rightarrow ((take?>0) \wedge (2*take? = pile \, p?) \wedge (pile \in pileid \twoheadrightarrow \mathbb{N}_1))$$

which, using that $p \Rightarrow q$ is equivalent to $\neg p \vee q$, is the same as

$$(pile \notin pileid \twoheadrightarrow \mathbb{N}_1)$$
$$\vee$$
$$((pile \, p?) \bmod 2 \neq 0)$$
$$\vee$$
$$((take? > 0) \wedge (2*take? = pile \, p?) \wedge (pile \in pileid \twoheadrightarrow \mathbb{N}_1))$$

Conjoining this with the property of *PlayOK* eliminates the cases where $(take?>0)$ or $(pile \in pileid \twoheadrightarrow \mathbb{N}_1)$ fail to hold, so that

$$PlayOK \wedge (EvenPile \Rightarrow EvenTake)$$

reduces to

```
ΔGame
p? : pileid
take? : ℕ₁
rc! : code
─────────────────────
pile p? ≥ take?
pile′ = pile ⊕ {p? ↦ (pile p? − take?)}
((pile p?) mod 2 = 0) ⇒ (2*take? = pile p?)
```

Of course, another way to answer this exercise would be to write

$$(\neg \, EvenPile \wedge PlayOK) \vee (EvenPile \wedge PlayOK \wedge HalfTake)$$

which is just as much an 'expansion' as the schema above.

Answer 10.8

The equivalence reduces to the same one for predicates, which can be demonstrated by truth tables. The interpretation is more difficult, but it can be phrased thus: the schema '*S* if and only if *T*' allows states which are *either* both *S* and *T* or both non-*S* and non-*T*, and disallows all other states. In other words, states of *S* and *T* occur (or do not occur) together.

Answer 10.9

The signature is $start : POINT;\ join : POINT\leftrightarrow POINT$ and the property is

$$\forall place : points \bullet start \in points \ \wedge\ join \in points\leftrightarrow points \ \wedge\ start\ join^{*}\ place$$

which, combined, allows us to deduce that *ConnectedGraph* is equivalent to

---
start : *points*
Graph

$\forall place : points \bullet start\ join^{*}\ place$

Answer 10.10

The signature is sig *PlayOK* \ sig *Ended'*, which reduces to $pile{:}\mathbb{P}\,(pileid\times\mathbb{Z})$; $p?{:}pileid;\ take!{:}\mathbb{Z};\ rc!{:}code$, and the property is

$pile\ p? = take?\ \wedge\ \mathrm{ran}(\{p?\}\lhd pile) = \{0\}$
$pile \in pileid \nrightarrow \mathbb{N}_1$
$take? \in \mathbb{N}_1$

Of course this is not as easy to read as

Game
Parameters

$pile\ p? = take?$
$\mathrm{ran}(\{p?\}\lhd pile) = \{0\}$

---

which says quite clearly that the last *take?* must be the whole of the last remaining pile of sticks (all other piles being empty).

Answer 10.11

Since its components were not renamed in *OtherPlayOK*, the *Parameters* schema is the same in both parts of SuperNIM. Thus, in *SuperPlayOK*, *p?*, *take?* and *rc!* are the only input and output parameters still. The value of *rc!* is unconstrained by any of the schemas making up *SuperPlayOK*.

Answer 10.12

The player needs to provide another parameter indicating which group is which. *This?* and *That?* express the parameter and the value for each case, so a suitable play schema might be:

$HyperPlayOK \ \hat{=}\ (This? \wedge PlayOK \wedge \Xi OtherGame)$
$\qquad\qquad\quad \vee\ (That? \wedge OtherPlayOK \wedge \Xi Game)$

Answer 10.13

pre *PlayLast* is

Game
p? : *pileid*
take? : $\mathbb{N}_1$

∃ *Game'*; *rc!* : *code* •
   pile p? ≥ *take?*
  ∧ *pile'* = *pile* ⊕ {*p?* ↦ (*pile p?* − *take?*)}
  ∧ *rc!* = *fin*
  ∧ ran *pile'* = {0}

---

which, because the value of *rc!* is immaterial and the constraints on *pile'* and *take?* combine to reduce the options drastically, can be reduced to

---

Game
p? : *pileid*
take? : $\mathbb{N}_1$

---

pile p? = *take?*
ran({*p?*} ⊲ *pile*) = {0}

SPECIFICATION PROBLEMS

This final set of specification problems differs from the others in that the problems are less constrained and we have not provided solutions. You should freely invent extra requirements and, if possible, collaborate with colleagues on solutions of your own. They are in no particular order.

Write formal specifications for any of the following:

(1) A set of traffic lights.

(2) The interface for a video cassette recorder (VCR).

(3) The interface for an actual car radio.

(4) Chess: try a game position; the intial position; valid moves.

(5) Bridge: evaluation of a Bridge hand.

(6) Poker: the rules for ranking a hand.

(7) GO: the rules of GO.

(8) Othello (Reversi): try a game position; the rules; a move.

(9) A warehouse stock control system.

(10) A college timetabling system; difficult one this – try a simple state first of all.

(11) A diary and calendar system supporting multiple users which allows each person to inspect anyone's diary (unless it is restricted) and to update their own diary (and any others for which they are authorized).

(12) An estate agent's system for storing house details and supporting on-line enquiries to find houses matching a purchaser's requirements and other query and update transactions.

(13) A flexible working hours system (allowing employees to choose their own hours of work within certain constraints).

(14) A cash issuing terminal system.

(15) A text editor.

(16) A cross reference program.

(17) A computer instruction set.

(18) The syntax rules for a high level language (such as BASIC or Pascal).

(19) A compiler.

(20) A lending library system.

(21) A source code library control system.

Appendix A

Summary of Notation

This Appendix contains two parts:

- a summary of the syntax rules;
- tables summarising the language constructs, including what we have assumed to be in the basic library.

These tables are intended as a quick reference section, and we show simple illustrative definitions of most constructs. A full formal definition of many of them would be in *generic* form (see Chapter 9).

Throughout the definitions, we use the following abbreviations:

D	a declaration
P	a predicate
E	an expression

SYNTAX RULES

In this section we summarize the syntax rules for identifiers and declarations and the rules of scope.

An **identifier** consists of a **base-name** preceded by an optional **prefix** and followed by an optional series of **decorations**.

A **base-name** is a sequence of letters, digits and underscore characters. Uppercase letters are distinct from lowercase letters and the first character of a base-name must be a letter.

A **prefix** is either Δ (Delta) or Ξ (Xi). A prefix can be used only with a schema name.

A **decoration** is:

- a dash (');
- a question mark (?);
- an exclamation mark (!);
- a superscript;
- a subscript.

An **identifier-list** is:

identifier, identifier, ...

A **declaration** is:

identifier-list : set-expression

The declaration asserts that the value of each of the variables in identifier-list is in the set set-expression.

A *declaration-list* is:

declaration; declaration; ...

Scope rules

The *scope* of a variable depends on the sort of definition that introduces it and where that definition occurs.

Given set and axiomatic definitions introduce *global* variables. The predicate part of an axiomatic definition can also introduce local variables known only in the constraint.

An abbreviation is equivalent to an axiomatic definition, so it too introduces a *global* variable.

A data-type definition is equivalent to a given set definition together with an axiomatic definition, so it introduces *global* variables.

A schema definition introduces the schema name, which is *global*, and the schema components which are *local* to the schema (they are known only in the predicate part of the schema).

Z phrases

There are five sorts of Z phrase:

- given set definition;
- axiomatic definition;
- abbreviation;
- data-type definition;
- schema definition.

A *given set definition* is:

[identifier-list]

This introduces a global variable for each identifier in the list.
An *axiomatic definition* is

> declaration-list
> _____
> predicate

or

declaration-list | predicate

This introduces a global variable for each identifier in the declaration-list and the predicate expresses constraints on these values.
An *abbreviation* is:

identifier == expression

which introduces the identifier as equivalent to the value of expression.

It is equivalent to the following axiomatic definition:

identifier : set-expresssion | identifier = expression

A *data-type definition* is

identifier ::= branch | branch | ...

where branch is either

- an identifier, or
- function-name ≪ set-expression ≫

The identifiers used for each branch must be distinct from the others in the same data-type definition.

The data-type definition introduces its identifier as a new type which is made up of a series of disjoint sets of values, one set for each branch in the definition. If the branch is a simple identifier, then the corresponding set contains only one value. If the branch is function-name ≪ set-expression ≫, then the set can contain several elements.

The data-type definition also introduces each branch identifier and function-name as a global variable. Each function-name is defined to be an *injection* from the set specified by set-expression to the set identifier. Thus the data-type definition is equivalent to:

[identifier]
function-name : set-expression ↣ identifier

(and similar declarations for all branches) together with various constraints.

If several constructor functions are defined in one data-type, then the ranges of the constructor functions are disjoint and the values of each simple identifier may not be in any of these ranges.

Each variable introduced by a data-type definition (the data-type name and each name in the branches) has *global* scope.

A *schema definition* is:

```
┌schema-name───────────────────────────────
│ declaration-part
│ ─────────────
│ predicate-part
└───────────────────────────────────────────
```

or:

schema-name ≙ [declaration-part | predicate part]

The schema-name has *global* scope.

The variables declared in the declaration-part (the schema *components*) have *local* scope (they are known only within the predicate-part).

SUMMARY TABLES

Table A.1. Definitions and declarations.

abbreviation ==	$t ==$ expression Introduces a global variable, t, whose value and type are given by expression.
schema definition ≙	$S ≙$ schema-expression Introduces a schema name, S, whose value and type are given by schema-expression.
given set [ ]	[S] Introduces a *given set* called S. A given set is a type.
declaration :	$x :$ set-expression Introduces a variable, x, whose value is declared to be in the set given by set-expression.
multiple declaration ,	$x, y, z :$ set-expression Introduces variables x, y and z, each of whose values are declared to be in the set given by set-expression.
declaration list ;	$x, y :$ set-expr$_1$; $u, v :$ set-expr$_2$ Introduces variables x, y, u and v. The values of x and y are declared to be in the set given by set-expr$_1$, and the values of u and v are declared to be in the set given by set-expr$_2$.
datatype definition ::= |	$T ::= a \mid b \mid c$ Introduces T as a *given set* and global variables a, b and c as the (sole) members of T. Their values are distinct. The definition is equivalent to $\quad [T]$ $\quad a, b, c : T$ $\quad a \neq b \neq c \neq a$
constructor ≪ ≫	$T ::= f ≪$set-expression$≫$ Introduces T as a *given set* and a global variable f as a total injection from the set given by set-expression to T. This definition is equivalent to $\quad [T]$ $\quad f :$ set-expression$\rightarrowtail T$

Table A.2. Logic.

not ¬	¬p *True* if p is *False*; *False* if p is *True*.
and ∧	$p \wedge q$ *True* if both p and q are *True*; *False* if either p or q is *False* (or if both are *False*).
or ∨	$p \vee q$ *True* if either p or q is *True* (or if both are *True*); *False* if both p and q are *False*.
implies ⇒	$p \Rightarrow q$ *True* if both p and q are *True*; *True* if p is *False* (irrespective of the truth of q); *False* if p is *True* and q is *False*.
equivalence ⇔	$p \Leftrightarrow q$ The same as $(p \Rightarrow q) \wedge (q \Rightarrow p)$, thus *True* if both p and q are *True*; *True* if both p and q are *False*; *False* if p is *True* and q is *False*; *False* if p is *False* and q is *True*.
there exists ∃	∃ $x : S$ | constraint • predicate *True* if at least one element of the set S subject to constraint satisfies predicate. The variable x is *bound*.
there exists one ∃$_1$	∃$_1$ $x : S$ | constraint • predicate *True* if exactly one element of the set S subject to constraint satisfies predicate. The variable x is *bound*.
for all ∀	∀ $x : S$ | constraint • predicate *True* if all elements of the set S subject to constraint satisfy predicate. The variable x is *bound*.

Table A.3. Numbers.

integers $\mathbb{Z}$	The set of integers. ($\mathbb{Z}$ is a given set, and hence a type, defined in the basic library.)
natural numbers $\mathbb{N}$	The set of non-negative integers. ($\mathbb{N}$ is *not* a given set.) $\mathbb{N} == \{x : \mathbb{Z} \mid x \geq 0\}$
positive numbers $\mathbb{N}_1$	The set of positive integers. ($\mathbb{N}_1$ is *not* a given set.) $\mathbb{N}_1 == \{x : \mathbb{Z} \mid x > 0\}$
integers m to n $m..n$	The set of integers from m to n inclusive. $m..n == \{x : \mathbb{Z} \mid m \leq x \leq n\}$ (If $m>n$, then the set is empty.)
minimum min	$\min S$ If S is a set of integers, then $\min S$ is the element of S which is smaller than any other. min is defined for all sets that have such a minimum and S need not be finite, although it must be non-empty. $(\min S \in S) \wedge (\forall x : S \bullet \min S \leq x)$
maximum max	$\max S$ If S is a set of integers, then $\max S$ is the element of S which is larger than any other. max is defined for all sets that have such a maximum and S need not be finite, although it must be non-empty. $(\max S \in S) \wedge (\forall x : S \bullet \max S \geq x)$
arithmetic operators **+ − ∗**	$m{+}n \quad m{-}n \quad m{*}n$ Addition, subtraction and multiplication of integers: $\_+\_, \ \_-\_, \ \_*\_ : (\mathbb{Z}\times\mathbb{Z})\rightarrow\mathbb{Z}$
prefix minus −	$-n$ Negation of integers declared as: $- : \mathbb{Z}\rightarrow\mathbb{Z}$
quotient ÷	$n{\div}m$ The quotient n divided by m declared as: $\_\div\_ : \mathbb{Z}\times (\mathbb{Z}\backslash\{0\}) \rightarrow \mathbb{Z}$
remainder mod	$n \bmod m$ The remainder of n divided by m declared as: $\_\bmod\_ : \mathbb{Z}\times(\mathbb{Z}\backslash\{0\}) \rightarrow \mathbb{Z}$ Note $m*(n{\div}n) + n \bmod m = n$.
comparison ≤ < = > ≥	$m{\leq}n \quad m{<}n \quad m{=}n \quad m{>}n \quad m{\geq}n$ Numeric comparisons between integers declared as: $\_\leq\_, \ \_<\_, \ \_=\_, \ \_>\_, \ \_\geq\_ : \mathbb{Z}\leftrightarrow\mathbb{Z}$

Table A.4 (Page 1 of 2). Sets.

enumeration { }	$\{a, b, ..., z\}$ The set containing the elements a, b, ..., z. (a, b, ..., z must all be of the same type.)
comprehension | •	$\{x : S \mid \text{predicate}\}$ The set containing those elements of S that satisfy predicate. $\{x : S \mid \text{predicate} \bullet \text{expression}\}$ The set of values of expression for all values of x in S which satisfy predicate.
member of ∈	$x \in S$ *True* if x is a member of the set S; *False* if x is not a member of the set S.
not member of ∉	$x \notin S$ *True* if x is not a member of the set S; *False* if x is a member of the set S.
empty set ∅	A set containing no members. ∅ is generically defined, for it must have a *type* and this is determined from context just as for all generic definitions. This means there are several empty sets, one for each type.
set equality =	$S = T$ *True* if S and T have the same members; *False* if either has a member that the other does not. $S = T \;==\; (\forall s : S \bullet s \in T) \wedge (\forall t : T \bullet t \in S)$
set inequality ≠	$S \neq T$ *True* if S and T do not have the same members; *False* if they have the same members. $S \neq T \;==\; (\exists s : S \bullet s \notin T) \vee (\exists t : T \bullet t \notin S)$
subset ⊆	$S \subseteq T$ *True* if each member of S is also a member of T; *False* if there is a member of S which is not in T. $S \subseteq T \;==\; \forall s : S \bullet s \in T$
proper subset ⊂	$S \subset T$ *True* if $S \subseteq T$ and $S \neq T$; *False* if $S = T$ or if S is not a subset of T.

Table A.4 (Page 2 of 2). Sets.

union ∪	$S \cup T$ The set of elements that belong to either S or T, or both. $S \cup T == \{x : X \mid x \in S \vee x \in T\}$ where X is the underlying type of both S and T.
intersection ∩	$S \cap T$ The set of elements that belong to both S and T. $S \cap T == \{x : X \mid x \in S \wedge x \in T\}$ where X is the underlying type of both S and T.
difference \\	$S \setminus T$ The set of elements that belong to S but not to T. $S \setminus T == \{x : X \mid x \in S \wedge x \notin T\}$ where X is the underlying type of both S and T.
size #	$\#S$ The number of elements in the set S. This is meaningful only if S is finite.
power set ℙ	$\mathbb{P}S$ The set of all subsets of S.
non-empty power set $\mathbb{P}_1$	$\mathbb{P}_1 S$ The set of all subsets of S excluding the empty set. $\mathbb{P}_1 S == \mathbb{P}S \setminus \{\emptyset\}$
finite subset 𝔽	$\mathbb{F}S$ The set of all finite subsets of S (precisely the ones with a *size*).
non-empty finite subset $\mathbb{F}_1$	$\mathbb{F}_1 S$ The set of all finite subsets of S excluding the empty set. $\mathbb{F}_1 S == \mathbb{F}S \setminus \{\emptyset\}$
distributed union ∪	$\bigcup S$ If S is a set of *sets* then $\bigcup S$ is the set of all the members of the sets in S. $\bigcup S == \{x{:}T \mid (\exists s : S \bullet x \in s)\}$ where S is of type $\mathbb{P}(\mathbb{P}T)$.
distributed intersection ∩	$\bigcap S$ If S is a set of *sets*, then $\bigcap S$ is the set of members common to all sets in S. $\bigcap S == \{x : T \mid (\forall s : S \bullet x \in s)\}$ where S is of type $\mathbb{P}(\mathbb{P}T)$.

Table A.5 (Page 1 of 3). Relations.

cartesian product ×	A×B The set of ordered pairs whose first member is in *A* and whose second member is in *B*. $A×B == \{a:A;\ b:B \bullet (a,b)\}$
relation ↔	A↔B The set of all subsets of A×B. Each subset is a *relation* between elements in *A* and *B*, and this is the set of all such relations. $A↔B == \mathbb{P}(A×B)$
maps to ↦	a ↦ b Another notation for the ordered pair (a, b). $a ↦ b == (a, b)$
domain dom	dom R The set of all elements of the *from-set* of R which are related (by R) to members of the *to-set*. R must be a relation. $dom\ R == \{a:A;\ b:B \mid (a,b) \in R \bullet a\}$ where $R : A↔B$.
range ran	ran R The set of all elements of the *to-set* of R which are related (by R) to members of the *from-set*. R must be a relation. $ran\ R == \{a:A;\ b:B \mid (a,b) \in R \bullet b\}$ where $R : A↔B$.
inverse ⁻¹	R^{-1} The relation in which all the pairs of R appear, but with their components reversed. R must be a relation. $R^{-1} == \{a:A;\ b:B \mid (a,b) \in R \bullet (b,a)\}$ where $R : A↔B$.
composition ;	R;S The relation between the *from-set* of R and the *to-set* of S which relates elements only if there is an intermediate value in the *to-set* of R (also in the *from-set* of S) to which both elements relate. $R;S == \{a:A;\ b:B;\ c:C \mid (a,b) \in R \land (b,c) \in S \bullet (a,c)\}$ where $R : A↔B$ and $S : B↔C$.

Table A.5 (Page 2 of 3). Relations.

backward *composition* ∘	R∘S The relation between the *from-set* of S and the *to-set* of R which relates elements only if there is an intermediate value in the *to-set* of S (also in the *from-set* of R) to which both elements relate. $\quad$ R∘S == {a : A; b : B; c : C | (a,b) ∈ S ∧ (b,c) ∈ R • (a,c)} where R : B↔C and S : A↔B. Note that R∘S == S;R.
domain restriction ◁	S◁R The relation which is a subset of R, containing just those pairs with first elements in the set S. $\quad$ S◁R == {a : A; b : B | (a,b) ∈ R ∧ a ∈ S} where R : A↔B and S ⊆ A.
domain *subtraction* ◁	S◁R The relation which is a subset of R, containing just those pairs with first elements *not* in the set S. $\quad$ S◁R == {a : A; b : B | (a,b) ∈ R ∧ a ∉ S} where R : A↔B and S ⊆ A.
range restriction ▷	R▷S The relation which is a subset of R, containing just those pairs with second elements in the set S. $\quad$ R▷S == {a : A; b : B | (a,b) ∈ R ∧ b ∈ S} where R : A↔B and S ⊆ B.
range *subtraction* ▷	R▷S The relation which is a subset of R, containing just those pairs with second elements *not* in the set S. $\quad$ R▷S == {a : A; b : B | (a,b) ∈ R ∧ b ∉ S} where R : A↔B and S ⊆ B.
relational image (||)	R(|S|) The set of elements related to elements of S by R. $\quad$ R(|S|) == {a : A; b : B | (a,b) ∈ R ∧ a ∈ S • b} where R : A↔B and S ⊆ A.
identity *id*	id S The relation that (only) relates each member of S to itself. $\quad$ id S == {s : S • s ↦ s}

Table A.5 (Page 3 of 3). Relations.

transitive closure $+$	R^+ The smallest transitive relation containing R. $\quad R^+ \;==\; \bigcap \{S : A \leftrightarrow A \mid R \subseteq S \wedge (S \,;\, S \subseteq S)\}$ where the type of R is $\mathbb{P}(A \times A)$.
reflexive *transitive* *closure* $*$	R^* The smallest reflexive transitive relation containing R. $\quad R^* \;==\; R^+ \cup id\,A$ where the type of R is $\mathbb{P}(A \times A)$.

Table A.6 (Page 1 of 2). Functions.

function ⇸	$A \nrightarrow B$ The set of relations between A and B where, for each element in A there is *at most one* corresponding element in B. $A \nrightarrow B == \{r : A \leftrightarrow B \mid$ $(\forall a : A; \; b_1, b_2 : B \mid (a,b_1) \in r \wedge (a,b_2) \in r \bullet b_1 = b_2)\}$
total function →	$A \rightarrow B$ The set of functions from A to B whose domains are the whole of A. $A \rightarrow B == \{f : A \nrightarrow B \mid \operatorname{dom} f = A\}$
finite function ⇻	$A \nrightarrow\!\!\!\!\nrightarrow B$ The set of functions from A to B whose domains are finite subsets of A. $A \nrightarrow\!\!\!\!\nrightarrow B == \{f : A \nrightarrow B \mid \operatorname{dom} f \in \mathbb{F}A\}$
injection ↣	$A \rightarrowtail B$ The set of functions from A to B in which distinct elements of the domain correspond to distinct elements of the range. $A \rightarrowtail B == \{f : A \nrightarrow B \mid f^{1} \in B \nrightarrow A\}$
total injection ↣	$A \rightarrowtail B$ The set of injections from A to B which are also *total* functions. $A \rightarrowtail B == A \rightarrowtail B \cap A \rightarrow B$
finite injection ⤔	$A \rightarrowtail\!\!\!\!\rightarrowtail B$ The set of injections from A to B which are also *finite* functions. $A \rightarrowtail\!\!\!\!\rightarrowtail B == A \rightarrowtail B \cap A \nrightarrow\!\!\!\!\nrightarrow B$
surjection ⤀	$A \nrightarrow\!\!\!\twoheadrightarrow B$ The set of functions from A to B whose range is the whole of B. $A \nrightarrow\!\!\!\twoheadrightarrow B == \{f : A \nrightarrow B \mid \operatorname{ran} f = B\}$
total surjection ↠	$A \twoheadrightarrow B$ The set of surjections from A to B which are also total functions. $A \twoheadrightarrow B == \{f : A \nrightarrow\!\!\!\twoheadrightarrow B \mid f \in A \rightarrow B\}$
bijection ⤖	$A \rightarrowtail\!\!\!\twoheadrightarrow B$ The set of one-to-one mappings from A to B. (The set of total injections that are also surjections.) $A \rightarrowtail\!\!\!\twoheadrightarrow B == \{f : A \rightarrowtail B \mid f \in A \twoheadrightarrow B\}$

Table A.6 (Page 2 of 2). Functions.

override $\oplus$	$f \oplus g$ The function f overridden by the function g. $\quad f \oplus g == ((\text{dom } g \lessdot f) \cup g)$ (The definition of override applies equally well to relations.)
lambda λ	$\lambda D \mid P \bullet E$ The function formed by mapping the characteristic tuple of the declaration D (constrained by predicate P) to the expression E $\quad \lambda D \mid P \bullet E == \{D \mid P \bullet t \mapsto E\}$ where t is the characteristic tuple of the declaration D.
choice (*mu*) μ	$\mu D \mid P \bullet E$ The value of the expression E where the variables of the declaration D have values determined by predicate P. P (with D) must *completely* determine the values of the variables, otherwise the value of the choice expression is not defined.

Table A.7 (Page 1 of 2). Sequences.

enumeration $\langle \rangle$	$\langle a,b,...,z \rangle$ The sequence a, followed by b, ..., followed by z. $\langle a,b,...,z \rangle == \{1 \mapsto a, 2 \mapsto b, ..., n \mapsto z\}$
sequence seq	seq X The set of all sequences of elements of X. seq $X == \{f : \mathbb{N} \nrightarrow X \mid \text{dom } f = 1..\#f\}$
non-empty *sequence* seq_1	$\text{seq}_1 X$ The set of all non-empty sequences of elements of X. $\text{seq}_1 X == \text{seq } X \setminus \{\emptyset\}$
size $\#$	$\#s$ The number of elements in the sequence s.
concatenate $\wedge$	$s^\wedge t$ The sequence formed by appending the sequence t to the sequence s. $s^\wedge t == s \cup (\lambda i : \#s+1..\#s+\#t \bullet t(i-\#s))$
head head	*head* s The first element of the non-empty sequence s. head $s == s\,1$
last last	*last* s The last element of the non-empty sequence s. last $s == s\,(\#s)$
squash squash	*squash* f The sequence formed by arranging the elements of ran f in ascending order of their corresponding domain values. (f must be a finite function whose domain is a set of integers.) $f \neq \{\} \Rightarrow$ squash $s = \langle f \min(\text{dom } f) \rangle \;^\wedge\; \text{squash}(\{\min(\text{dom } f)\} \lhd f)$
index restriction $\upharpoonleft$	$A \upharpoonleft s$ The sequence s restricted to just those indexes that appear in the set A. (A must be a set of integers.) $A \upharpoonleft s == \text{squash}(A \lhd s)$
sequence *restriction* $\upharpoonright$	$s \upharpoonright B$ The sequence s restricted to just those elements that appear in the set B. (B must be a set of elements of the same type as ran s.) $s \upharpoonright B == \text{squash}(s \rhd B)$

Table A.7 (Page 2 of 2). Sequences.

tail *tail*	tail s The sequence consisting of all elements of s except the first. tail s == $2..\#s \uparrow s$
front *front*	front s The sequence consisting of all elements of s except the last. front s $^\wedge$ last s = s front s == $1..(\#s-1) \uparrow s$
reverse rev	rev s The sequence formed by reversing the sequence s. $s \neq \langle \rangle \Rightarrow$ rev s = $\langle$last s$\rangle$ $^\wedge$ rev (front s)
distributed *concatenation* $^\wedge/$	$^\wedge/ss$ The sequence consisting of all the elements of the sequences in ss taken in order. (ss is a sequence of sequences.) If s is a sequence, then $^\wedge/\langle s\rangle = \langle s\rangle$. If ss_1 and ss_2 are sequences of sequences, then $^\wedge/ (ss_1 ^\wedge ss_2) = (^\wedge/ ss_1) ^\wedge (^\wedge/ ss_2)$.
distributed *composition* $;/$	$;/sr$ A relation consisting of the members of the sequence of relations, sr, taken in order and combined with the composition operator. For example, $;/ \langle r_1, r_2 \rangle == r_1 ; r_2$ $;/ \langle r_1, r_2, r_3 \rangle == r_1 ; r_2 ; r_3$ where r_1, r_2 and r_3 are relations.
distributed *override* $\oplus/$	$\oplus/sr$ A relation consisting of the members of the sequence of relations, sr, taken in order and combined with the override operator. For example, $\oplus/ \langle r_1, r_2 \rangle == r_1 \oplus r_2$ $\oplus/ \langle r_1, r_2, r_3 \rangle == r_1 \oplus r_2 \oplus r_3$ where r_1, r_2 and r_3 are relations.

Table A.8 (Page 1 of 3). Schemas.

horizontal *definition* $\hat{=}$	$S \hat{=} [D \mid P]$ Introduces S as a schema with declaration part D and predicate part P.
decoration $' ? !$	S' Introduces S' as a schema that is the same as S except that each variable name in the signature of S is decorated with a dash (similar remarks apply to ? and ! decorations).
binding θ	θS A binding between the components of S and their current values (see Chapter 6).
Delta Δ	ΔS A schema consisting of the schema S conjoined with schema S'. $\Delta S == S \wedge S'$
Xi Ξ	ΞS A schema consisting of the schema S conjoined with schema S' where the value of each dashed component is the same as the value of the corresponding undashed component. $\Xi S == [\Delta S \mid \theta S' = \theta S]$
conjunction $\wedge$	$S \wedge T$ A schema consisting of the signatures of S and T merged and their properties conjoined. $S \wedge T == [\, sigS; \; sigT \mid propS \wedge propT\,]$
disjunction $\vee$	$S \vee T$ A schema consisting of the signatures of S and T merged and the disjunction of their properties. $S \vee T == [\, sigS; \; sigT \mid propS \vee propT\,]$
negation $\neg$	$\neg S$ A schema consisting of the signature of S and the negation of its property. $\neg S == [\, sigS \mid \neg propS\,]$
implication $\Rightarrow$	$S \Rightarrow T$ A schema consisting of the signatures of S and T merged and a property that is *True* if the property of S implies the property of T. $S \Rightarrow T == [\, sigS; \; sigT \mid propS \Rightarrow propT\,]$

Table A.8 (Page 2 of 3). Schemas.

equivalence ⇔	$S \Leftrightarrow T$ A schema consisting of the signatures of S and T merged and a property that is *True* if the property of S is equivalent to the property of T. $S \Leftrightarrow T == [sigS; sigT \mid propS \Leftrightarrow propT]$
there exists ∃	$\exists D \mid P \bullet S$ A schema whose signature is the signature of S without the variables introduced in the declaration D and whose property is the property of S existentially quantified using the variables in D as bound variables. $\exists D \mid P \bullet S == [sigS \setminus sigD \mid (\exists D \mid P \bullet propS)]$ Also, with schema T, we can write $\exists T \bullet S$
for all ∀	$\forall D \mid P \bullet S$ A schema whose signature is the signature of S without the variables introduced in the declaration D and whose property is the property of S universally quantified using the variables in D as bound variables. $\forall D \mid P \bullet S == [sigS \setminus sigD \mid (\forall D \mid P \bullet propS)]$ Also, with schema T, we can write $\forall T \bullet S$
rename [/]	$S[new/old]$ A schema consisting of schema S with component *old* renamed *new*.
schema hiding \ ( )	$S \setminus (v_1, v_2, \ldots)$ A schema consisting of schema S with variables v_1, v_2, ... removed from the signature and existentially quantified in the property. Also, with schema T, we can write $\forall S \setminus T$
pre-condition pre	pre S The pre-condition of schema S. This is formed by hiding all the components of S that are decorated with a dash or an exclamation mark. The use of pre-condition is usually restricted to schemas that describe an "operation". Then pre S describes the minimum condition for the operation to be defined.

Table A.8 (Page 3 of 3). Schemas.

composition $\overset{\circ}{,}$	$S\overset{\circ}{,}T$ If S and T describe "operations", then $S\overset{\circ}{,}T$ can be thought of as "operation S followed by operation T". $S\overset{\circ}{,}T$ can be formed by decorating the components of T with a dash, hiding the single dashed variables and removing a dash from each double-dashed variable. $\quad S\overset{\circ}{,}T == S\wedge T' \setminus (v_1', v_2', ...) [v_1'/v_1'', v_2'/v_2'', ...]$ where $v_1, v_2, ...$ are the components of T. See Chapter 10 for an alternative definition.
overriding $\oplus$	$S \oplus T$ If S and T describe operations, then $S \oplus T$ is the operation "T, except where T does not apply, in which case S". $S \oplus T$ is the disjunction of T and (S wherever pre T is *False*). $\quad S \oplus T == T \vee (\neg \text{pre } T \wedge S)$

Appendix B

Answers to Problems

"It's time for you to answer now," the Queen said, looking at her watch.
Lewis Carroll, Through the Looking-Glass

4.1 CENTRAL HEATING STATE DESCRIPTION

The system can be in any one of four modes:

sysmode ::= *cont* | *off* | *once* | *twice*

and the current mode is represented by *mode*

mode : *sysmode*

We do not need to know what units are used to measure temperatures so we will treat them as natural numbers:

temperature == $\mathbb{N}$

The thermostat setting, *roomstat*, is a temperature:

roomstat : *temperature*

roomtemp is the current temperature:

roomtemp : *temperature*

The *pump* can be *ON* or *OFF*

OnOff ::= *ON* | *OFF*
pump : *OnOff*

Time is measured in minutes in the range *mintime* to *maxtime*:

mintime == 0
maxtime == 60*24 − 1

currtime is the current time:

currtime : *mintime..maxtime*

The four times set on the control clock are *t1*, *t2*, *t3* and *t4*

$t1, t2, t3, t4$: *mintime..maxtime*

$t2 - t1 \geq 10$
$t3 - t2 \geq 10$
$t4 - t3 \geq 10$
$(maxtime - t4) + (t1 - mintime) \geq 10$

and each time interval is at least 10 minutes.

The thermostat is on if the room temperature exceeds the room thermostat setting:

stat : *OnOff*

stat = *ON* $\Leftrightarrow$ *roomstat* < *roomtemp*

The clock is on depending on the *mode*, the timer settings and *currtime*:

clock, mode0, mode1, mode2 : *OnOff*

mode0 = *ON* $\Leftrightarrow$ *mode* = *cont*
mode1 = *ON* $\Leftrightarrow$ (*mode* = *once*) $\wedge$ ($t1 \leq$ *currtime* $\leq t4$)
mode2 = *ON* $\Leftrightarrow$
  (*mode* = *twice*) $\wedge$ (($t1 \leq$ *currtime* $\leq t2$) $\vee$ ($t3 \leq$ *currtime* $\leq t4$))
clock = *ON* $\Leftrightarrow$ (*mode0* = *ON*) $\vee$ (*mode1* = *ON*) $\vee$ (*mode2* = *ON*)

The *pump* is on if both the clock and the *roomstat* are on, otherwise it is off.

clock = *ON* $\wedge$ *stat* = *ON* $\Leftrightarrow$ *pump* = *ON*
$\neg$ (*clock* = *ON* $\wedge$ *stat* = *ON*) $\Leftrightarrow$ *pump* = *OFF*

4.2 CENTRAL HEATING STATE EXTENDED

There are now three thermostats:

roomstat : *temperature*
tankstat : *temperature*
boilerstat : *temperature*

and three temperatures to consider:

roomtemp : *temperature*
tanktemp : *temperature*
boilertemp : *temperature*

boiler, water, heat : *OnOff*

The boiler will be on if:

boiler = *ON* $\Leftrightarrow$ *boilerstat* < *boilertemp*

The water will be on if:

water = ON ⇔ roomstat < roomtemp

The central heating will be on if:

heat = ON ⇔ tankstat < tanktemp

The *valve* can have one of four positions:

valveposn ::= *waterflow | heatflow | both | neither*
valve : valveposn

The *valve* position is determined by the tank thermostat and room thermostat

water = ON ∧ heat = OFF ⇒ valve = waterflow
water = OFF ∧ heat = ON ⇒ valve = heatflow
water = OFF ∧ heat = OFF ⇒ valve = neither
water = ON ∧ heat = ON ⇒ valve = both

This same information could be presented in a table (Table B.1).

Table B.1. Central heating *valve*.

	water=ON	*water=OFF*
heat=ON	*both*	*heatflow*
heat=OFF	*waterflow*	*neither*

5.1 SUBSTRINGS

[CHAR]
string == seq *CHAR*

The *substr* function maps a triple of the form (s, p, n) to a *string*

s is the input *string*.
p specifies the starting position within s: it is a number in the range *1..#s*.
n specifies the length.

> *substr : (string×ℕ₁×ℕ) ⇸ string*
>
> ∀ s : *string*; $p : ℕ_1$; $n : ℕ$ • *substr*$(s, p, n) = \{i : p..p+n-1 • (i-p+1, s\ i)\}$

The value of *substr(s,p,n)* is a string – that is, a sequence of characters. Thus we can describe it as a set of ordered pairs of the form (x,ch) where x is a number *1..m* and *ch* is a character of the string s. So we write $\{i:p..p+n-1 • (i-p+1, s\ i)\}$. As i ranges from p to $p+n-1$, the first term, $i-p+1$, ranges from *1* to *n*. The second term, $(s\ i)$, is, of course, simply the ith character of s. So the set expression simply 'renumbers' the n characters, starting at p, in s.   (Later, we will see how the *squash* function could be used for this definition.)

We see that $substr(s,0,n)$ is not defined because the second parameter should be in $\mathbb{N}_1$.

The value of $substr(s,p,0)$ is an empty sequence and the value of $substr('abc',2,4)$ is

$\{i : 2..6 \bullet (i-1, s\,i)\}$

However, $s\,4$ and $s\,5$ are meaningless, (because neither 4 nor 5 is in the domain of s), so the set expression is meaningless.   That is, $substr('abc',2,4)$ is not defined. If we wish it to have a defined value, for instance '*bc*', then we need to extend our definition of *substr*

$p+n-1 \le \#s \Rightarrow ...$
$p+n-1 > \#s \Rightarrow ...$

The *IsIn* relation is a correspondence between strings.

> $\_IsIn\_ : string \leftrightarrow string$
>
> ---
>
> $\forall s1, s2 : string \bullet s1\ IsIn\ s2 \Leftrightarrow (\exists\ bef, aft : string \bullet bef\char`^s1\char`^aft = s2)$

The substring *s1* is in string *s2* if (and only if) we can find two strings *bef* and *aft* such that *bef^s1^aft* is the same as *s2*.

We could have used *substr* to define *IsIn*.   We need to say that we can find a position, p, such that $substr(s2,p,\#s1)=s1$.

5.2 PERMUTE AND SORT

$\_IsPermOf\_$ is a relation between two sequences of natural numbers:

> $\_IsPermOf\_ : (seq\ \mathbb{N}) \leftrightarrow (seq\ \mathbb{N})$
>
> ---
>
> $\forall a, b : seq\ \mathbb{N} \bullet (a\ IsPermOf\ b \Leftrightarrow$
> $(\exists p : dom\ a \rightarrowtail dom\ b \bullet$
> $(\forall i, j : dom\ p \mid i \ne j \bullet p\,i \ne p\,j) \land$
> $(\forall i : dom\ p \bullet a\,i = b\,(p\,i))))$

Sequence a is a permutation of sequence b if (and only if) we can find a permutation, p, of the indexes of a (i.e. of $dom\,a$) that produces the indexes of b, such that corresponding values are the same (that is, $a\,i = b(p\,i)$).   A concrete example is shown in Figure B.1.

In this case, p could be

$\{1 \mapsto 3, 2 \mapsto 4, 3 \mapsto 1, 4 \mapsto 2, 5 \mapsto 6, 6 \mapsto 5\}$

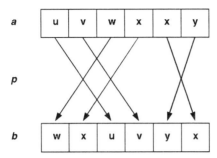

Fig B.1. Permutation example

or, because there is a duplicate value, 'x', *p* could be:

$$\{1 \mapsto 3, 2 \mapsto 4, 3 \mapsto 1, 4 \mapsto 6, 5 \mapsto 2, 6 \mapsto 5\}$$

The same values are produced by yet a third function

$$\{1 \mapsto 3, 2 \mapsto 4, 3 \mapsto 1, 4 \mapsto 6, 5 \mapsto 6, 6 \mapsto 5\}$$

but this is not a permutation: to ensure that we use one, we needed the constraint

$$\forall i, j : \text{dom } p \mid i \neq j \bullet p\, i \neq p\, j$$

which requires *p* to be an 'injection'. In Chapter 8, we see how relational composition and an injection notation can be used to greatly simplify this definition.

Now we see how we can express the condition that *listB* is a sorted version of *listA*:

> *listA, listB* : seq $\mathbb{N}$
>
> ---
>
> *listA IsPermOf listB*
> $\forall i, j : \text{dom } listB \mid i < j \bullet listB\, i \leq listB\, j$

5.3 RIGHT ADJUSTED LINE

[*CHAR*]
blank : *CHAR*
wid : $\mathbb{N}$
string == seq *CHAR*

words is a set of *string* (*CHAR* sequences)

> *words* : $\mathbb{P}$ *string*
>
> ---
>
> $\forall w : word \bullet blank \notin \text{ran } w$

where each *w* in *words* contains no blank characters. We note that
$\langle\rangle \in$ *words*.

blanks is a set of *string*

---
blanks : $\mathbb{P}$*string*

$\forall\, b$: *blanks* • ran $b = \{blank\}$

---

where each *b* in *blanks* contains *only* blank characters. In this case
$\langle\rangle \notin$ *blanks*.

full_lines is a set of *string*

---
full_lines : $\mathbb{P}$*string*

$\forall\, fl$: *full_lines* •
$(\neg\, \exists\, b$: *blanks* | $\#b > 1$ • b *IsIn* fl)
$(fl \neq \langle\rangle \Rightarrow$ head $fl \neq blank\, \wedge$ last $fl \neq blank)$

---

where each *fl* in *full_lines* contains no *b* in *blanks* longer than one and
neither starts nor ends with a *blank* character. Perhaps surprisingly,
$\langle\rangle \in$ *full_lines*.

right_adjusted_lines is a set of *string*

---
right_adjusted_lines : $\mathbb{P}$*string*

$\forall\, ral$: *right_adjusted_lines* •
$\#ral = wid$
(*ral* $\in$ *full_lines*
$\vee\, \exists\, b$: *blanks*; *fl* : *full_lines* • $ral = b^\frown fl)$

---

where each *ral* in *right_adjusted_lines* is *wid* characters long. It is either in
full_lines, or is formed from a member of *full_lines* 'padded on the left' with a
member of *blanks*.

If *wid* is greater than zero, then the empty sequence is not a member of
right_adjusted_lines; however, if *wid=0*, the *only* element of *right_adjusted_lines*
is the empty sequence, $\langle\rangle$.

5.4 CROSS REFERENCE TABLE

A *StmtNum* is a non-zero positive number that uniquely identifies a
statement:

StmtNum == $\mathbb{N}_1$

The variable names (or 'identifiers') we take to be a given set:

[*IDENT*]

At a high level of abstraction suitable for our purposes, we can think of such a program as a mapping (function) from *StmtNum* to a set of *IDENT*:

program : *StmtNum*→→ℙ*IDENT*

This is not a total function, because there will be 'unused' statement numbers.

Our *crossref* table is a mapping from *IDENT* to a set of *StmtNum*:

---

crossref : *IDENT*→→ℙ*StmtNum*

∀ *st* : *StmtNum*; *id* : *IDENT* •
  (*id* ∈ dom *crossref* ∧ *st* ∈ *crossref id*)
    ⇔ (*st* ∈ dom *program* ∧ *id* ∈ *program st*)

For each possible statement number, *st*, and each possible identifier, *id*, there is an entry in the *crossref* table containing *id* and *st* if (and only if) *id* appears in statement *st* of the program.

We had to take care in this formulation to correctly specify the *domain* of *crossref*. It is easy to mistakenly allow *crossref s* = {} for statements numbered s that don't appear in the *program* at all!

Here is another possible solution:

---

crossref : *IDENT*→→ℙ*StmtNum*

---

crossref =
  { *id* : *IDENT*; *sst* : ℙ*StmtNum*
    | *sst* = {s : dom *program* | *id* ∈ *program s*} ≠ {}
    • *id* ↦ *sst*}

---

where the set of pairs which is *crossref* is made explicit, including an extra condition for the range element to be non-empty.

6.1 CROSS REFERENCE

This answer is based on the answer to Specification Problem 5.4.

A *StmtNum* is a non-zero positive number that uniquely identifies a statement:

StmtNum == ℕ$_1$

The variable names (or 'identifiers') we take to be a given set:

[*IDENT*]

We reformulate our model so that a program line, *ProgLine*, has an *IDENT* on the left-hand side (*LHS*) and a *set* of *IDENT* on the right-hand side (*RHS*):

```
┌─ ProgLine ────────────────────────────────────────
│  LHS : IDENT
│  RHS : ℙIDENT
└
```

XrefLine, a line in the cross reference table, contains two sets of *StmtNum*, namely *whereset* and *whereused*:

```
┌─ XrefLine ────────────────────────────────────────
│  whereset : ℙStmtNum
│  whereused : ℙStmtNum
└
```

The *program* is now a mapping from *StmtNum* to *ProgLine*, and the cross reference table, *crossref*, is a mapping from *IDENT* to *XrefLine*:

```
┌
│  program : StmtNum↣ProgLine
│  crossref : IDENT↣XrefLine
│ ────────────────────────────────────────
│  crossref =
│  { id : IDENT;  x : XrefLine
│   | x.whereset = {s : dom program | id = (program s).LHS}
│    ∧ x.whereused = {s : dom program | id ∈ (program s).RHS}
│    ∧ (x.whereset ≠ {} ∨ x.whereused ≠ {})
│  • id ↦ x}
└
```

where we have adopted the same style as the second solution to Specification Problem 5.4. Notice how subtle the non-empty condition is in this case.

The constraints on the identifiers and cross-reference lines we are to relate are:

• *whereset* should be the set of all statement numbers with *id* on the left.
• *whereused* should be the set of all statement numbers with *id* appearing on the right.
• And that these two sets cannot both be empty.

Notice that, throughout this formulation, we have made no reference to *how* this cross reference table should be constructed.

6.2 CHECKERS

The schema descriptions from Exercise 6.4 are reproduced below:

```
BW ::= black | white
YN ::= yes | no
Place ≙ [row, col : 1..8 | (row + col) mod 2 = 1]
PieceType ≙ [colour : BW;  queen : YN]
Checker ≙ [Place; PieceType]
```

We will now use these to describe the board.

The black pieces consist of a set of pieces which includes their positions. However, for convenience the positions are also identified as *bpos*.

```
┌─BlackPieces ─────────────────────────────────────
│ bp : ℙChecker
│ bpos : ℙ(ℕ×ℕ)
├───────────────────────────────────────────────────
│ ∀ p : bp • p.colour = black
│ #bp ≤ 8
│ bpos = {p : bp • (p.row,p.col)}
│ ∀ p1, p2 : bp | p1 ≠ p2 • p1.row ≠ p2.row ∨ p1.col ≠ p2.col
└───────────────────────────────────────────────────
```

All the checkers are black; there cannot be more than eight; the setof 'positions', *bpos*, is the set of pairs of rows and columns from the pieces in *bp*; no two pieces can be in the same position.

We needed to say that each piece had a different position because pieces may differ in any one of position, colour or 'queenliness'. Of course, we have insisted that they are all black pieces, but there remains the possibility of a queen and one of her subjects booking the same square.

Another way to express this condition would be to use the set of positions and to insist that there are the same number in this set as pieces in *bp*. We would say $\#bpos = \#bp$. This would force a distinct position for each piece, otherwise *#bpos* would be smaller. It is not obvious, however, that this way of expressing it would be easier to understand.

The white pieces can be similarly described:

```
┌─WhitePieces ─────────────────────────────────────
│ wp : ℙChecker
│ wpos : ℙ(ℕ×ℕ)
├───────────────────────────────────────────────────
│ ∀ p : wp • p.colour = white
│ #wp ≤ 8
│ wpos = {p : wp • (p.row,p.col)}
│ ∀ p1, p2 : wp | p1 ≠ p2 • p1.row ≠ p2.row ∨ p1.col ≠ p2.col
└───────────────────────────────────────────────────
```

with the same conditions on positions.

The *Board* consists of all the black and white pieces. For convenience, we have called this set *dp*:

```
┌─Board ───────────────────────────────────────────
│ dp : ℙChecker
│ BlackPieces
│ WhitePieces
├───────────────────────────────────────────────────
│ bpos ∩ wpos = ∅
│ dp = bp ∪ wp
└───────────────────────────────────────────────────
```

There are no positions in common between *bpos* and *wpos* because black and white pieces stay apart. The ease of expressing this condition is the reason we invented *bpos* and *wpos* in the first place. *dp* is the whole set of pieces.

The initial board, *InitBoard*, is a *Board*:

```
┌─ InitBoard ──────────────────────────────────────────
│  Board
│ ────────────────────────────────────────────────────
│  bpos = {(1,2), (1,4), (1,6), (1,8), (2,1), (2,3), (2,5), (2,7)}
│  wpos = {(7,2), (7,4), (7,6), (7,8), (8,1), (8,3), (8,5), (8,7)}
│  ∀ p : dp • p.queen = No
```

in which the initial positions are given by the two set expressions. None of the pieces are regal.

6.3 FILENAMES

(1) Using schemas

We assume a given set of characters:

[*CHAR*]

Alpha is the set of alphabetic characters, a subset of *CHAR*:

Alpha : $\mathbb{P}$*CHAR*

Numeric is the set of numeric characters, a subset of *CHAR*:

Numeric : $\mathbb{P}$*CHAR*

Alpha and *Numeric* have no characters in common:

Alpha ∩ *Numeric* = $\emptyset$

AlphaNumeric is the set of alpha and numeric characters, a subset of *CHAR*:

```
│  AlphaNumeric : ℙCHAR
│ ──────────────────────────
│  AlphaNumeric = Alpha ∪ Numeric
```

CHAR contains a *dot* character which is neither alphabetic nor numeric:

```
│  dot : CHAR
│ ──────────────────
│  dot ∉ AlphaNumeric
```

These are the only elements of *CHAR*:

CHAR = *AlphaNumeric* ∪ {*dot*}

A simple name is a non-empty sequence of alphanumeric characters

```
┌─Name────────────────────────────────────────
│ nm : seq₁ AlphaNumeric
├──────────────────────
│ #nm ≤ 8
│ head nm ∈ Alpha
└──────────────────────────────────────────────
```

no more than eight characters long; the first is alphabetic.
An extension is a non-empty sequence of alphanumeric characters

```
┌─Extn────────────────────────────────────────
│ ex : seq₁ AlphaNumeric
├──────────────────────
│ #ex ≤ 3
└──────────────────────────────────────────────
```

no more than three characters long.
An extended name is a sequence of characters

```
┌─ExtendedName─────────────────────────────────
│ efn : seq CHAR
│ Name
│ Extn
├──────────────────────
│ efn = nm ⌢ ⟨dot⟩ ⌢ ex
└──────────────────────────────────────────────
```

consisting of a name followed by a dot followed by an extension.
A *Filename* is a sequence of characters

```
┌─Filename─────────────────────────────────────
│ fn : seq CHAR
│ ExtendedName
├──────────────────────
│ fn = nm ∨ fn = efn
└──────────────────────────────────────────────
```

either a simple name or an extended name.
(2) Using sets
We use *CHAR*, *Alpha*, *AlphaNumeric* and *dot* as before.

$Name == \{nm : \text{seq}_1 \, AlphaNumeric \mid \#nm \leq 8 \land \text{head } nm \in Alpha\}$

Name is the set of all non-empty character strings consisting of not more than eight *AlphaNumeric* characters and whose first character is in *Alpha*.

$Extn == \{ex : \text{seq}_1 \, AlphaNumeric \mid \#ex \leq 3\}$

Extn is the set of all non-empty character strings consisting of not more than three *AlphaNumeric* characters.

$ExtendedName == \{nm : Name; \, ex : Extn \bullet nm \, ⌢ \, \langle dot \rangle \, ⌢ \, ex\}$

ExtendedName is the set of all character strings consisting of a *Name* followed by a *dot* followed by an *Extn*.

FileName == *Name* ∪ *ExtendedName*

A *FileName* is either a *Name* or an *ExtendedName*.

You should notice that we were able to form *FileName* so readily only because we took care to make *Name* and *ExtendedName* have the same underlying type, based upon *CHAR*.

7.1 CASH DISPENSER

The customer data includes descriptive information that consists of *String*s of *CHAR*acters:

[*CHAR*]
String == seq *CHAR*

We are told nothing about account numbers so we will treat them as a given set:

[*ACCNUM*]

PIN numbers have four digits, the first of which cannot be zero:

PIN == *1000..9999*

A customer account contains *Fixed* data that is unaffected by cash dispenser transactions:

```
┌─ Fixed ─────────────────────────
│ name : String
│ address : String
│ pinlist : seq PIN
├─────────────────────────────────
│ #pinlist ≤ 3
```

An account also contains *Status* information that shows whether or not the customer has requested a cheque book or statement:

OnOff ::= *On* | *Off*

```
┌─ Status ────────────────────────
│ CBreq : OnOff
│ stmtreq : OnOff
```

These details, together with the current *balance*, make up an *Account*:

```
┌─ Account ───────────────────────
│ fxd : Fixed
│ stat : Status
│ balance : ℕ
```

The central *AccountFile* is a collection of accounts indexed by account number:

```
┌─ AccountFile ─────────────────────────────
│ cust : ACCNUM ⇸ Account
└
```

A cash dispenser *Card* contains an account number, *accno*, and a card number, *cardno*:

```
┌─ Card ────────────────────────────────────
│ accno : ACCNUM
│ cardno : 1..3
└
```

All transactions require a *ValidPin* which requires a *Card* and a *PIN*:

```
┌─ ValidPin ────────────────────────────────
│ AccountFile
│ Card?
│ pin? : PIN
├───────────────────────────────────────────
│ pin? = (cust accno?).fxd.pinlist cardno?
└
```

To identify the various situations we introduce a return code:

RetCode ::= *OK* | *toomuch* | *PINerr*

The *QueryBalance* transaction changes nothing:

```
┌─ ChangeNowt ──────────────────────────────
│ ValidPin
│ ΞAccountFile
└
```

The *WithDraw* transaction changes only the *balance*:

```
┌─ ChangeBalance ───────────────────────────
│ ValidPin
│ ΔAccountFile
├───────────────────────────────────────────
│ ∀ user : dom cust •
│   ( (cust' user).fxd = (cust user).fxd
│   ∧ (cust' user).stat = (cust user).stat)
└
```

The *RequestStmt* and *RequestChequeBook* transactions change only the *Status* information:

```
┌─ ChangeStatus ──────────────────────────────────────┐
│ ValidPin                                             │
│ ΔAccountFile                                         │
├──────────────────────────────────────────────────────┤
│ ∀ user : dom cust •                                  │
│   ( (cust' user).balance  =  (cust user).balance     │
│   ∧  (cust' user).fxd  =  (cust user).fxd)           │
└──────────────────────────────────────────────────────┘
```

A successful cheque book request, *RequestCBOK*, sets the *CBreq* flag:

```
┌─ RequestCBOK ───────────────────────────────────────┐
│ ChangeStatus                                         │
│ rc! : RetCode                                        │
├──────────────────────────────────────────────────────┤
│ (cust' accno?).stat.CBreq = On                       │
│ ∀ n : dom cust | n ≠ accno? • (cust' n).stat.CBreq = (cust n).stat.CBreq │
│ ∀ n : dom cust • (cust' n).stat.stmtreq = (cust n).stat.stmtreq │
│ rc! = OK                                             │
└──────────────────────────────────────────────────────┘
```

Only the *CBreq* status of the specified customer is changed.
A successful statement request, *RequestStmtOK*, sets the *stmtreq* flag:

```
┌─ RequestStmtOK ─────────────────────────────────────┐
│ ChangeStatus                                         │
│ rc! : RetCode                                        │
├──────────────────────────────────────────────────────┤
│ (cust' accno?).stat.stmtreq = On                     │
│ ∀ n : dom cust | n ≠ accno? • (cust' n).stat.stmtreq = (cust n).stat.stmtreq │
│ ∀ n : dom cust • (cust' n).stat.CBreq = (cust n).stat.CBreq │
│ rc! = OK                                             │
└──────────────────────────────────────────────────────┘
```

Only the *stmtreq* status of the specified customer is changed.
A successful withdrawal, *WithDrawOK*, decrements the *balance*:

```
┌─ WithDrawOK ────────────────────────────────────────┐
│ ChangeBalance                                        │
│ amt? : ℕ                                             │
│ rc! : RetCode                                        │
├──────────────────────────────────────────────────────┤
│ amt? ≤ 100                                           │
│ amt? ≤ (cust accno?).balance                         │
│ (cust' accno?).balance = (cust accno?).balance − amt? │
│ ∀ n : dom cust | n ≠ accno? • (cust' n).balance = (cust n).balance │
│ rc! = OK                                             │
└──────────────────────────────────────────────────────┘
```

If the specified amount, *amt?*, is not greater than £100 and does not exceed
the current *balance*, then the new *balance* is the old *balance* decremented by
amt?.

The *balance* in all other accounts is unchanged. The return code shows the result.

Next we consider a request for *TooMuch*:

```
┌─ TooMuch ─────────────────────────────────────────────
│ ΞAccountFile
│ ValidPin
│ amt? : ℕ
│ rc! : RetCode
├───────────────────────────────────────────────────────
│ (amt? > 100) ∨ (amt? > (cust accno?).balance)
│ rc! = toomuch
└
```

If the specified amount, *amt?*, is greater than £100 or exceeds the current *balance*, then no change is made.

Finally we consider what happens if the specified PIN is invalid. We first describe the conditions that characterize an *InvalidPin*:

```
┌─ InvalidPin ──────────────────────────────────────────
│ AccountFile
│ Card?
│ pin? : PIN
├───────────────────────────────────────────────────────
│ pin? ≠ (cust accno?).fxd.pinlist cardno?
└
```

The specified PIN, *pin?*, does not match that on file.

Now we consider a *RejectPin* operation:

```
┌─ RejectPin ───────────────────────────────────────────
│ InvalidPin
│ ΞAccountFile
│ rc! : RetCode
├───────────────────────────────────────────────────────
│ rc! = PINerr
└
```

If the specified PIN is invalid, then no change is made, and the return code shows the reason.

We can now specify the 'robust' transactions:

QueryBalance ≙ *ChangeNowt* ∨ *RejectPin*
RequestCB ≙ *RequestCBOK* ∨ *RejectPin*
RequestStmt ≙ *RequestStmtOK* ∨ *RejectPin*
WithDraw ≙ *WithDrawOK* ∨ *RejectPin* ∨ *TooMuch*

In Chapter 9 we will see how the 'theta' notation (θ) can be used to simplify some of the expressions in this solution.

7.2 CALL AND RETURN

An *Address* is simply a natural number:

Address == $\mathbb{N}$

The *bootaddr* is an *Address*:

bootaddr : *Address*

The machine state, *MC*, is described by the address of the next instruction to be executed, which we shall call *NI*, and a stack of return addresses, *RS*.

```
┌─MC────────────────────────────────────────────────
│ NI : Address
│ RS : seq Address
└────────────────────────────────────────────────────
```

Initially, execution starts at the 'boot address' and the stack is empty:

```
┌─Init──────────────────────────────────────────────
│ MC'
│ ───────────
│ NI' = bootaddr
│ RS' = ⟨⟩
└────────────────────────────────────────────────────
```

The *CALL* instruction specifies a target address, *addr?*:

```
┌─CALL──────────────────────────────────────────────
│ ΔMC
│ addr? : Address
│ ───────────
│ RS' = ⟨(NI+5)⟩ ⌒ RS
│ NI' = addr?
└────────────────────────────────────────────────────
```

The effect is to stack the address of the next instruction, namely 5 bytes beyond the current address, and put the specified address in the instruction register.

The *RETURN* instruction will 'succeed' if the stack is not empty:

```
┌─RetOK─────────────────────────────────────────────
│ ΔMC
│ ───────────
│ RS ≠ ⟨⟩
│ NI' = head RS
│ RS' = tail RS
└────────────────────────────────────────────────────
```

The next instruction becomes the one at the top of the stack and the top stack entry is 'popped'.

Otherwise, it will behave as a 'no-op', that is, it will simply increment the instruction counter:

```
┌─RetNoop ──────────────────────────────
│ ΔMC
├───────────────────────────────────────
│ RS = ⟨⟩
│ NI′ = NI + 1
│ RS′ = RS
└───────────────────────────────────────
```

The *RETURN* instruction is either *RetOK* or *RetNoop*:

RETURN ≙ *RetOK* ∨ *RetNoop*

We now modify the solution to cope with a finite stack. We introduce a maximum stack size:

```
│ maxstacksize : ℕ
├──────────────────
│ maxstacksize > 10
```

We decide that if we can't have a stack of at least 10 addresses, it's not worth building the machine!

The machine description is much the same

```
┌─MC ───────────────────────────────────
│ NI : Address
│ RS : seq Address
├───────────────────────────────────────
│ #RS ≤ maxstacksize
└───────────────────────────────────────
```

except for a limit on the stack size.

There is no change to the *Init* schema.

A new possibility, 'stack overflow' arises:

RetCode ::= *OK* | *oflow*

The *CALL* instruction is now a bit more complicated:

```
┌─CallOK ────────────────────────────────
│ ΔMC
│ addr? : Address
│ rc! : RetCode
├───────────────────────────────────────
│ #RS < maxstacksize
│ NI′ = addr?
│ RS′ = ⟨(NI + 5)⟩ ⌢ RS
│ rc! = OK
└───────────────────────────────────────
```

If there is space on the stack, the *CALL* instruction behaves as before, but

```
┌─CallOflow────────────────────────────────────
│ ΔMC
│ addr? : Address
│ rc! : RetCode
├───────────────────────────────────────────────
│ #RS = maxstacksize
│ NI' = NI + 5
│ RS' = RS
│ rc! = oflow
└───────────────────────────────────────────────
```

if the stack is full, the *CALL* instruction simply increments the instruction counter to the next instruction. The return code distinguishes these two situations.

$CALL \triangleq CallOK \lor CallOflow$

The *RETURN* schema is unchanged.

7.3 NIM

We will call the piles *A*, *B* and *C*.

$pileid ::= A \mid B \mid C$

The *Game* state is a mapping from *pileid* to the number of sticks in that pile:

```
┌─Game──────────────────────────────────────────
│ pile : pileid ↦ ℕ
└───────────────────────────────────────────────
```

A player may make a valid or invalid move (requesting too many sticks). A valid move will complete the game or will leave sticks still available:

$code ::= ok \mid error \mid fin$

The input values for *Play* are a pile identity, *p?*, and the number of sticks the player wishes to take, *take?*. A return code, *rc!*, shows the result:

```
┌─Parameters────────────────────────────────────
│ p? : pileid
│ take? : ℕ₁
│ rc! : code
└───────────────────────────────────────────────
```

The play is permitted if there are enough sticks:

```
┌─ PlayOK ──────────────────────────────────
│ ΔGame
│ Parameters
│ ─────────────────
│ pile p? ≥ take?
│ pile' = pile ⊕ {p? ↦ (pile p? − take?)}
└─
```

The set of piles is updated by decrementing the count for *p?* by *take?*.
The play is prohibited if there are too few sticks:

```
┌─ PlayErr ─────────────────────────────────
│ ΞGame
│ Parameters
│ ─────────────────
│ pile p? < take?
│ rc! = error
└─
```

The game is complete when all piles are empty:

Ended ≙ [*Game* | ran *pile* = {0}]

Any intermediate state (that is, where there are sticks on the table) we
will call *Open*:

Open ≙ [*Game* | ran *pile* ≠ {0}]

(In Chapter 10 we see how schema negation can be used here.)
  A play that leaves the game in an *Open* state can be described thus:

PlayMore ≙ [*PlayOK* | *Open'* ∧ *rc!* = *ok*]

A play that ends the game can be described thus:

PlayLast ≙ [*PlayOK* | *Ended'* ∧ *rc!* = *fin*]

We can now describe a play:

Play ≙ *PlayMore* ∨ *PlayLast* ∨ *PlayErr*

7.4 TEXT EDITOR

One way to model a sequence with a 'current place' is with a position
number:

[*THING*]

```
┌─ Seq ─────────────────────────────────────
│ tot : seq THING
│ pos : ℕ
│ ─────────────────
│ 0 ≤ pos ≤ #tot
└─
```

where we have to allow the position to be one of *#tot+1* possibilities, to account successfully for the empty sequence and for the start and end positions.

Another way is to break the sequence at the current position so that the sequence splits into two parts:

```
┌─Seq2──────────────────────────
│ bef, aft, tot : seq THING
├───────────────────────────────
│ tot = bef ^ aft
└───────────────────────────────
```

where we again have *#tot+1* possibilities for the placement of the 'break'.

In the solution to this problem we illustrate both of these techniques.

A text file contains lines that consist of strings of characters:

[CHAR]
string == seq CHAR

The *text* consists of a sequence of strings. The current line within the text file is identified by a *row* (line number).

The current line, *curlin*, consists of two parts: *bef* is the text before the current position; *aft* is the remainder. Thus head *aft* is the current character and tail *aft* is the text after the current character.

```
┌─TextFile──────────────────────
│ text : seq string
│ row : ℕ
│ bef : string
│ aft : string
│ curlin : string
├───────────────────────────────
│ 0 ≤ row ≤ #text
│ row ≠ 0 ⇒ (curlin = text row = bef ^ aft)
└───────────────────────────────
```

This model of a line, and the delete and insert operations, are illustrated in Figure B.2.

Notice that, when *row=0* there is no 'current line' and so the conditions are avoided by 'protecting' them with an implication. When *row=0* the predicate is automatically satisfied.

Initially, the text file is empty and there is no line current:

```
┌─Init──────────────────────────
│ TextFile'
├───────────────────────────────
│ text' = ⟨⟩
│ row' = 0
└───────────────────────────────
```

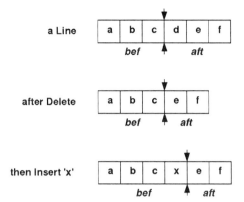

Fig B.2. A line, delete and insert.

Insert a line (CR)

The CR key inserts an empty line after the current row

```
┌─InsertLine ──────────────────────────────
│ ΔTextFile
├────────────────────────────────────────
│ ∀ i : 1..row • text′ i = text i
│ row′ = row + 1
│ text′ row′ = ⟨⟩
│ ∀ i : row′..#text • text′(i + 1) = text i
```

and makes the new line the current one. All rows up to and including the current one are unchanged. The next row is empty. All remaining rows are 'shifted down by one'.

Cursor movement

Moving the cursor (left, right, up or down) does not change the text file content (the text):

$MoveCursor \ \hat{=} \ [\Delta TextFile \mid text′ = text]$

Up and down

Moving the cursor up or down can change the current row and positions the cursor at the start of the new current row.

$UpDown \ \hat{=} \ [MoveCursor \mid bef′ = ⟨⟩]$

The cursor cannot be moved up beyond row zero.

$Up \ \hat{=} \ [\Xi TextFile \mid row = 0] \lor [UpDown \mid row \neq 0 \land row′ = row - 1]$

The cursor cannot be moved down beyond the last row:

Down ≙ [Ξ*TextFile* | *row* = #*text*] ∨ [*UpDown* | *row* < #*text* ∧ *row'* = *row* + 1]

Left and right

Moving the cursor left or right does not change the current row, and only happens if we are 'at a line':

LeftRight ≙ [*MoveCursor* | *row'* = *row* ≠ 0]

If there is text to the left of the current position, then the cursor is moved left:

┌─ *LeftMove* ────────────────────────────
│ *LeftRight*
├──
│ *bef* ≠ ⟨⟩
│ *bef'* = front *bef*
└──

If there is no text to the left, or we are not at a line, then no action is taken:

Left ≙ *LeftMove* ∨ [Ξ*TextFile* | *bef* = ⟨⟩ ∨ *row* = 0]

If there is text to the right of the current position, then the cursor is moved right:

┌─ *RightMove* ───────────────────────────
│ *LeftRight*
├──
│ *aft* ≠ ⟨⟩
│ *aft'* = tail *aft*
└──

If there is no text to the right, or we are not at a line, then no action is taken:

Right ≙ *RightMove* ∨ [Ξ*TextFile* | *aft* = ⟨⟩ ∨ *row* = 0]

Insert and delete character

Character insert and delete only happens when there is a current line (*row*≠0), and only alters the current line:

┌─ *InsertDeleteChar* ─────────────────────
│ Δ*TextFile*
├──
│ *row* ≠ 0
│ *row'* = *row*
│ *text'* = *text* ⊕ {*row* ↦ *curlin'*}
└──

DeleteChar removes the character (if any) to the right of the current position:

DeleteOK $\hat{=}$ [*InsertDeleteChar* | *aft'* ≠ ⟨⟩ ∧ *bef'* = *bef* ∧ *aft'* = tail *aft*]

If there *are* any characters to the right of the current position (that is *aft*≠⟨⟩), then: the characters before the current position are unchanged; the character at the current position is deleted; and the remaining characters are shifted left by one position.

If there are no characters to the right, or we are not at a line, then no action is taken:

DeleteChar $\hat{=}$ *DeleteOK* ∨ [*ΞTextFile* | *aft* = ⟨⟩ ∨ *row* = 0]

The *InsertChar* operation takes a character input and inserts it into the current line:

```
┌─InsertOK ─────────────────────────────────
│ InsertDeleteChar
│ chr? : CHAR
│ ─────────────────
│ bef' = bef ^ ⟨chr?⟩
│ aft' = aft
└────────────────────────────────────────────
```

The new character is appended to those before the current position; the remaining characters are unchanged.

Where there is no current line, then no action is taken:

InsertChar $\hat{=}$ *InsertOK* ∨ [*ΞTextFile* | *row* = 0]

7.5 EVENT HANDLER

There are three different types of event: mouse movement, a key press or a mouse button press or release.

EventType ::= *Mouse* | *Key* | *Button*

The amount of mouse movement is a value ranging from −128 to 127:

mousedelta == −128..127

The screen addresses range from 0 to 1023 in both X and Y directions:

screenlowX == 0
screenlowY == 0
screenhiX == 1023
screenhiY == 1023
screenX == *screenlowX..screenhiX*
screenY == *screenlowY..screenhiY*

Interrupt addresses are simply positive numbers:

address == $\mathbb{N}_1$
V1 : address
V2 : address

Event data

The data available when each kind of event occurs is described below.

Mouse movement

If the mouse is moved (more than 2mm):

┌─*MouseData*────────────────────
│ *x,y : mousedelta*
└──────────────────────────────

Mouse button

There are two mouse buttons and we detect 'down' and 'up' on each:

but1down == *1*
but1up   == *129*
but2down == *2*
but2up   == *130*
ButtonValue == {*but1down, but1up, but2down, but2up*}

Key press

There are 127 keys:

KeyValue == *1..127*

An event

An event is identified by an *EventType*, and has corresponding data values:

┌─*Event*────────────────────────
│ *type : EventType*
│ *mou : MouseData*
│ *but : ButtonValue*
│ *key : KeyValue*
└──────────────────────────────

Workstation state

The state of the workstation can be represented by five registers:

```
┌─CtlRegs─────────────────────────────────────
│ Xreg : screenX
│ Yreg : screenY
│ Creg : KeyValue
│ Dreg : KeyValue
│ Preg : address
└──────────────────────────────
```

Keyboard events

Whichever sort of key is pressed, the control registers are changed. The input values are an *EventType* and a *KeyValue*:

```
┌─KeyCommon───────────────────────────────────
│ ΔCtlRegs
│ evt? : EventType
│ key? : KeyValue
├──────────────────────────────
│ evt? = Key
│ Xreg' = Xreg
│ Yreg' = Yreg
│ Preg' = V2
└──────────────────────────────
```

The event is a *KeyEvent*; the XY registers are unchanged; the program register is set to vector 2.

For a control key

```
┌─CtlKey──────────────────────────────────────
│ KeyCommon
├──────────────────────────────
│ Creg' = key?
│ Dreg' = 0
└──────────────────────────────
```

the key value is placed in the control register and the data register is set to zero.

For any other key

```
┌─OtherKey────────────────────────────────────
│ KeyCommon
├──────────────────────────────
│ Creg' = 0
│ Dreg' = key?
└──────────────────────────────
```

the key value is placed in the data register and the control register is set to zero.

A *KeyHit* event is either a *CtlKey* or an *OtherKey*:

$KeyHit \mathrel{\hat{=}} CtlKey \lor OtherKey$

Mouse button events

When a mouse button is pressed, the control registers are changed. The
input values are an *EventType* and a *ButtonValue*:

```
┌─ ButtonPress ─────────────────────────────────────
│ ΔCtlRegs
│ evt? : EventType
│ but? : ButtonValue
├───────────────────────────────────────────────────
│ evt? = Button
│ Xreg' = Xreg
│ Yreg' = Yreg
│ Preg' = V1
│ Creg' = Creg
│ Dreg' = but?
└───────────────────────────────────────────────────
```

The event is a *Button* event; the XY registers are unchanged; the program
register is set to vector 1; the control register is unchanged; the data register is set to the value associated with the button.

Mouse movement

When the mouse is moved, the control registers are changed. The input
values are an *EventType*, an *Xdelta* and a *Ydelta*. New values, *newx* and
newy are computed:

```
┌─ MMcommon ────────────────────────────────────────
│ ΔCtlRegs
│ evt? : EventType
│ xval? : mousedelta
│ yval? : mousedelta
│ newx,newy : ℤ
├───────────────────────────────────────────────────
│ evt? = Mouse
│ Creg' = Creg
│ Dreg' = Dreg
│ newx = Xreg + xval?
│ newy = Yreg + yval?
└───────────────────────────────────────────────────
```

The event is a *Mouse* event; the control and data registers are unchanged;
the *newx* and *newy* values are the old values plus the deltas.

The *Xreg* will be changed only if *newx* lies within the screen boundaries:

```
┌─MMX────────────────────────────────────────────────
│ MMcommon
│ ─────────────
│ ((screenlowX ≤ newx ≤ screenhiX)  ∧  Xreg' = newx)
│ ∨
│ (¬ (screenlowX ≤ newx ≤ screenhiX)  ∧  Xreg' = Xreg)
└──────────────────────────────────────────────────────
```

The *Yreg* will be changed only if *newy* lies within the screen boundaries:

```
┌─MMY────────────────────────────────────────────────
│ MMcommon
│ ─────────────
│ ((screenlowY ≤ newy ≤ screenhiY)  ∧  Yreg' = newy)
│ ∨
│ (¬ (screenlowY ≤ newy ≤ screenhiX) ∧ Yreg' = Yreg)
└──────────────────────────────────────────────────────
```

A mouse movement results in a possible change to *Xreg* and a possible change to *Yreg*:

MouseMove $\triangleq$ *MMX* ∧ *MMY*

In fact, the values *newx* and *newy* are not needed in the description of *MouseMove* (we need only *Xreg'* and *Yreg'*). In Chapter 9 we see how such intermediate values can be hidden.

An *InputEvent* is a *KeyHit*, a *ButtonHit* or a *MouseMove*:

InputEvent $\triangleq$ *KeyHit* ∨ *ButtonPress* ∨ *MouseMove*

8.1 SUBSTRINGS

The *substr* function defines a substring of a string given a starting position and a length:

```
[CHAR]
string == seq CHAR
```

```
│ substr : (string × ℕ₁ × ℕ)⇸string
│ ──────────────────────────────────────────────
│ ∀ s : string;  p : ℕ₁;  n : ℕ  •  substr(s,p,n) = squash((p..p+n)◁s)
```

The expression $p..p+n◁s$ defines those characters of s in which we are interested, but associates them with their positions in s. For instance, if s is $\langle h,o,l,i,d,a,y \rangle$ then $3..5◁s$ is $\{3 \mapsto l, 4 \mapsto i, 5 \mapsto d\}$.

This is 'squashed' down to $\{1 \mapsto l, 2 \mapsto i, 3 \mapsto d\}$, that is $\langle l,i,d \rangle$.

8.2 PERMUTE

This answer is a restatement of the Answer 5.2, now using more powerful mathematical models.

$$\_IsPermOf\_ : \text{seq } \mathbb{N} \leftrightarrow \text{seq } \mathbb{N}$$

$$\forall a, b : \text{seq}\mathbb{N} \bullet (a \text{ } IsPermOf \text{ } b \Leftrightarrow (\exists p : \text{dom } a \rightarrowtail\!\!\!\rightarrow \text{dom } b \bullet p \text{ ; } b = a))$$

p is a permutation from a to b, that is, it is a 1-1 onto mapping from dom a, the indexes of a, to dom b, the indexes of b.

8.3 CAR RADIO

Main switch

The radio has a main switch that can be

$$OnOff ::= \text{ } ON \mid OFF$$

and a volume control, whose maximum value is

$$maxvol : \mathbb{N}_1$$

The *volume* control and *main* switch are combined:

┌─ Volume ─────────────────────────────────
│ volume : 0..maxvol
│ main : OnOff
├──
│ main = OFF $\Leftrightarrow$ volume = 0
│ main = ON $\Leftrightarrow$ volume > 0
└──

Wavebands

A *WaveLength* (radio station) is simply a non-zero natural number:

$$WaveLength == \mathbb{N}_1$$

A *WaveBand* is a sequence of *WaveLength*

$$WaveBand : \mathbb{P}(\text{seq } WaveLength)$$

$$\forall w : WaveBand \bullet (\forall i, j : \text{dom } w \mid i < j \bullet w \text{ } i < w \text{ } j)$$

in ascending order.

There are three wavebands:

$\lfloor$ *medium, long, UHF* : *WaveBand*

WaveBand = {*medium,long,UHF*}
medium ≠ *long* ≠ *UHF* ≠ *medium*

In the radio, *band* is the currently selected waveband and *station* is the selected station. Its position in *band* is identified by *stanum*:

```
┌─ Bands ─────────────────────────────────────
│ band : WaveBand
│ station : WaveLength
│ stanum : ℕ₁
│ ──────────────────────────
│ station = band stanum
│ stanum ≤ #band
└──────────────────────────────────────────────
```

The radio state

The state of the *Radio* is identified by *Volume* and *Bands*:

```
┌─ Radio ─────────────────────────────────────
│ Volume
│ Bands
└──────────────────────────────────────────────
```

Initial state

Initially

```
┌─ InitRadio ─────────────────────────────────
│ Radio′
│ ──────────────────────────
│ main′ = OFF
│ stanum′ = 1
│ station′ = medium 1
│ band′ = medium
└──────────────────────────────────────────────
```

the *main* switch is *OFF* and the lowest *station* on the medium *band* is selected.

The other controls have no effect when the main switch is *OFF*:

NoOp ≙ [Ξ*Radio* | *main* = *OFF*]

Volume

The volume control (and combined ON/OFF switch) does not change the *band* or *station*:

ChgVol ≙ [Δ*Radio* | *band*′ = *band* ∧ *station*′ = *station*]

The *volume* can be increased, up to the maximum:

```
┌─IncVol────────────────────────────────────────
│ ChgVol
│ ────────
│ (volume < maxvol ∧ volume' = volume + 1
│ ∨
│ (volume = maxvol ∧ volume' = volume)
└────────────────────────────────────────────────
```

and can be decreased down to zero:

```
┌─DecVol────────────────────────────────────────
│ ChgVol
│ ────────
│ (volume > 0 ∧ volume' = volume − 1)
│ ∨
│ (volume = 0 ∧ volume' = volume)
└────────────────────────────────────────────────
```

(zero is the same as *OFF*.)

Change station (UP/DOWN buttons)

The UP/DOWN buttons take effect only if the radio is *ON* and they do not affect *volume*, *main* switch or *waveband*:

```
┌─ChgSta─────────────────────────────────────────
│ ΔRadio
│ ────────
│ main = ON
│ volume' = volume
│ main' = main
│ band' = band
└────────────────────────────────────────────────
```

UpSta describes moving to the 'next' *station* on the current *band*:

```
┌─UpSta──────────────────────────────────────────
│ ChgSta
│ ────────
│ stanum < #band  ⇒  stanum' = stanum + 1
│ stanum = #band  ⇒  stanum' = 1
└────────────────────────────────────────────────
```

which cycles round the stations.

The UP button will change to the next higher station on the current *band* if the radio is *ON*, otherwise it will do nothing:

UP ≙ *UpSta* ∨ *NoOp*

DownSta describes moving to the 'previous' *station* on the current *waveband*:

```
┌─ DownSta ──────────────────────────────────────
│  ChgSta
│ ────────────────────────────────────
│  stanum > 1  ⇒  stanum' = stanum − 1
│  stanum = 1  ⇒  stanum' = #band
└────────────────────────────────────
```

The DOWN button will change to the next lower station on the current *waveband* if the radio is *ON*, otherwise it will do nothing:

$DOWN \triangleq DownSta \vee NoOp$

The MLU button

The *Cycle* schema describes the effect of 'cycling' round the three wavebands:

```
┌─ Cycle ─────────────────────────────────
│  ΔRadio
│ ────────────────────────────────────
│  main = ON
│  volume' = volume
│  main' = main
│  stanum' = 1
│  band = medium  ⇒  band' = long
│  band = long  ⇒  band' = UHF
│  band = UHF  ⇒  band' = medium
└────────────────────────────────────
```

If the radio is *ON*, cycling consists of changing from Medium to Long to UHF to Medium. The lowest station on the new waveband is selected. The *volume* is unchanged.

If the radio is *ON*, the MLU button cyles round the wavebands, otherwise it has no effect:

$MLU \triangleq Cycle \vee NoOp$

The radio and its permitted operations are summarized below:

Radio
InitRadio
IncVol
DecVol
UP
DOWN
MLU

Footnote

In first postulating this problem, I had in mind the radio in my own car. In trying to produce a formal specification, I began to realize that I really didn't know how that radio behaved. That Saturday afternoon involved many trips between the car and my desk! The resulting specification is actually a simplification of the real radio and took upwards of eight hours (plus an independent review) to produce. If you would like a more demanding challenge than the problem above, find such a real radio and produce a specification for it.

8.4 GO

The stones are black or white:

colour $::=$ *black | white*

The game is played on a square board, any *size* from 11x11 up to 19x19:

$$\begin{array}{|l} size : \mathbb{N} \\ \hline 11 \leq size \leq 19 \end{array}$$

A *stone* is characterized by its position and colour:

stone $\hat{=}$ [*x, y : 1..size; clr : colour*]

In the definitions that follow we find a need to use the 'positive difference' between two integers. We call this *abs*:

$$\begin{array}{|l} abs : (\mathbb{Z} \times \mathbb{Z}) \to \mathbb{N} \\ \hline \forall i, j : \mathbb{Z} \bullet ((i \leq j \wedge abs(i,j) = j - i) \vee (i = j \wedge abs(i,j) = i - j)) \end{array}$$

Two stones are *touching* if they are in the same row and adjacent columns, or in the same column and adjacent rows:

$$\begin{array}{|l} touching : stone \leftrightarrow stone \\ \hline touching = \{a, b : stone \mid \\ \quad ((a.x = b.x \wedge abs(a.y, b.y) = 1) \vee \\ \quad (a.y = b.y \wedge abs(a.x, b.x) = 1))\} \end{array}$$

Two stones *a* and *b* are *joined* if it is possible to get from *a* to *b* via *touching* stones. This is expressed by the transitive closure of *touching*. We want to consider any stone to be joined to itself, so we will define *joined* as the *reflexive* transitive closure of *touching*:

joined $==$ *touching**

A collection of stones is *Connected* if they are all the same colour and are all *joined* to each other:

```
┌─ Connected ──────────────────────────────────
│ gp_col : colour
│ stones : ℙstone
├──────────────────────────────────────────────
│ ∀ s : stones  •  s.clr = gp_col
│ ∀ a, b : stones  •  (a,b) ∈ joined
└──────────────────────────────────────────────
```

A *Group* is a maximal collection of *Connected* stones:

```
┌─ Group ──────────────────────────────────────
│ Connected
├──────────────────────────────────────────────
│ ∀ g : Connected | stones ∩ g.stones ≠ ∅ • g.stones ⊆ stones
└──────────────────────────────────────────────
```

That is, it is a collection for which there is no superset that is also *Connected*.

Footnote

Like the radio specification, this answer took many hours of thought. The result is deceptively simple and elegant – the reader cannot see our overflowing wastebin!

9.1 PHONE DIRECTORY SYSTEM

To remind us of the context, we reproduce the *PhoneDir* schema, its initial state, and one operation on it here. (The complete description can be found in Chapter 7.)

```
┌─ PhoneDir ───────────────────────────────────
│ addr : NAME⇸ADDRESS
│ phone : NAME⇸NUMBER
├──────────────────────────────────────────────
│ dom addr = dom phone
└──────────────────────────────────────────────
```

```
┌─ InitPD ─────────────────────────────────────
│ PhoneDir′
├──────────────────────────────────────────────
│ addr′ = ∅
│ phone′ = ∅
└──────────────────────────────────────────────
```

```
┌─ AddOK ──────────────────────────────────────
│ ΔPhoneDir
│ name? : NAME
│ addr? : ADDRESS
│ phone? : NUMBER
│ rc! : RetCode
│──────────────────────────────────────────────
│ name? ∉ dom addr
│ addr' = addr ∪ {name? ↦ addr?}
│ phone' = phone ∪ {name? ↦ phone?}
│ rc! = OK
└──────────────────────────────────────────────
```

```
┌─ AddDuplicate ───────────────────────────────
│ ΞPhoneDir
│ name? : NAME
│ addr? : ADDRESS
│ phone? : NUMBER
│ rc! : RetCode
│──────────────────────────────────────────────
│ name? ∈ dom addr
│ rc! = duplicate
└──────────────────────────────────────────────
```

$Add \triangleq AddOK \lor AddDuplicate$

We now show how these can be promoted to a *PDS*.

The directory system contains one directory for each town. The names of towns are in the given set:

$[TOWN]$

The PDS consists of a mapping between town names and phone directories:

$PDS \triangleq [pd : TOWN \nrightarrow PhoneDir]$

Initially, the PDS is empty:

$InitPDS \triangleq [PDS' \mid pd' = \emptyset]$

The *AddTown* operation might specify an existing town and *DeleteTown* might specify an unknown town. To identify these situations, we introduce:

$RetCode ::= OK \mid duplicate \mid unknown$

AddTown

If the specified town does not exist already, then it is added to the PDS, with an empty directory:

```
┌─ AddTownOK ─────────────────────────────────────
│ ΔPDS
│ town? : TOWN
│ rc! : RetCode
│ InitPD
├─────────────────────────────────────────────────
│ town? ∉ dom pd
│ pd' = pd ∪ {town? ↦ θPhoneDir'}
│ rc! = OK
└─────────────────────────────────────────────────
```

The second predicate says that an element is added to *pd*. This element consists of the specified town mapped to the specified *PhoneDir*. *InitPD* in the declaration says that this *PhoneDir* is empty.

If the town exists already, then the PDS is unchanged:

```
┌─ DupTown ───────────────────────────────────────
│ ΞPDS
│ town? : TOWN
│ rc! : RetCode
├─────────────────────────────────────────────────
│ town? ∈ dom pd
│ rc! = duplicate
└─────────────────────────────────────────────────
```

The robust operation is:

$AddTown \;\hat{=}\; AddTownOK \lor DupTown$

DeleteTown

If the specified town exists, then it is deleted from the PDS:

```
┌─ DeleteTownOK ──────────────────────────────────
│ ΔPDS
│ town? : TOWN
│ rc! : RetCode
├─────────────────────────────────────────────────
│ town? ∈ dom pd
│ pd' = {town?} ⊲ pd
│ rc! = OK
└─────────────────────────────────────────────────
```

Otherwise, the PDS is unchanged:

```
┌─ NoTown ─────────────────────────────────────────
│ ΞPDS
│ town? : TOWN
│ rc! : RetCode
│ ────────────────────────────────────────────────
│ town? ∉ dom pd
│ rc! = unknown
└──────────────────────────────────────────────────
```

The robust operation is:

DeleteTown ≙ *AddTownOK* ∨ *NoTown*

ListTown

The set of existing towns is returned:

```
┌─ ListTown ───────────────────────────────────────
│ ΞPDS
│ townlist! : ℙ TOWN
│ ────────────────────────────────────────────────
│ townlist! = dom pd
└──────────────────────────────────────────────────
```

Promoted operations

We will now promote the operations on a single directory to the PDS:

```
┌─ PromotePD ──────────────────────────────────────
│ ΔPDS
│ ΔPhoneDir
│ town? : TOWN
│ ────────────────────────────────────────────────
│ θPhoneDir = pd town?
│ pd' = pd ⊕ {town? ↦ θPhoneDir'}
└──────────────────────────────────────────────────
```

The first predicate says that the *PhoneDir* we are talking about is in fact *pd town?*. The second predicate says that the new directory system (*pd'*) is the old one (*pd*) overridden by a new *PhoneDir* for the specified town, *town?*.

The promoted operations can now be simply described:

PDSAdd ≙ (*PromotePD* ∧ *Add*) \ *ΔPhoneDir*

PDSDelete ≙ (*PromotePD* ∧ *Delete*) \ *ΔPhoneDir*

PDSReplace ≙ (*PromotePD* ∧ *Replace*) \ *ΔPhoneDir*

PDSQueryPhoneNum ≙ (*PromotePD* ∧ *QueryPhoneNumber*) \ *ΔPhoneDir*

Index